WHEN FRIDAY COMES

James Montague is a 29-year-old journalist from Chelmsford, Essex. His work has appeared in the *New Statesman*, *GQ*, *Arena*, *Marie Claire*, *FourFourTwo*, *World Soccer*, *Observer Sports Monthly*, *Jerusalem Post*, *Time Out Dubai*, *The Guardian* and the *International Herald Tribune*. He supports West Ham United. *When Friday Comes* is his first book.

WHEN
FRIDAY
COMES

Football in the War Zone

JAMES MONTAGUE

**MAINSTREAM
PUBLISHING**

EDINBURGH AND LONDON

To Alison, still

First published in Great Britain in 2008 by
MAINSTREAM PUBLISHING COMPANY
(EDINBURGH) LTD
7 Albany Street
Edinburgh EH1 3UG

All internal photographs courtesy of the author

ISBN 9781845963699

This book is a work of non-fiction based on the life, experiences
and recollections of the author. In some instances, names of people,
places, dates, sequences or the detail of events have been changed
to protect the privacy of others. The author has stated to the
publishers that, except in such respects, not affecting the substantial
accuracy of the work, the contents of this book are true

A catalogue record for this book is available
from the British Library

Typeset in Bembo and Century Gothic

Printed in Great Britain by
CPI Mackays of Chatham Ltd, Chatham, ME5 8TD

ACKNOWLEDGEMENTS

I owe so many people a debt of gratitude – and in some cases simply a debt – that it is almost impossible to know where to start. My agent, Rebecca Winfield at Luxton Harris, deserves to be top of the list. Without her sometimes holding my hand, I simply would not have been able to finish this book. And neither would you be reading a copy if Iain MacGregor – Associate Publisher of Mainstream Publishing – hadn't taken a punt on me and believed in the proposal, even when I was being tardy.

For advice and support when it was needed most: Mum, Dad, Laura, Keith Colley, Rob Reddy, who came up with the sub-title, Fyfe Hutchings, Simon Loydall, Anthony Edward Lawson, Caru Sanders and Amy Sargeant. Thank you Ben. If it weren't for you this book wouldn't exist. Simple as that. For commissioning various pieces which allowed me to explore the region and research the book whilst feeding and clothing myself: Barbara Gunnell, Paul Henderson, Jason Cowley, Hugh Sleight, Louis Massarella, Sean Ingle, Bridget Freer, Will Storr and John Kampfner.

In Israel: Jeremy Last, Amir Ben David, Ahikam Seri and Yossi Benayoun. and Adriana Rodriquez In Lebanon: Emile Rustom. In Jordan: Eddie Taylor, who coined the phrase 'the Jordanian Silvio Berlusconi'. In Iraq: Waleed Tabra. In Syria: Toufik Sarhan.

In Egypt: Jonathan Spollen. In the UAE: a huge thank you to Rob Orchard, John and Victoria Hazell-Thatcher and Marcus Webb. Not forgetting Matthew Lee and Matthew Pomroy. I also shouldn't forget the huge assistance I was given by the football associations of Lebanon, Palestine, Jordan, Egypt, Yemen and Syria. Apologies to Saudi Arabia, Bahrain, Oman, Kuwait and Libya. There will be more on you in the next one.

But most importantly, I'd like to thank all the people I met on the way, who pointed me in the right direction, translated conversations, gave me tea and – when I ran out of money – waved aside border tolls, shared their lunch with me, let me sleep on their sofas and generally dispelled every stereotype you can imagine about the Middle East. I will never forget the kindness of strangers. Finally, thank you to everyone I have shamefully forgotten.

James Montague,
25 June 2008

CONTENTS

INTRODUCTION

All that I know most surely about morality and the obligations, I owe it to football.

Albert Camus

He's hiding near Kabul, he loves the Arsenal, Osama wooh, oh, Osama, wooh, oh, oh, oh.

Arsenal fans chant the name of (allegedly)
their most famous supporter, Osama Bin Laden

The shisha café in the quiet, overlooked suburb of Hor Al Anz in Dubai was the only sign of life on the street. It was late, past midnight, and the sticky humidity that always followed a searing Gulf summer's day coated everyone, and everything, in a thin layer of perspiration. My bed was enticing me home, but I still felt the pull of unfinished business. The lone yellow light along the concrete row of shops and shwarma stands threw itself enticingly onto the pavement in front. A distant clatter of porcelain cups and raised male voices in a foreign tongue wafted over. I instinctively moved towards the light. Inside, the harsh white glow from the strip lighting mixed with the fog-thick fug of sweet apple tobacco and strong, dark cigarettes. It stung the eyes momentarily until a few moments of blinking acclimatised you to the toxic atmosphere. It was standing room only. Every available seat was taken, the space tightly packed together by white-robed Emiratis wearing the traditional dish dasha. More stood in any available place they could find. I inched along the back wall and found the solitary last seat. A young Pakistani boy worked the cracks, emptying ashtrays and refilling tiny thimbles full of thick Turkish coffee as his Egyptian colleague slalomed around the chairs with his metal ladle of hot coals, replacing the dying embers from atop each customer's billowing water pipe. The crowd was oblivious to their services. Tactics had to be discussed and players rated. All eyes were stuck on the television in the corner for the big match. The appearance of white uniformity from the back of the room was a myth. Two tribes had emerged from Dubai's darkness to watch their respective teams do battle. An invisible line had been drawn in the sand, the room divided. To the right, the supporters of France, to the left, Brazil. The only way to differentiate the two was the hastily hung flags in each corner. It was the 2006 World Cup quarter-final and neither side could contemplate going home saddled with defeat. Arguments started to break out between the sets of fans over who was truly the greatest player in the world: Ronaldinho or Zidane. One had to be pulled back by his friends, so incensed was he that Zizou had been defamed. And the match hadn't even started yet.

Fights, devotion and obsession over faraway players and footballing nations was something I had quickly got used to when I accidentally stumbled into Dubai nearly two years previously. I hadn't even known for sure where Dubai was on the map when the email arrived in my inbox advertising a job on the city's *Time Out* magazine. The timing was almost suspiciously good. That morning I'd heard that *Jack* – the magazine I had just started writing for – was being shut with immediate effect. Two weeks later I was stepping out of an air-conditioned arrivals lounge into a brick wall of humidity. It was August and a thick, moist air had emptied my lungs the moment I stepped out of the controlled environment of the airport. Dubai was noisy, brash and hellishly hot. I had seen many new arrivals react in different ways upon arriving in such an alien place. Some flew back home in a matter of days. Most stayed, but stuck to their own in expat communities, replicating the life they had enjoyed back home oblivious to their surroundings and refusing to mix with the locals to acclimatise. I had put my faith in football. In the beginning, I would walk to my local shisha café late at night to watch Premiership matches. More often than not the Egyptian manager would show only Tottenham games, no matter who else was on, given that Mido was turning out for them at the time. But soon I started to pick up little threads of the local football stories: a World Cup qualifier against the UAE where the mysterious North Korean national team were in town; the struggles of the Palestinian national football team to try, but ultimately fail, to qualify for the 2006 World Cup; riots in the Lebanese league between supporters representing competing sectarian interests; in Yemen footballers were struggling to kick the habit of their national drug *khat*. I devoured each and every story I could find. They were reported matter of factly, as if this kind of thing was perfectly normal in the Middle East. In a way, it was. But each story held something of wider significance. At its root football seemed to embody something about the country's psyche, its national character, its place in the world and where it was heading. I wanted to find out more about the Middle East, its mysteries and its contradictions, and football seemed the perfect platform. My catalyst was the news that French World Cup winner Marcel Desailly had signed to play in the Qatari league. Qatari was a barren, inoffensive country whose recent discoveries of gas had given it phenomenal wealth. Some of this money was being pumped into sport, especially football, in an attempt to raise its international profile. Without thinking or having any particular plan I booked my flight to Doha. It was the start of a journey that would take me to terraces and football pitches as far south as Sana'a, to Tehran in the east, to Cairo in the west and to Damascus in the north. In all these places I discovered the same thing: a deep and passionate love for the beautiful game and a window of wider understanding.

Of course, the globalisation of football isn't anything new. After all, it was predicted eight in every ten people in the world would watch some part of the last World Cup. Neither is it particularly illuminating that passion is something the Middle East has in abundance, though there is a messianic reverence for the game that matches anything in Europe or South America. Yet, in theory, it shouldn't be like this. The Middle East isn't a place predisposed to successful Western interventions. Tragedy has stalked every corner of the region and when I first arrived the West's standing couldn't have been lower. Decades of nefarious interference in Iran, Lebanon, Saudi Arabia, Egypt, Israel and Jordan to name a few, had created a toxic mix of corrupt regimes, Islamic fundamentalism, poverty, anger and disillusionment. The duplicity and betrayal reached its nadir after the disastrous second Gulf War and the dismantling of Iraq. As the veteran war correspondent Robert Fisk wrote:

> From the borders of Hindu Kush to the Mediterranean, we – we Westerners that is – are creating . . . a hell disaster.

The chaos and the confusion had been a boon for Islamic fundamentalists seeking to paint the world in black and white, in us versus them rhetoric. More than ever the Middle East's jaded subjects rejected the ideals that had once been heralded as the force of modernity. As a Westerner, an outsider trying to make sense of it all, taking the pulse of a region would be nigh on impossible normally. Yet despite all this, one Western cultural export had achieved something that no amount of American missiles, aggressive foreign policy or attempted subjugation could. Football has without doubt won hearts and minds in the Middle East with every country in the region obsessed with the beautiful game. A weekend of Premiership or *Serie A* or *La Liga* football had the power to momentarily disable the most unforgiving jihadist: even Osama Bin Laden couldn't resist. It is alleged that during his time in London in the 1980s he developed a deep and lasting love for the game, and for Arsenal.

How had this happened? After all, the document that brought the game to life, arguably one of the only documents that has universal and unwavering approval across the region and across sectarian lines, was set down in a smoke-filled room by English public school masters in the nineteenth century. In his *Twelve Books That Changed the World*, which rightly heralded the *Rule Book of Association Football* as one of the most inspirational tomes ever written, Melvyn Bragg wrote that football:

> Has caused at least one war and many battles, often tragic, off the pitch. It has always triggered outbursts of local and national joy, pride and unity . . . and it all flowed from the meeting of a few Victorian Oxbridge graduates in a pub in Lincoln's Inn Fields in London 1863. Before the afternoon was out they had called themselves 'the football association' and the Rule Book was on its way.

It was perhaps the greatest imperialist document ever written, allowing the British Empire to successfully spread the footballing gospel. When the British forces retreated, momentum did the rest. Today, whether I was in Amman or Erbil, the first question I was asked in cafés and on street corners wasn't about George Bush or Tony Blair, or the war or Israel. I wasn't spat at in the street or harangued for my country's complicity in very bad things. Rather, it was: 'Manchester United or Chelsea?' with the more sophisticated barracking me for supporting such a bunch of underachievers as West Ham United. One Lebanese international footballer in his late 20s even went as far as conceding that the 3–3 FA Cup final against Liverpool in 2006 was interesting to watch, but that West Ham were a shadow of the 1966 team, with Moore and Peters. I watched avowed Hezbollah members profess their undying love for Steven Gerrard, and spoke to Syrians who were livid – angrier than me, certainly – with Steve McClaren for not steering England to the finals of Euro 2008. Simply put, football is the Middle East's great unifying thread. More so, you could argue, than Islam, divided as it is, sometimes violently, between Shia and Sunni, and certainly more than the failed forces of Arab nationalism.

Even language fails the test when you throw the *Farsi* speaking Iranians and the Hebrew speaking Israelis into the mix.

Despite its ubiquity, some had sought to drive a wedge between football and Islam, the most famous being the 2003 football fatwa issued by a Saudi cleric Sheikh Abdallah Al-Najdi, which signified a strange attempt to Islamify football. In it the Sheikh gave a 15-point plan of how to rid the game of Western influence. These included only punishing transgressions, not by red or yellow cards, but by Sharia law; playing only one half; not playing in front of crowds; and urging followers to use the game only to strengthen the body for *jihad*. My favourite, though, was point nine:

> You should spit in the face of whoever puts the ball between the posts or uprights and then runs in order to get his friends to follow him and hug him like players in America or France do, and you should punish him, for what is the relationship between celebrating, hugging and kissing and the sports that you are practising?

According to the Middle Eastern Media Research Institute in Washington, Saudi newspaper *Al Watan* had reported that the fatwas had provoked three players from Al Rashid football club to leave and join the insurgency in Iraq, even though the fatwas were roundly condemned in Saudi Arabia. The Grand Mufti of Saudi Arabia, Sheikh Abdul Ibn Abdallah Aal-Sheikh, who was also an adviser for the Saudi Justice Department, told *Al Watan*:

> [The authorities needed to] prosecute those involved in the publishing of these fatwas in a Sharia court for the crime they have committed [and to] track down those involved and prosecute them, in view of the dangers and the venom with which they are trying to influence society.

Neither was there anything wrong with the heathen rules that had been incorporated from the West.

> There is nothing wrong with . . . the soccer rules. All
> things that come from the West but are not unique to
> it are permitted. Soccer has become a world sport and
> does not belong only to the non-believers.

Moqtada Al Sadr, the Iraqi Shia cleric so hated by the US,
also took umbrage at the beautiful game in 2006. 'Sharia
also prohibits such activities which keep the followers too
occupied for worshipping, keep people from remembering [to
worship].' The interesting thing in both cases was the furious,
incredulous reaction by both the authorities and the average
fan on the street. In the end, Saudi Arabia qualified with flying
colours for Germany 2006, and Iraq would win the Asian Cup
in 2007. No football fatwas have been heard of since.

When Friday Comes isn't a book with a happy ending, where
football provides some kind of silver bullet to solve the region's
seemingly intractable problems. Football doesn't change things
by and in of itself. A two-state solution won't be kick-started by
the Palestinian national team playing Israel. Currently neither
team would even dream of playing the other. No, football is
a mirror that reflects the zeitgeist; a sponge that soaks up the
tensions, the flaws, the frustrations and the hopes of society. For
those involved it is one of the few forms of catharsis. Which might
give another explanation as to why, every Friday from Aden to
Aleppo, millions of fans leave the mosque and head straight
for their local football club. In the absence of true democracy
and a genuine public space, the terraces provide a forum for
dissent. In Jordan, the songs for a free Palestine sung by the
fans of the football team from Wihdat refugee camp wouldn't
be accepted by the police on the street. In Iran the frustrations
of the women's rights movement are vented, not outside the
Majlis, but outside the Azadi national football stadium before
every home international.

But above all else, football is about passionately appreciating
guile wherever it may be found. The crowd watching the World
Cup quarter-final in Dubai understood that better than most.
France famously dispensed with Brazil 1–0 thanks to a Thierry

Henry goal. The French contingent celebrated as if the United Arab Emirates had themselves put the Brazilians out. They ran into the street and mounted a fleet of expensive, powerful 4x4s before driving them out onto a patch of sandy waste ground, spinning doughnuts and blaring their horns whilst hanging a French flag out of a blacked-out window. The Brazilian fans quickly walked away, heads down, in silence – the defeat tasting every bit as bitter as it did in Rio.

ONE

Qatar

'Excuse me, are you Manfred Hoener?' The rotund, dark-skinned pensioner wearing long, white flowing robes and a face that looked like it had been disfigured from years of chewing on ball bearings was obviously struggling with my feeble and slightly desperate request. 'Manfred Hoener, he was supposed to meet me here,' I persisted in vain. 'You wan' taxi?' came the confused response. The Qatari man was clearly not the middle-aged German football coach I had been instructed to meet at Doha International Airport. But after running around the brand new arrivals terminal for an hour asking anyone vaguely blond, over five-foot-ten or with a square jaw whether they were the only person in the country who could save me from a night of vagrancy, I had started to become desperate. By 9.30 p.m., and with the last stragglers from my inbound Dubai flight leaving the hall in the smug knowledge that they would indeed be lying down under a roof, with air con, I still had no idea what Manfred Hoener looked like. I'd even begun to doubt his existence.

Manfred had assumed something of a mythical status in my world. We had first made contact with each other when I came across an old story in the Scottish newspaper the *Daily Record*. They had reported that legendary Dutch World Cup midfielder Ronald De Boer was close to signing a shock, big money deal for one last huzzah after falling out of favour at Glasgow Rangers. But rather than choose one of a host of mid-table Premiership urchins like Tottenham or Aston Villa, he had opted to decamp to the footballing powerhouse of Qatar on a whopping tax-free salary, with a nice villa and all-year-round sunshine. And he wasn't the first. Dozens of players, Batistuta, Dugary, Caniggia, Sonny Anderson and Romario, to name a few, had gone before him to play football in a country where the local population was just under a million, the stadiums were rarely quarter-full and the nearest neighbours for your forthcoming pre-season friendlies would be insurgent-riddled Saudi Arabia or soon-to-be-nuclear Iran. Still, Ron wasn't upset in the slightest. In fact, he had managed to talk his brother Frank into joining him in the ageing footballer exodus east. Or, more accurately, Manfred Hoener had convinced Ronald De Boer to convince his brother to join him. Hoener was, according to the *Daily Record*, Qatar's 'Mr Fix it', the man who worked on behalf of the Qatar FA to bring high profile, big name players nearing the end of their careers to the tiny Gulf state to play in the Q League, no expense spared. His success had been legion, tempting players who could expect at least a season or two more in *La Liga* or the Premiership to give up their plush, continental lifestyles in some of the world's greatest cities to move to Doha, a city of such monumental dullness that the US military based their entire Asian Central Command, CENTCOM, here. After all, if your troops have nowhere to rip apart after a few Budweisers on the town, you're unlikely to upset the locals. The man was quite clearly a genius, or a retired double-glazing salesman – or both – and I had arranged to meet him at the airport in the hope he could put me in touch with some of his success stories. But he clearly had more important things to do. As I sat on the deserted kerb outside Doha International Airport in the oppressive humidity, I cursed his father's good name and wondered whether Ronald De Boer had been in the same position just weeks earlier, gently perspiring into his Armani suit as he stalked the arrivals lounge asking anyone male, 'Are you Manfred Hoener?'

Manfred was supposed to escort me to a Q League match that night to see one of his charges in action. Josep Guardiola, the cultured Catalan midfielder who used to play for Barcelona and was now turning out for Al Ahli Doha. I could, Manfred reasoned, catch up with Josep after the game and interview him then. The interview was the last thing on my mind but in desperation I jumped into a shabby, orange and white Datsun taxi and took the short ride to Al Ahli's stadium. When I got there it was clear something was wrong. The floodlights were on but there was no sound. The stadium was a huge concrete bowl that had probably never seen the tens of thousands of fans that could fill it up. Inside the main foyer was abuzz with obscenely tall Qatari teenagers who had obviously just finished playing basketball. If any football had taken place here, I'd missed it. But then someone who could only be Manfred appeared, striding towards me with a maniacal grin, arm outstretched. He was a big, perma-tanned, silver-haired fox of a man with a handshake like a malfunctioning robot. And not unlike a Teutonic Robert Kilroy-Silk. 'Yes, yes, I'm sorry, but the interview is off,' he spat in a manner that confusingly seemed to be both dismissive and friendly at the same time. 'The team was playing in Morocco and got caught in the worst snowstorms in 20 years.' Snowstorms? In North Africa? I'd clearly underestimated Manfred. 'Never mind, I will drive you to a hotel.' On the way downtown Manfred regaled me with his life story. In coaching terms he was something of a mercenary, a figure you often came across when at the coal face of international football – a journeyman who had travelled three continents coaching football from his first job teaching Peruvian jungle kids the finer technique of the beautiful game in the 1960s, to today where he was arguably the most important person in Qatari football. 'Yes, yes, it's all very good but the head, he doesn't want to talk to the press. But I don't tell him! Ha!' The boss was the head of the Qatari National Olympic Committee, Sheikh Tamim Bin Hamad Al-Thani. Between them they oversaw an odd transfer system where the committee directed Manfred to sign the players they wanted and then, in turn, doled them out to the clubs that deserved them. Sheikh Tamim was also a member of the Thani royal family, son of the emir and nominated crown prince no less, that had ruled for a hundred years and of whom criticism was still taboo. Manfred seemed to revel in his dissent, giving out a little whoop as we approached my shabby hotel. 'OK, OK. Call me tomorrow and we'll arrange something with Marcel.' Tomorrow I was to meet Manfred's greatest triumph thus far, the crowning glory of all his veteran baiting achievements: French World Cup winner Marcel Desailly.

Somewhere along the line I had gone horribly wrong. Manfred had told me to go right at the mangled car on a podium. I hadn't a clue what he meant until my taxi dropped me off in front of a gleaming new shopping mall. In front a large podium overlooked a large roundabout. Atop sat a mangled car from a fatal car accident, a shock tactic to encourage young Qataris to stop speeding in their unfeasibly powerful 4x4s. It was one of the unfortunate by-products of the Gulf's explosion of oil and gas wealth. All I could see for miles around was flat, shimmering desert. Qatar didn't have much variety in terrain. The tiny Gulf state is almost 100 per cent desert and it has the heat to match – in summer, the thermometer rarely drops below 40 degrees. Each road seemed to lead into a mirage of nothingness. I chose one at random and walked under the blazing midday sun. Just as I was about to give up, the gleaming new stadium loomed into view – the ground of Al Gharrafa. For one season at least it was to be home for Marcel Desailly. The ground was magnificent, a steel-and-glass edifice that wouldn't have looked out of place in Manchester, Munich or Marseilles. But there was something of the *Marie Celeste* about it: a beautiful ship prepared for a sumptuous feast, in the middle of nowhere with no sign of life. The place was deserted but rather stranger was the fact that I could just walk into the grounds of the biggest club in the country and poke around the changing rooms and offices totally unmolested. This despite the fact that Qatar was high up on the Foreign Office's list of places likely to experience a terrorist attack, in one of the most volatile regions of the world. In Europe I'd have been garrotted by a phalanx of burly security guards before I'd even got out of the taxi. Eventually a curious secretary, wondering who the sunburnt blond man ambling around was, informed me that the players would be back from training any minute and that I should wait in the canteen. The players streamed in – largely African men in their early 20s sprinkled with a few Arabs – for their buffet lunch of chicken and rice before the star attraction arrived. Quietly and without a word to the other players, Marcel filled his plate, retired to a table on his own and silently went about chewing on the gristly meat. I watched for a while, too nervous to approach him at first, and thought just how lonely he looked, in his training ground tracksuit – stripped of fame and notoriety – yet aesthetically appearing no different from the Desailly that had picked up the World Cup for France in 1998. It was as if, rather than moving to the Middle East for one last bumper pay day, this was the place where football souls came to die.

'Sit down. I don't mind if you eat with me.' After staring at him for so long that other players were beginning to think I was some kind of infatuated stalker, I plucked up the courage to pick up a plate, slop on some of the goo and invite myself for lunch with Desailly. I tried asking him politely why he had come out here. Although, after years of media training in Italy and England, the subtext was clear: why are you pissing the rest of your career away by playing in the middle of nowhere in a league where you're head and shoulders above your team-mates? 'Well, I would say it's no different from the second tier in a European league,' he replied, smiling. Clearly it was an incredulous query he had fielded a lot. 'I was offered the chance to be coach of the Ghanaian national team but I could follow my passion, being paid what I was earning at Chelsea and I said: "Yes, why not?" New experience, new people, new traditions, another mentality, a sunny place.' And in Qatari terms, Marcel was thriving. Gharrafa was top of the league and with his being the most technically gifted player within a thousand-mile radius, he had begun to loosen the defensive shackles and maraud up field, playing as an attacking midfielder and scoring regularly.

The Qataris loved him. As I was getting ready for our meeting in the hotel, the local television station was replaying Desailly's two headed goals from the weekend over and over and over. But Desailly – a French Catholic who found himself in a staunchly Sunni Muslim state – was finding it a little hard to get used to. 'I am surprised when they go to pray. I never knew that Ramadan was so respected. It's the little details you discover. Training is at six o'clock and I am on the field ready to train and there's nobody – why? Because they are praying. Little things like that. But you have to accept it because it's their traditions and culture without judging them. We are not in Europe. I realised that they are not really lazy. I thought I was going to get into a country where, you know, maybe sometimes in Africa you get lazy and relaxed. They are kind of lazy. But here they are still motivated to do things. And also they are really educated. I thought I was going to come to a country where they didn't really care. You are from Europe, you are stupid, they speak badly to you. But no.' Despite Marcel's protestations that all was gravy, something didn't sit right. He just didn't look like the brash, chin-thrusting central defender that had smothered wave after wave of attacks in the red and black of AC Milan and latterly the blue and white of Chelsea. But then it became clear why. Anywhere else but on the football pitch, things weren't going well. 'My family, they're in France. I had moved from England to France to settle down but then I signed for Qatar and thought about moving everybody here, the kids, wife, nanny. I have a great wife and my last-born is six months old. I wanted to enjoy it and be with him because with my career I really didn't have the time to give to my kids. But my wife saw that I needed to play on. She said: "Go on, we lose one year and we'll gain twenty." People are working until they are 55 years old and I can give up after one year and start a new life.' I wasn't surprised to hear that six months later, Marcel had quit Qatar and gone back home to France. After all, he was here for the same reason that 80 per cent of Qatar's population – mostly labourers from the Indian subcontinent who build the country's stadiums, skyscrapers and hotels – were here: to put hardship away from your family to one side, save your wages and send them back in hope of a better future. Qatar is a transitory place, whether you're a world famous footballer or an Indian taxi driver. I was even more surprised to read that, with Portsmouth struggling to survive in the Premiership, returning manager Harry Redknapp had enquired as to Marcel's availability, in the hope that the Frenchman would plug the gaps in his leaky defence. And Marcel was considering it, albeit briefly. As I left the dinner table and thanked him for his hospitality, I asked about such a scenario: what if a European club came back in for you, as Bolton did when they signed former Real Madrid great Fernando Hierro from the Qatari wilderness. Surely you'd give all this up in a shot? 'No, not at my age. It's finished for me. I realised that I still wanted to play football and that's why I came here. But I would go back to Europe for what? I know everything from Europe. The crowd, the pressure. I did it for 20 years and it's enough. It's enough.' Despite his bluster face-to-face, you can understand why the prospect of playing in the Premiership, even for Portsmouth, still appealed. Perhaps the fire hadn't burnt out after all.

One thing Desailly was worried about was the rumblings over the Arabian Gulf in Iran. The Iranians actually call the stretch of water separating Persia from the Arab Middle East, two empires that badly disguise a certain degree of dislike for each other, the Persian Gulf and wranglings over its name had got to the diplomatic level. Iran threatened to pull out of the 2006 Asian Games in Doha due to the fact that the event's promotional material called it the Arabian Gulf. Regardless of the gulf (ahem) in agreement, the distance between Qatar and Iran is obscenely short and the election of firebrand ex-Tehran mayor Mahmoud Ahmadinejad – an avowed Shiite who proclaimed that, much like George W. Bush, God had guided him to the presidency – had got pulses racing from Yemen to Iraq, not least as one of his first dictates was to restate Iran's right to nuclear power. In Qatar, Ahmadinejad's chest beating was felt more keenly than anywhere else in the Gulf. The country had only existed as an independent entity since 1971. When the British pulled out of the Gulf in that year, Qatar had a decision to make: join the Emirates of Dubai and Abu Dhabi, amongst others, that had made up the tiny Trucial coast in a pan-Gulf Arab union, or go it alone. Qatar chose independence. The bulbous outcrop that juts out into the Gulf, dwarfing nearby Bahrain, wasn't the richest of Arab states as it didn't have the oil reserves of neighbours in the newly formed United Arab Emirates or the economic and military might of Saudi Arabia. But whilst the West allowed Saudi Arabia to degenerate – economically and politically – in a corrupt, oil-funded fog that helped sow the seeds of Islamic militancy and gave birth to Osama Bin Laden and Al Qaeda, Qatar took a far more enlightened route to development.

Since independence the country had been ruled by Emir Khalifa bin Hamad al-Thani, a playboy who didn't rock the boat, kept a tight lid on any dissent and spent most of his time holidaying in Switzerland. It was on one of his jaunts to the Swiss Alps in 1995 that his idealistic eldest son, Hamad bin Khalifa al-Thani, decided that he was tired of waiting for his old man to die and seized control of the country in a bloodless palace coup. Internecine warfare and benevolent dictators aren't unusual in this part of the world but what was surprising was the path that the new Emir decided to take. Shunning his materialistic peers, one of Emir Thani's first moves was to abolish the Ministry of Information – effectively ending censorship in the country. Not content with that, he decided to bankroll Al Jazeera, a new Arab owned television network that wouldn't be hamstrung by the clumsy censoring of its state-owned, Middle Eastern brethren, infuriating his neighbours – and later its allies in the West – with its uncompromising reporting. The money came from Qatar's newly found gas deposits which overnight thrusted them to the top of the world's GDP per capita chart. Even more surprising was his decision to introduce democracy to Qatar – becoming the first Gulf state to grant universal suffrage – and invite the US military to base its entire regional nerve centre on its northern shore. The Qataris had also come across a cunning plan. Rather than pump billions into expensive advertising campaigns, allow sport to promote your country's brand for you. The UAE, and especially Dubai, has been particularly successful in doing this, hosting the world's

most expensive horse race – the Dubai World Cup; a PGA
tour event where Tiger Woods regularly appeared; and the
Dubai Tennis Championship, where Roger Federer turned up
every year to pick up his trophy with depressing regularity.
Thanks in no small part to celebrity sporting endorsements,
Dubai had put itself on the map and, jealously coveting its
success, Qatar decided to follow suit with its own tennis
championship (another glorified Federer inauguration); golf
tournament; and, most importantly of all, its star-packed
football league. It even managed to win the bid for the 2006
Asian Games, the smallest country ever to do so. So proud
were they of their Asian Games achievement that they threw
billions of gas dollars into developing sport in the country,
building the dozen or so brand new, gleaming stadiums that
each Doha-based club now played in, including a scaled-down
replica of Old Trafford. The jewel in the crown was to be
the Aspire academy, which – if the spin was to be believed
– hoped to be the biggest, most comprehensive incubator for
sporting talent in the world, all hosted in the state-of-the-
art, Wembley-esque, 45,000-seater Khalifa Stadium. What the
Qataris hoped to achieve most out of the investment, and
the presence of superstar footballers, was to qualify for the
World Cup. Languishing close to three figures on the FIFA
rankings hit parade and struggling in their qualifying group
for Germany 2006, it was a tall order, but Manfred and the
Qatari FA reasoned that the influx of talented, experienced
foreigners could only improve Qatar's national players in their
push towards the finals. And if that failed they could always
attempt to buy players to play for the national team. After
knocking in a hatful of goals in the *Bundesliga* for Werder
Bremen, Brazilian striker Ailton was approached by the Qatari
FA to take up Qatari citizenship – taking advantage of FIFA's
relaxed rules on nationality – in exchange for a huge bag
of cash. After being inexplicably shunned by the Brazilians,
Ailton was seriously considering it. At 29, he didn't have
many more shots at playing in the World Cup. Even the
national coach, Frenchman Philippe Troussier, was in favour.
'[Naturalisation was] probably the only means to one day

qualify Qatar for a World Cup,' he told French newspaper *L'Equipe*. 'Naturalisations are nothing new to Qatar, 80 per cent of my squad were not born in Qatar.' FIFA, appalled that a rudimentary transfer system akin to club football was developing, stamped down on the practice – much to the embarrassment of the Qataris. Given his expertise in this field, you sensed that if a forensic scientist went through the paperwork, Manfred's fingerprints would be all over it. But the surreal meeting with Marcel in Gharrafa's futuristic stadium had made me wonder about some of the other players who had come out to Qatar. Surely money wasn't the only thing that had persuaded them all to move themselves and their families to within an hour's flight of Baghdad? I decided to phone Manfred and see if he could hook me up with anybody else. 'Yes, yes, I know Gabriel [Batistuta] is in the country, maybe you can call him. But be careful, he hates journalists,' he helpfully obliged before handing out Batistuta's mobile number anyway. 'You should speak to Ronald [De Boer] as well. He's very friendly.'

There's a strange slowness to Qatar that doesn't seem to affect the other Gulf states. Whilst the hyperactive capitalism of Dubai in particular and the UAE in general regularly appear in neo-liberals' wet dreams, and with Bahrain racked with poverty and internal political struggles between the Sunni royal family and its restless Shia majority, life in Qatar is quieter, more spread out and far more relaxed. Certainly that's how Ronald De Boer had found it. 'There are some great golf courses here and I play with Batistuta, Guardiola, Frank LeBoeuf, my brother, every week. It's great fun. You feel safe in the country and there's no pressure. The papers aren't on you every day. And anyway, it's in Arabic, so you can't read what they say!' Ronald chortled into his delicate porcelain cup at his last joke, as if his ignorance of the world's fourth biggest language was a pre-conceived foolproof way of avoiding bad press. With Batistuta's phone off, I'd speculatively called him and was surprised when he had agreed to meet me straight away for a cup of tea in the lobby of the Ritz Carlton hotel. Obviously he was at a loose end. But rather than seem glum, resigned and insular like Marcel did earlier, Ronald had adjusted to the role of the rich, Western expat with too much time on his hands rather easily. 'The life here, I love it. Dubai is nearby and that's like New York. For me if I could get another year and move to Dubai for another two I would love to do it.' Ronald was happily playing for Rangers when the first call from Manfred came and, after agreeing to bring his brother Frank with him, they signed lucrative two-year contracts. The football, he explained, wasn't exactly *La Liga* standard but his team Al Rayyan could give most Scottish teams a run for their money. 'The standard is a little bit higher in Scotland but I don't think any of the lower teams would beat us. I must say, when I look at Rangers now, I think they might struggle against us,' he said. 'I mean, the last game we played to 12,000 people, and then you play some weak teams and only your wife and mother-in-law turn up. But they have some big rivalries like Al Rayyan versus Al Sadd. Sadd is like Ajax and Rayyan more Feyenoord, more with the working-class people, whilst Al Sadd is from the upper-class people. They don't have hooligans, though. They all want to make music.' Clearly, Ronald and Frank were loving their new surroundings, and the proximity of some of the most dangerous countries in the world didn't faze them. But Qatar offered them both something much more than money, although it clearly helped. It was a chance to play without the intense pressure, from the media, from the fans and from their managers that had sullied the most productive years of their careers. 'After all those years of pressure, it makes sense,' he explained, finishing his tea and smoothing down his expensive jeans. 'Of course your level goes down at the end of your career. I've had six operations on my knee and can now only bend it half-way. I couldn't crouch down properly even when I was at Barcelona for the team photograph. Here you get well paid and do what you like, no stress. Of course it's a graveyard of European footballers at the end of their careers. I don't want to make myself crazy with a second ranked team [in Europe]. They expect so much from you because you are their big star and you probably can't do it. But why do that when you can come here and relax?'

With the exception of Steve Claridge and Teddy Sheringham, losing one's motivation for the beautiful game through injury, time, or bitterness is an inevitable part of a footballer's evolutionary cycle – like dating a glamour model or buying a baby Bentley. But as someone who never had the talent to even hold down a regular berth in my primary school's starting XI something still rankled that these talented individuals had chosen not to nobly play for one final shot at meaningful glory but instead had taken the safe option for anonymity and a large pay cheque. Perhaps it was my latent rancour that Gabriel Batistuta had picked up on when I called him later that night from my hotel room. 'Hello Gabriel, Manfred Hoener has given me your number, I'm a journalist ...', I regaled authoritatively, before being cut down. Gabriel couldn't quite hide his anger. 'Manfred Hoener? Gragghh!' With that strangled scream, somewhere between rage and incredulity, Batistuta hung up and turned his phone off, lest I had the temerity to attempt to speak to him again. Later I discovered that he never played in Qatar again. I hoped that my phone call wasn't the straw that broke the camel's back, although by the sound of it things clearly weren't going well for Gabriel in Qatar – Manfred earlier complained that Batistuta had missed numerous league games on trips back to Argentina for treatment on a spurious 'injury'. Even the prospect of his weekly golf treat with Ronald, Frank and the boys wasn't enough to keep him there. Despite the money, privacy and his well-practised snake oil spiel, Manfred Hoener had at least one very unhappy customer.

Television has a horrible habit of fooling the mind's ability to judge distance and size. In *Top Gun*, for instance, Tom Cruise strides around like a six-foot, jet-flying colossus. It's only when you see him in real life, or up against something like a phone box that gives you a hint of relativity, that you realise that he's little taller than a garden gnome. The one person this does not apply to is Diego Armando Maradona. A ten-year-old Qatari boy lay prone on the floor in front of me clutching his ankle in agony with tears in his eyes. Diego's curly mop of hair barely grazed the referee's nipples as he was given a telling off for his reckless and slightly inappropriate tackle. He was every bit the midget you imagined he was from those images of football tournaments in balmy, faraway lands. There are some things as a football fan you resign yourself to never seeing. Bobby Moore effortlessly ushering out an overhit through ball, Puskas tormenting Barcelona's back line, Beckenbauer marauding across the pitch. But watching Maradona play football? In the flesh? In Qatar? Twelve months previously you'd have been pushing a bookmaker to take a bet that Maradona would still be alive by the end of the year. His was the classic – man plays game; man conquers game; man takes Herculean quantities of drugs, shoots journalists and balloons to the size of an ox – footballing story. After being slung out of USA 1994 for failing a drugs test, Maradona went into free-fall, unable to deal with his dwindling talent and no longer able to scratch a living from the game he had been obsessed with since crawling out of a Buenos Aires barrio 25 years previously. He had tried his hand at management in Argentina, business ventures, even endorsements, but nothing sat right. By the turn of the century, Maradona was morbidly obese, snorting lines of cocaine every morning and one more Cuban cigar away from an inevitable coronary. With his heart unable to take the strain of ten extra stone and enough nose candy to kill an elephant, Maradona had two heart attacks. Lying in the hospital and at his lowest ebb, salvation came from an unlikely source: Cuban dictator Fidel Castro. The pair had been friends for years, both sharing a fiery brand of left-wing politics and a mutual loathing for what they saw as American imperialism in South America. Sensing that his old friend was at death's door, Fidel offered to fly Diego to Cuba for a stomach stapling operation. Within weeks the Diego that had resembled a zeppelin had been replaced by a Diego that was svelte, half the size, and once again looking like the tiny wizard that had lit up two World Cups, and disgraced a third. It was the start of a long road to recovery that would see him embrace the world of television, fronting his own hit talk show entitled *The Night Of The Ten*, a reference to his famous number ten shirt, which embraced hard-left politics.

But the apex of his recovery was here, on a football pitch in Qatar, where he was once again kicking a ball, and young children, in anger.

At first I thought the email was a joke: Maradona and Pele, it read, would both be present in Qatar to open a new sports academy. Usually such an honour would be reserved for government ministers, or even minor royalty. But somehow someone, somewhere, had persuaded two of the world's most famous sportsmen to ,come to a quiet, inoffensive country in the Middle East to open a glorified leisure centre. For the first time in months I thought of Manfred. Surely not even Manfred could have pulled this one off, I thought – could he? The Qataris had pulled out all the stops to get them. Both were rumoured to have been paid half a million dollars just to turn up and the region's press would be flown in to witness the pair share a stage, putting their enmity behind them to discuss the footballing issues of the day. I didn't need to be asked twice. But as Qatar's policy of pumping huge sums into sport seemed to be continuing as normal, the country had changed since my last visit ten months previously. Six weeks after I'd left Manfred, Desailly and the De Boer brothers, Omar Ahmed Abdullah – a seemingly normal, friendly Egyptian computer programmer – packed his 4x4 with explosives and rammed into the Doha Players Theatre. Qatar's first suicide bombing killed one person and injured scores more. When viewed against the daily three-figure casualty numbers from Iraq, a single death in Qatar seemed tragically insignificant. But it had a far more damaging effect on Qatar's psyche. It shattered the idyllic complacency that had allowed life to go on as normal as the states around it degenerated into an internecine anarchy. Returning back to Doha International, it was clear that Qatar had lost something of its innocence. Every hotel now had metal detectors at its front door and huge concrete barriers had been universally erected to prevent suicide bombers from approaching by car. The government had been particularly worried that the bombing would jeopardise its huge investment in sporting set pieces, not least its hosting of the 2006 Asian Games, and had responded with police state measures to ensure that the bombing wasn't repeated. All this didn't seem to bother Maradona much as he careered around the Aspire training pitch, looking ten years younger than his forty-one, slide tackling boys a quarter of his age and still getting aerated enough to argue with the referee even though it was a kick around with kids. It was a Damascene recovery. Sure, some of his pace was gone, but that unmistakable, blurry-legged, barrel-chested gait was still there. He even had time to instinctively punch the ball into the net, much to the whooping delight of the English journalists assembled. I doubt they gave him the same honour when God intervened to score in the same manner against England in Mexico 20 years previously. Just as Fenwick and Butcher did back in 1986, the Qatari children looked on incredulously. Yet Maradona's impish charm beguiled all who encountered him — presidents, statesmen, royalty, even English journalists — which was never more evident than when, sweating from the 20-minute-long exertion, he decided to sign some autographs. The circle around him grew as Arab men in flowing white dish dashas and the previously restrained press corps literally threw children out of their path to get to their hero, to touch him, to feel his sweat on their hands. Eventually security guards had to intervene and hauled Maradona out of the ruck, beaming with the knowledge that — whatever FIFA thought — he was still number one. This issue had preoccupied him for some time. When FIFA offered the public the chance to vote for their player of the century, Maradona won hands down. But FIFA, fearing Maradona's exalted position would set a bad example to the kids, chose to give the award to Pele as well. Maradona was furious, debate raged from Sao Paulo to Manila and the two men's already strained relationship was all but destroyed. To say Maradona had a chip on his shoulder about it is like saying George W. Bush is indifferent to Al Qaeda. It consumed him and, if anything, has given him the impetus to turn his life around and to claim the legacy he sees as rightfully his.

'Who is the greatest? My mother says it's me. And you should always believe your mother.' The crowd of a dozen or so journalists ignited into spontaneous, sycophantic laughter. Maradona, now wearing a casual shirt and jeans, sat in front of us, slumped in a chair the same way a wayward schoolboy would confrontationally sit in the headmaster's office after he'd set fire to a classroom. He smiled at his ability to make a room of educated middle-aged men fawn at his feet and nonchalantly answered questions about football, drugs and his former life as a very fat man. Maradona was articulate in a rough, uncomplicated kind of way. After years of being barracked by the press, you would have thought that he would come across as guarded, even reticent. But he was the exact opposite, sitting for an hour talking about everything from Argentina's chances in the World Cup to how, despite all the money in the game, he would still choose to play for Napoli if he was 21 today. His most interesting moments came when he talked politics, openly criticising George W. Bush for the war in Iraq. '[Hugo] Chavez, Fidel [Castro] and Che Guevara they fought for their people, to give them more equality [and] they fought against the United States and anyone who fights against the US is good for me,' he said when asked about the influence of his friend Fidel. Maradona famously has a tattoo of Che on his shoulder, but few would have thought that it signified anything other than a pretty adornment rather than a deep affinity with left-wing politics. 'I was at the summit in Argentina two weeks ago and I know Bush commanded the war from Qatar. But I support Qatar and an assassin is an assassin anywhere. Every country has the freedom to make its own laws and make a decision and you must respect that. So even if he leaves Qatar, an assassin can kill from everywhere.' The summit he was referring to was the Summit of the Americas. Maradona had just been involved in his first act of political agitation. After securing a five-hour interview with Fidel on his talk show, Maradona decided that he was done talking, wanted to get active and decided to organise an anti-Bush protest. Bush was in town to thrash out free-trade agreements with governments increasingly turning leftwards and wary of the economic liberalism that their forebears had subscribed to in the 1990s. 'No to Bush!' Maradona declared to the local press after the Fidel interview. 'Fellow Argentines, we will be waiting for you at the march.' Thousands turned up for the march in Mar Del Plata and saw Maradona take to the stage wearing a 'Stop Bush' T-shirt and embracing current US pariah Venezuelan president Hugo Chavez in front of rapturous crowds. The entire event was dogged by protests, disrupted by arguments and sunk by political indifference. Bush left Argentina empty handed. It occurred to me that someone like Maradona would walk an election in Argentina. His talk show was the most watched on Argentine television, he's mobbed wherever he goes, can count on the vote of the politician-fatigued poor and can lean on some of the continent's political heavyweights for support. Imagine if a candidate emerged in British or American politics that had the same attributes – a universal popular touch, a clean slate (after all, his dirty linen had already been washed in public) and 100 per cent name recognition. It would be a cakewalk. Maybe, I asked, one day he'd consider running for office? Diego paused, the first time he had done so since entering the room. He began cautiously. 'You are . . . taking . . . from the pockets of the people,' he responded slowly before warming to his theme. 'It's like using the charm of those goals I scored against England just to get some votes from the people. I couldn't take advantage of that for a vote.' By the end he was smiling, without actually categorically denying anything. As was once famously said of Eisenhower's half-hearted denials that he would run for the White House, he slammed the door wide open. Clearly he had learned much from Fidel and Hugo. It was the perfect politician's answer.

Pele, on the other hand, had a strangely more subdued reception. He arrived at the training pitch where Maradona had previously wowed hundreds of onlookers with his newfound fitness in an electrically powered golf cart and wearing a blue 1970s safari suit that he'd obviously kept from his New York Cosmos days. We've got so used to seeing the replays of his magnificent career that you can forget that Brazil's greatest player is now a pensioner. He gingerly disembarked and wandered aimlessly around the pitch. He was too far gone to kick a ball, so small crowds of middle-aged men politely queued for his autograph. Compared to the histrionics of the previous day, you'd have thought that the Qataris had wheeled out a minor character in world football, but Pele has become strangely accustomed to indifference in recent years. Despite leading an exemplary life on and off the pitch as a clean cut, family-loving ambassador for the game – and a flawless example to generations of footballing hopefuls – even his countrymen hadn't been totally convinced by him. In Brazil he was mocked for not being very bright, lambasted for a disastrous but well-meaning tenure as Brazilian sports minister and derided for signing up to be the face of Brazilian Viagra. He quickly withdrew his support when the press began to question his virility. It probably wasn't the best move in a country gripped by machismo. Yet Maradona's failings are all but forgotten. Maybe it's because a flawed genius is someone who can be more easily empathised with. He's one of us, really. Or maybe it's because a flawed genius still leaves room for speculation. If he'd played like that half-cut, imagine what he'd have been like sober? For a true, unadulterated genius like Pele, it must be infuriating, although you wouldn't know that from the warm smiles that greeted the half-empty press conference. No one seemed that bothered and, besides, the Q&A session was cut short after fifteen minutes as the Emir had demanded luncheon with his two temporary charges. And no one can say no to the Emir. As Pele rose and walked to the exit, a journalist from the *Daily Mirror* dived at the Brazilian's feet. It was a fascinating sight, watching a British hack at work. He'd managed to put his arm around Pele's neck in such a way that he was unable to escape and his security couldn't prise the *Mirror* man off. I guess the 'Pele neck lock' is something you learn in your first week. He clung on for dear life, just long enough for his photographer to get a snap of the happy moment, to prove to the *Mirror*'s avid readers that the two had been friends all their lives: Pele grinning crazily, the hack smiling as if hugging his best man. When security had managed to lever him off, Pele's handler, puce with rage, admonished the *Mirror* man for disrespecting Pele. In the distance, Pele was disappearing down a corridor, still smiling and waving to no one in particular. You sensed that, after a weekend in Maradona's shadow, Pele was simply glad for some attention. Any attention.

The lights dimmed and the crowd were in their seats waiting

for the main event. In the main hall of Qatar's Aspire stadium, the local dignitaries in their white dish dashas chattered in animated Arabic at the front whilst journalists and photographers crowded around the hastily erected stage. Qatar's policy of sporting investment was about to reach its apex. First, Pele modestly sauntered in. Polite applause followed. Then Maradona entered. Perhaps it's the rabid welcoming from the crowd, or the fact that the spotlight sparkled off his white suit jacket adorned with bright silver thread, but the moment feels less like a meeting of two equals, and more like Diego's coronation. And then the two shook hands. A thousand flashes followed, capturing the moment when Pele and Diego buried the hatchet. Except this wasn't the moment they really buried the hatchet. Pele had been Maradona's first guest on his talk show debut earlier that year. There wasn't even any real warmth in their reconciliation but the Pele and Maradona show had become big business and useful for both men: a vehicle for Maradona's rehabilitation and an opportunity for Pele to counter his detractors whilst both were handsomely rewarded for their time. Maradona admitted as much when the discussion started – a supposedly adversarial 'debate' on sportsmanship. Presumably the Qataris had hoped that Pele would represent the fair-minded professional, with Maradona taking the role of the Machiavellian magician, willing to bend the rules and invoke God to get the right result. 'We just never clicked,' admitted Maradona, glancing over at Pele. 'We always rubbed each other up the wrong way. We would see each other and sparks would fly.' And he didn't stop there, kicking out against the press that hounded him and the football authorities that doubted him. 'I was addicted . . . drugging myself. Then I would play football without sleeping, eating or even drinking water,' he said, getting increasingly irate. 'The media really only emphasised my drug addiction – they wanted a drugs story. All they wanted to do was publicise drugs. They wanted to kill Maradona and I make no apologies for my behaviour to the press.' His behaviour related to the time he tried to shoot a couple of Argentinian journalists, who had been stationed outside his house. But then Maradona exceeded himself, comparing himself to the one person less popular than George W. Bush amongst the crowd. 'To defend my family I will become Bin Laden. And if that's what it takes I'll become the fiercest human being on the planet.' Everyone took an intake of breath, Maradona looked at Pele and they both laughed. The rest of the crowd laughed with them. The debate finished and, sensing that Qatar was unlikely to see the two greatest footballers of the 20th century ever again, the crowd rushed the stage. I followed but the crush took me to the right, where Maradona was standing. To the left, Pele stood on his own. The crowd clambered onto the stage and surrounded Diego, desperate for one last signature. A Qatari man with a walkie-talkie manfully tried to hold back the hordes, screaming for the crowd to get back. The stage was buckling under the collective weight of the scrum but all I could see in the melee was the top of Diego's unkempt hair, buried in a sea of adoring fans. Unable to move, I looked over to Pele. He was being ushered away. Not for the first time in Pele's life, not even for the first time in Qatar, Maradona had stolen the show.

It's not clear what Qatar gained from this set piece. Some journalists wrote stories of the strangeness of it all, others used it to make tenuous comparisons between Diego and Wayne Rooney, whilst the guy from the *Mirror* used the event as a Trojan horse to break a much larger story which appeared that weekend and made headlines across the world: that a memo had emerged where George W. Bush had allegedly contemplated bombing Qatar's meddlesome Al Jazeera television network to stop the bad news stories that had emerged out of Iraq. Whatever the benefit, it appeared slight and even the most enthusiastic of backers were now questioning whether Qatar's huge investment was a wise one. On my last day in Qatar, out on the training pitch, I spotted a familiar figure. A tall, silver-haired bear of a man. It was Manfred. Immediately he strode towards me and shook my hand, almost severing it at the wrist, whilst affectionately beating me on my back. 'Hello Manfred, I take it this is all your work then?' I asked, surveying the scene of journalists, PRs and world famous footballers. 'What, this? No, I've given that all up now. It wasn't working out.' As if on cue, one of Manfred's last signings ambled past, ex-Derby and West Ham striker Paolo Wanchope. As good a player as Paolo was, he was no Desailly. Manfred had suffered from the law of diminishing returns. Each month it had been harder and harder to attract the big names. The old guard of Desailly, LeBoeuf and Batistuta were gone and whilst World Cup winners could once be persuaded to come, now only mid-table journeymen like Wanchope and Jay Jay Okocha could be talked into the moneyed pilgrimage east. The Qatari government had even begun to lose patience. The whole point of the exercise was to raise the level of the league and its indigenous players so that Qatar might qualify for the World Cup for the first time in its history. That dream, for Germany 2006, was over long before when the national team succumbed meekly to Iran in Doha. To make matters worse, Qatar had now slid from 61st to 89th on the FIFA rankings between 2004 and 2006. The Asian Games, too, were an unfortunate failure after being washed out by unseasonable torrential rain and a series of bizarre incidents. To start with, the authorities had incorrectly calculated the number of beds needed for visiting athletes by at least 3,000 – leading to the unedifying sight of three cruise ships having to be towed in to make up the numbers. And arguably one of the strangest incidents in international sport occurred when Indian 800-metre runner Santhi Soundarajan was stripped of her silver medal, not for failing a drugs test, but for failing a gender test. Worse, the games were marred by the deaths of seven spectators and a sportsman due to the conditions. A South Korean equestrian rider, Kim Hyung-Chil, was killed after his horse slipped on the mud and fell, crushing him to death. 'The Death Games', as one local paper referred to them, had been a publicity disaster and Qatar's expensive experiment in footballing immigration and sporting PR had failed. I felt sorry for Qatar. Like a teenager who had unexpectedly won the lottery, Qatar had spent big on expensive, flashy accessories but to little reward. It was a shame because, as a young country, some of its other, more enlightened investments had paid off – like a fledgling democracy and its free media. As the veteran BBC journalist Tim Sebastian pointed out, when asked why he had moved to Doha to host a regular televised debate: 'Qatar is building institutions. Places like Dubai are building malls.' But that was cold comfort for the Emir when you compared the name recognition of Qatar's glitzy neighbour, which had neither democracy nor a free media. Seeing the writing on the wall, Manfred left the Q League and the FA before he was pushed. 'So what are you doing here then, Manfred?' I asked, confused. He pointed over towards two nervous-looking Indian men, one holding a sound boom and wearing headphones, the other with a large camera strapped to his shoulder. It was his film crew. 'I'm in television now, a football talk show. I talk, they listen. Ha!' I took it as an indelible sign of Qatar's sporting failure. When Manfred Hoener decided to jump ship, you really had to start worrying.

TWO

Iran

Outside Tehran's hulking, grey Azadi national football stadium a riot was fermenting. A mob, 70 strong, with whistles, drums and banners, pushed on the crush barriers and screamed slogans in strangulated *Farsi*. I hadn't expected my first taste of Iran to involve a loud and angry protest. Iran, we are led to believe, isn't a place where dissent is tolerated unless it's the power to 'dissent' against Western cultural imperialism, burn hastily constructed effigies of George W. Bush or protest vigorously in favour of the Iranian government's right to enrich nuclear fuel. Equally, I hadn't expected my first taste of Iran to involve a loud and angry protest exclusively made up of abaya-clad women, faces painted the colour of the Iranian flag and one and all clutching a national football team scarf. They berated the hundred or so riot officers who had constructed a Kevlar wall between themselves and the stadium, as dozens of men – only men – streamed past unmolested towards the stadium's huge gates and that afternoon's main event: a World Cup warm-up match between Iran and Costa Rica. No one looked surprised and no one looked back. The riot police looked on perplexed. You could almost see the dilemma etched into their faces: at riot police school they were taught how to deal with enemies of the state – wade in first and ask questions later. Instead they were frozen, stuck between a conservative culture where women were revered and protected from the wicked mores of the modern world and the demands of the state to crack some skull. Paralysis broke out. They looked impotently on as the women's angry cries broke on their body armour. Inside the car, our driver interrupted the silence. 'Not the women again,' he rasped as we slalomed past the protest and through the crowd. 'Again?' I asked, surprised. 'This is normal?' 'They come here before every game to protest in their scarves,' sighed Amir, my guide, of the familiar sight. I wanted to go and speak to them, ask them about their protest, but the doors were locked. Amir didn't think it was a good idea to try and talk to the women with police around. 'It's dangerous,' he said. I pulled the handle anyway. The doors stayed firmly shut as we glided past. 'It's not a religion thing why they can't come to a football match,' Amir hastily tried to explain, sensing my disappointment. 'They can go to a cinema with a man. But it's the atmosphere in the ground: the swearing, the bad language. It's just not suitable.'

Three hours before every home game the female fans of Team Melli – as the Iranian national football team is affectionately known – trudge to the Azadi Stadium in the western suburbs of Tehran. And every game they are denied entry and trudge back to whence they came, past a huge motivational sign that mockingly adorns the entrance. It reads:

> The Most Powerful Person is That That Can Keep Their Hunger

It's a hopeless, unrewarding task. But the protests – along with my arrival at Sharjah Airport in the United Arab Emirates – gave me a glimpse that everything in Iran wasn't what it seemed. British passport holders, and British journalists in particular, were persona non grata for the regime in Tehran and a few days before my flight I was denied a visa. After my time in Qatar, Iran was the next obvious destination to head for. The 2006 World Cup was but a few months away and Iran had assembled arguably the best team in its history.

For only the second time, a team in the region had a good chance of actually making the second round. But first I had to get in, which is where Amir came in. Amir was an Iranian who worked for the airline but seemed to have connections in the upper reaches of pretty much every Iranian institution: the Iranian FA, the police, even, it seemed, Iranian airport immigration. 'Don't worry, get on the flight and we'll sort out your visa at the other end,' he assured me confidently over the phone. 'Don't worry,' he repeated, sensing my fear of being stranded in an unfamiliar, unfriendly country. 'My father used to be a minister in the government.' I wasn't convinced.

We met the next day at the check-in desk. Amir was young, in his mid-20s, and handsome, a useful tool when flirting with the check-in girls when you have a long, suspicious-looking package to put in the hold. A few sweet words in *Farsi* and it was in. I looked at him suspiciously. 'Oh, it's a bumper for my BMW,' he replied nonchalantly. 'I went a little too fast in the snow and hit a kerb. It's cheaper if I buy it here.' Even in an Islamic theocracy, it seems, the appetite for luxury cars can't be suppressed. As we flew the short journey from the UAE to Iran, Amir took it upon himself to put the record straight on a few things. The West, he thought, had the wrong idea about Iran and it was his responsibility, nay, his duty as a proud Iranian to make sure I had the correct version of events. 'I'm not anti-Jewish, I'm anti-Zionist, which is what he [President Mahmoud Ahmadinejad] was trying to say,' he explained cheerily when we discussed the Iranian president's recent calls for Israel to be pushed into the sea and his desire for a debate on whether or not the Holocaust actually happened. I had the feeling that Amir had had to account for the president's behaviour to foreign friends on more than one occasion since his accidental election eight months previously. Sure, he won the election but not without a little help from Iran's Guardian Council. The body of unelected, hard-line clerics – led by Iran's spiritual leader Ayatollah Khamenei – sits atop the Iranian political system like a brooding, mute ape. They have the power to veto everything from legislation to presidential candidates, which they did during the 2005 presidential election, barring dozens of reformist candidates from standing. The liberals shunned the poll in protest and Mahmoud Ahmadinejad, the ultra-conservative former mayor of Tehran, was voted in on a low turnout. The gentle-looking, lounge-suit-wearing President quickly made a name for himself in the West thanks to his anti-Israel pronouncements and his quest for nuclear power. Now Amir and the rest of the population were waiting for some Israeli retribution. 'If they [Israel] try to bomb us,' he said forebodingly whilst fiddling with the straw in his coke can, 'it will be the spark that lit a room full of gas. It will explode. I truly believe that it would be the end of the world.'

Few in the West knew of Ahmadinejad's existence before his shock election. The Americans initially accused him (falsely) of being the mastermind behind the 1979 American Embassy siege. Several of the American hostages still maintain he was present. What we do know is that his only earthly possession is a 1976 Peugeot, he has some dodgy views on the Holocaust and he doesn't wear ties, which, like the George Michael songs he banned from the nation's airwaves, he sees as a tool of Western cultural imperialism. His one weakness, which seems to be a blind spot in his distaste for western cultural exports, is football. The Iranian love of football is so pronounced that even the theocrats couldn't control it. Instead, Ahmadinejad sought to use it for his own means. Iran had qualified strongly for the World Cup and were preparing for the biggest tournament in their sporting history. But the preparations weren't going well. I had come to Iran to watch one of their final home warm-up games: a mid-afternoon clash with fellow qualifiers Costa Rica. It was one of the few times a non-Asian team had made the trip to Tehran. It was supposed to be Ukraine but they pulled out, citing the spurious excuse that Iran was too good for a friendly. Amir was livid. 'They said we should go to Ukraine, but why? There really is no problem here,' he spat as the plane began its descent. All around, women stood and fixed on their headscarves, covering the long dark hair that had been tolerated in the UAE but would be tolerated no longer.

Unsurprisingly, Tehran hadn't been a favoured destination

for international friendlies and after failing to entice Italy, Germany and England to the world's largest pariah state, they plumped for Costa Rica to work out arguably the greatest crop of players the country had ever seen: Ali Karimi – Iran's cultured midfielder – had become the latest Iranian player to sign for a *Bundesliga* club after inking a contract with Bayern Munich whilst Ali Daei, their 38-year-old centre-forward, held the world's international goal-scoring record. The team's popularity and imminent appearance on the world's biggest stage hadn't escaped Ahmadinejad. After landing at Imam Khomeini airport I picked up a copy of Tehran's English-language newspaper. On the front page was a picture of Ahmadinejad, meeting the players before training. Initially it looked like your standard statesman-meets-the-team picture. But closer inspection revealed a telling difference. The squad, including the talismanic Daei, was rapt, sitting legs crossed and intently soaking up the president's motivational words. It looked less like a meeting of adults and more like a gaggle of subservient boarding-school children following a particularly taxing nursery rhyme. 'Excuse me, can you step forward?' My concentration was broken by a border guard politely ushering me towards passport control. As Amir pontificated with the man holding the stamp, I waited. I sensed his colleague eyeing me up and down before he leant forward. Looking down, I feared the worse – handcuffs; a fist; an open palm demanding to be filled with a bribe? Instead, I saw a polystyrene plate full of meat and rice. 'You want?' he offered with a smile on his face. Not wanting to appear rude, I agreed, grabbed a fork and gobbled a mouth full of the gristly mess, forcing a smile. Lamb and gravy with sultanas – it was surprisingly good. His colleague cheerily stamped my passport whilst a glass of cold water was pushed in front of me, which I gulped before being genially waved off. Confronted by arguably the most hostile border police in the world, I was offered dinner, pleasantries and a drink. No, Iran wasn't supposed to be like this.

Even the most fervently nationalistic Iranian would admit that Tehran looks like a failed Soviet-era experiment in communal living. As our battered Paykan taxi veered around other battered Paykans towards Tehran city proper, you're hit by monochrome blandness: rows and rows of stumpy, identikit, grey concrete tower blocks. The bleak urban cityscape is only broken by the huge, colourful murals that cover the sides of whole tower blocks, eulogising the martyrs from the Iran-Iraq war – images of young, handsome soldiers standing in wheat fields, handing poppies to carefree, patriotic children. But like trying to hang an Ikea copy of a Rothko in a squat, it's a futile attempt at self-improvement. Yet there are nods to the Persian empire's glorious past: a complex network of channels – full of melting snow water from the nearby Alborz Mountains – laces the city, an ancient anti-flood mechanism invented when the tribes of Western Europe were still working out how to stop their mud huts from collapsing in the rain. Iran's modern-day attempt at creating a working network has been less successful. Tehran's roads are some of the most dangerous in the world and are constantly jammed by state-made Paykans and Sepands, flagrant copies of hardy European models like the Hillman Hunter and the Renault 5. Traffic accidents were so frequent that Tehran's drivers had given up caring about the dinks and scratches and thought nothing of bumping or scraping you accidentally before driving off without a second thought. Rush hour can resemble a ride on the dodgems. Whilst Tehran lacks the aesthetics of Shiraz, or the cultural riches of Isfahan, the capital is at the centre of every political and social fad, its delayed ripples inevitably reaching its vast borders. It's Iran's beating heart and a microcosm of a huge country that holds 69 million ethically divergent people, stretches from Afghanistan to Turkey and has the world's oldest continuously existing borders. The north of the city is dominated by the rich, middle-class intelligentsia who hate Ahmadinejad with a passion. The south is Ahmadinejad territory; deeply devout and poor, this was the electorate that carried their devout Shia candidate to the presidency. The physical division between reformists and traditionalists that bisects Tehran has shaped modern Iranian society. But it wasn't until a little-heard-of liberal cleric called Mohammad Khatami snuck past the Guardian Council censors and won a landslide election in 1997 that the reformist movement really had a voice. Preaching moderation, economic liberalisation and greater individual freedom for its people, Khatami rose to office on a tidal wave of optimism from Iran's young population. In fact, it has the youngest population in the world: nearly 70 per cent are under the age of 30. The theocrats in the Guardian Council – never for a moment thinking that such a man was electable – were red-faced. The powers that kept the spirit of the Islamic revolution alive vowed never to allow such a mistake to happen again, and subsequently at every turn, Khatami was met with obstruction and hurdles, while his innate caution in rocking the boat saw the conservatives take control again. In the end his government was so paralysed by inaction and bureaucracy, and the people so weary of big promises that were never met, that his popularity collapsed, laying the foundations for Ahmadinejad's red-letter day. It's no surprise then, given this schism and the political sensitivity that his post has, that Branko Ivankovic – Iran's coach – chose to live neither north nor south but in the centre of Tehran. He had made Iran his home since being appointed in 2001 after Iran's failure to make the finals in South Korea and Japan. After being an assistant coach for Croatia during their World Cup bow in 1998, and taking them to the semi-finals, Branko had a strong reputation and was quickly snapped up on a five-year contract. He had fulfilled his obligation, qualifying with a game to spare after drawing against Japan in front of 100,000 fans at the Azadi – officially the highest attendance of any World Cup qualifier although most fans suspect as many as 120,000 were crammed inside – and was now one of the most popular men in the country. Dressed in a preppy outfit of jumper, shirt and slacks and sporting expensive glasses, 51-year-old Branko looked more like a university don than a national coach and seemed much younger than his age betrayed, remarkable given the pressure and that the average life expectancy of a coach in Asia is shorter than that of a fruit fly. 'With my job, you don't know what's going to happen the next morning, especially in the Middle East,' he grinned as we sat down in the lobby of his plush hotel apartment. 'In the World Cup in France, after just three games, Brazilian coach Carlos

Alberto Parreira was sacked by Saudi Arabia. This is the destiny of our job and we can't make plans for our future. Sometimes one centimetre is all that matters. The ball might go one centimetre left, go out and I'm terrible, but it goes one centimetre right into the goal I am a hero. Just one centimetre defines my destiny.' Branko's objective, qualification for Germany 2006, had been made easier by the footballing riches that had been bestowed on him. Iran was experiencing something of a golden generation in footballing terms and a number of their key players had already been acclimatised to playing in Germany for a number of *Bundesliga* clubs – Karimi as Michael Ballack's understudy at Bayern Munich; Mahdavikia at Hamburg; Hashemian at Hannover 96; and Zandi at Kaiserslautern. 'We can beat any side in the world,' Branko declared confidently when I asked about his team's chances. But once the final whistle went against Japan, Branko's job became a little harder. With Ahmadinejad making trouble at the UN, foreign FAs stopped taking the Iranian FA's calls. Friendlies were called off and a tour of England's championship clubs, held in the aftermath of the 7 July bombings, was cancelled half-way through. It wasn't, given the political climate in England, deemed appropriate that Iran continued. As Ahmadinejad's rhetoric grew, so did the possible sanctions. Western politicians started calling for Iran to be thrown out of the World Cup. German and Israeli lawmakers tabled motions in their respective parliaments, calling for a ban after Ahmadinejad, in one of his fiery speeches, called for Israel to be 'wiped off the map'. There was also the issue of Iran's continuing uranium enrichment programme. Throwing Iran out of the World Cup, reasoned British Conservative party politician Michael Ancram, '. . . would give a very, very clear signal to Iran that the international community will not accept what they are doing'. Even the friendly against Costa Rica had attracted media attention, taking place as it did on the eve of a crucial International Atomic Energy Agency report on Iran's nuclear programme. If Iran was deemed to have shown sufficient doubt that its programme was anything but peaceful, it would set Iran on the road towards sanctions, further isolation and possibly war. Branko, like Ahmadinejad, wasn't too concerned.

'One of the very important rules of football is that politics is one side and sport is the other side so I'm sure we will go to the World Cup.' Branko may have rejected the link between sport and politics in Iran, but few politicians in Tehran, Washington or London saw the difference, not least Ahmadinejad, whose visit to the squad was loaded with 'us versus them' symbolism. The national team provided an opportunity for Iran to be seen as equals on the international stage and to prove that, despite the privations and isolation of the past 25 years, the country was strong. The 11 men on the pitch represented what Iran really was, not the fiction peddled by the West's media lies. This nationalism held common currency in Iran. Ahmadinejad may not be liked by all in Iran, but he had tapped into a strong emotion that resonates with all Iranians, one which he saw embodied in the national team – resilience, independence and national, if not political, pride. Branko was just happy to be taking care of footballing matters, even if his meeting with one of the world's most reviled politicians gave him a somewhat dubious honour: he became one of the few westerners to warmly shake the hand of the Iranian President. 'He's a big supporter of the team,' Branko explained, proud of the memory. 'He told us that football is very important to the country, especially at the moment because the image of Iran is not too good. He expects the players to do their best but that this is sport and everything can happen. He's happy with the players and that we won't have any problems going anywhere in the world.'

The inside of the Azadi Stadium is dominated by two, equal-sized portraits hoisted high up on the west stand. One shows Iran's future, the other its past. To the left was Imam Khomeini, the ayatollah who shattered Western complacency towards Iran when he assumed control after the 1979 revolution and irrevocably changed the way his country would be viewed by the rest of the world. To the right, Ayatollah Khamenei, his replacement at the apex of Iran's spiritual hierarchy and perhaps the only man who can control Ahmadinejad and either steer his country through the current choppy waters or lead it into oblivion. The stadium was a third full with 40,000 spectators, a remarkable number given that the match was being played mid-afternoon on a Wednesday. After driving past the doomed female protests we parked and entered through large metal doors into the east stand. 'Here, you'll need this.' Amir thrust a bib and a pass into my hand, a hastily constructed piece of laminated plastic with a black-and-white photograph cribbed from my passport. It read: 'Photographer.' Amir shrugged apologetically. 'At short notice, it was the best I could do.' I had never been pitch side for a football match before, unless you count being an unused substitute in a Sunday league match. Making the most of my chance brush with privilege, and using my old-fashioned camera to try and achieve a modicum of professionalism, I walked around the pitch taking pictures of nothing in particular. The crowd opposite the murals of the two ayatollahs banged on drums and chanted the name of Imam Hussein, whose contested status as the true heir to the Prophet Mohammed's legacy is at the root of the region's Shia-Sunni schism. Placards were waved in a language I didn't understand. One, on brightly coloured paper, had been written in English and was cheerily waved by two smiling teenagers. It read: 'Don't With the US.' Just before the match started, a television crew approached. 'Can we speak to you, on camera?' the excitable presenter asked. I couldn't work out why the opinion of a fake photographer would mean anything to anyone. He filled me in. 'We don't see many Westerners here. It's on satellite, please?' I had my misgivings. Television did me no favours. My only appearance, other than a shambolic attempt at the now defunct quiz show 15–1 where I technically came last, was as a pundit on ART's English Premiership show, a Dubai-based *Match of the Day*-style programme that went out to the Middle East and North Africa – a potential viewership of 400 million people. I was pontificating on the merits of Tottenham's game with Portsmouth whilst various fans from Lagos, Abidjan and Abu Dhabi sent in abusive text messages – 'Do you not have any make up in your studio?'; 'He looks like a ghost!'; 'Why have you let this loser on your show!' I gamely rode the hits and felt satisfied that my analysis of the 1–1 draw had risen above the boo-boy taunts. It was only when I looked back at the show on repeat that I realised I had swivelled on my chair so excessively I looked epileptic whilst my constant nervous blinking came across as coquettish flirting with the gruff Geordie presenter. I wasn't asked back. But, seeing that no one was likely to see it, and in the interest of Anglo-Iranian peace, I agreed. 'How are you liking Iran?' Easy. 'It's very nice and the people are very friendly.' 'Why does George Bush want to invade us?' Ahh. 'Well, erm, I'm not sure . . .' Flummoxed, I couldn't find an answer. Why did George W. Bush want to invade? I wasn't sure that he did, although the press had speculated that the White House had been putting together contingency plans for an attack. Sensing that the dead air time of me lost in thought didn't make good television, the presenter changed tack. 'How do you rate Iran's chances in the World Cup?' This was slightly easier to answer. The Iranians had pulled a hard group – Portugal, Mexico and Angola – but if they beat Angola and drew against Mexico, I offered, they might finish second. The presenter beamed, thanked me and walked off. It was what he wanted to hear, a Westerner giving his team the stamp of approval. The interview, though, had only sparked off the curiosity of other television crews, who rushed over just to make sure their rival hadn't scooped them. By the time the two teams came on the pitch for the national anthems, I was on my fourth interview, and had become an expert on Iranian football, firing off clichés and platitudes that would have made John Motson weep with pride: 'Of course, it all depends on the form of Ali Karimi'; 'If Branko can keep his team injury free, they have a great chance'; 'You know there are no easy games in international football any more, Mohammed, but . . .'

Iran were sublime. Within ten minutes they were ahead thanks to the best player on the pitch. Ali Karimi scored with a deft shot across the keeper from the outside of his left boot, and set up the next two, including Ali Daei's 109th international goal. The team tore their Central American rivals apart, who were just four places below them in the FIFA rankings, with Ali Karimi pulling the strings. You could see why the former Asian Player of the Year, dubbed the Asian Maradona, had been snapped up by Bayern Munich. They had a perfectly good fourth goal disallowed before Costa Rica scored against the run of play. Half-time arrived and the Costa Ricans couldn't get off the pitch quick enough. The Iranian media were ecstatic and jumped towards me, one by one, pointing at the empty pitch as if it were proof of Iran's inevitable World Cup success. Arash, a young French-Iranian journalist who lived in Tehran and wrote for *L'Equipe*, was a little more circumspect. 'Yes, it was a good half. But they have a small squad. Any injuries and we would really be in trouble.' Arash had lived in Tehran for the best part of a year, taking advantage of his dual citizenship to file stories from a country where western journalists weren't particularly liked. 'I still need a permit,' he replied. 'But it helps that I write stories for France. They couldn't be published here.' The news had been full of pictures in the weeks before my trip showing the Iranian government's opinions on Western ideals of freedom of speech. The caricatures of the Prophet Mohammed in the Danish paper *Jyllands-Posten* – an act that is haram (prohibited under Islam) – had sparked violent protest in the Iranian capital. The Danish embassy was attacked and burning barricades were erected. Television pictures bounced around the globe entrenching the view that all Iranians were theocratic maniacs. 'Oh no, that [the rioters] was the Basiji, everyone hates them,' Arash explained. The Basiji, he went on, were a government-funded religious militia who were set up during the Iran-Iraq war. It was a favourite regiment of the ayatollah, and renowned for being made up of devout Shia willing to do anything for the ecclesiastical cause. Some would even volunteer to walk through minefields to clear them. The ayatollah had promised them a quicker route to paradise for their sacrifice. With the Iran-Iraq war a fading memory, and Khatami's reformist revolution in the ascendancy in the late 1990s, the Basiji had impotently tried to reinvent itself as a moral guardian of the theocratic revolution on the street, harassing women for not covering up enough or for holding hands with men in public. Tehran's young population saw them as a joke. But with the rise of Ahmadinejad, their usefulness as a highly visible example of Iranian indignation at Western arrogance was recognised, and their power was on the rise. 'They are the people you see on television,' said Arash as the second half got underway. 'They are not normal Iranians.' Arash's pessimism proved correct. Ali Karimi had picked up a knock and was taken off at half-time, whilst Daei and the *Bundesliga* contingent were rested as a precautionary measure. Branko patrolled his dugout studiously throughout, his bald assistant shouting his instructions to the pitch in *Farsi*. The crowd chanted his name: 'Branko, Branko, Branko.' The most popular foreigner in Iran smiled and waved back. With a weakened team, Costa Rica fought back strongly, and could have grabbed a draw. In the end it finished 3–2. As Arash and I filed out of the stadium we talked about football's importance in Iranian society. Much like Catholicism in 1970s Poland, football was one area of Iranian life that even the ayatollah couldn't interfere with, although he did try. The league was suspended in the wake of the revolution, but the clubs quickly set up their own city leagues, albeit purged of pro-Western and pro-Shah sympathisers. Iran had just flown the country's flag for the first time in the 1978 World Cup in Argentina, securing a historic draw with Scotland. Yet six months later that team was dead. Many of those players fled to the US, including defender Andranik Eskandarian, who found himself playing in the same New York Cosmos side as Carlos Alberto and Franz Beckenbauer and eventually became an American citizen. Others simply vanished. After surviving the dissolution of the league, the clubs were then faced with another challenge. The Iran-Iraq war saw the availability of healthy young men collapse, meaning the football league couldn't continue. But the clubs soldiered on with an annual cup competition that drew huge attendances until the war ended and the national league could start up again in 1989, eleven years after the shah's final football season was cut short, never to be finished. Football boomed in the 1990s, mainly because the terraces of clubs like Pas, a team traditionally funded by the police; Persepolis, Iran's most popular team; and Esteghlal FC, formerly known until the revolution as Taj (which means crown in *Farsi*) but which had to change its name to Esteghlal FC to break its previous connections with the shah, were the only places where a frustrated population, tired of the revolution's economic failure, could vent their spleen. The climax came in 1997. Buoyed by the success of the reformist movement, Iran qualified for France 1998 on a wave of euphoria and a million people took to the streets. It was the first time in 18 years that women had been seen in Tehran uncovered. And whilst now the Iranian government look to football to give it a shred of legitimacy internationally whilst securing support at home, the authorities have paradoxically always feared its power. 'Football is the only place where people let go and those in power fear the power football has,' explained Arash as we said our goodbyes. 'Football is a threat to their authority. When a million people took to the streets, women were dancing and throwing off their *hijabs*. The authorities are scared of that, scared of losing control.'

I didn't have to travel far to my hotel. The Olympic was Tehran's finest, the place where visiting football teams would stay, attached as it was to the national stadium like an angular, drab carbuncle. When the ayatollah's forces took over the country, they did more than occupy the institutions of power. The city's hotels – the Sheratons, Hyatts and Hiltons – had also been forcibly nationalised, stripped of their insignia and given more Persian names. Cutting off Western companies also meant isolating Iran from the rest of the financial world – ATMs didn't work and neither did credit cards. The exchange rate from rial to sterling was so high (£1=IRR18,100) that most Iranians simply dropped the last few zeros to combat inflation. Not surprisingly, Iranian luxury hotels were hard to come by and the Olympic marked the upper class. My wood-panelled room was sparse but comfortable with little in the way of entertainment. After flicking through the *Farsi* television channels to see if I'd made it onto the 9 o'clock news – I hadn't – and making a stab of reading the Koran, I was bored senseless. By 9.15 p.m. I was climbing the walls. I called Armin, and went to see what Tehran's nightlife had to offer.

I wasn't expecting much. Being a dry Islamic country, Iran was always going to be one of the world's few countries not to have an Irish bar but I wanted to find out what young Iranians – and there were a lot of them – did at night. I met Arash at Vanak Square, the Piccadilly Circus of northern

Tehran where handsome twentysomethings with duck-fin haircuts and turned up jeans strolled the streets hand-in-hand with girlfriends sporting *hijabs* so far back they only stayed on by virtue of a stiff pony tail, making them almost redundant. Arash provided me with my answer. 'The youth are so bored, they don't have anywhere to go,' he said as we walked down to a local restaurant he had recommended. 'Especially the middle class. They have money, but nothing to do. So they sit around and take drugs.' It's hard to imagine somewhere like Iran having a drug problem, but all the vices that are open to the youth of the west also seem to be prevalent in Tehran. 'There are no nightclubs but people have parties at home and drink or take drugs. Tehran has a really big crystal meth problem.' I was incredulous. 'Crystal meth? How the hell do you find that here?' I asked, making it clear I had no interest in scoring a drug better known for making your face cave in after a few hits. 'You have to remember, Iran has some of the best scientists in the world! Last year, the city was full of heroin and everyone would go to "ex parties". They would give you ecstasy at the door and let you loose.' Arash didn't take drugs, and I got the impression he didn't overly approve. But I thought of my lonely room at the Olympic and secretly wished that an opportunity to attend an impromptu 'ex party' would present itself. We arrived at the restaurant, a small, strip-lit affair that sold Iranian staples like lamb with rice and sultanas and iced vermicelli, where Pegah was waiting for us. She was studying art at Tehran University and wore a brown *hijab* adorned with intricate stitching at the edges. Again, it hung off the back of her head, as if wearing it was little more than fulfilling a technicality. 'Most would probably say they'd rather not,' she admitted when I asked whether Iranian women resented having to cover up all the time. 'It's just the fashion, the way people wear it a little further back every year.' The incremental inching back of the *hijab* could be a metaphor for the increasing social freedoms that Iran's under-30s enjoy. Even under Ahmadinejad and an increasingly conservative political culture, the small gains that make a young person's life tolerable go on unabated. 'They (the police) know that they can't turn things back,' agreed Arash. One area where this had been put to the test on a nightly basis was in the field of dating. Although bluetooth technology had helped people to flirt more easily, explained Roxanna, there was an automobile version going on up and down Jordan Street every night. Known as the 'Jordan Game', cars full of single men and women would cruise up and down looking for prospective partners whilst the police sat in their patrol cars and did nothing. We climbed into Pegah's small battered car to take the short drive to Jordan Street. 'I like this a lot,' she smiled, as she pulled out a well-used tape and jammed it into the dusty car radio. Chris Rea replied back. 'Do you like it?' I've never been much of a Chris Rea fan but I didn't have the heart to tell the truth. 'I love him.' With 'Road to Hell' blaring, we hit Jordan Street and the throng of horny Iranians looking for a date. Dozens of cars inched slowly up the hill full of expectant cargo: groups of men hoping to get lucky for a quick fumble streamed by and shouted bawdy slogans in *Farsi*. One group, spotting me, shouted something in unison in their mother tongue before the entire car collapsed in laughter. 'What did he say?' I asked Arash. 'He said: "Nuclear energy is our right". It is supposed to be a joke.' Ahmadinejad's much-used slogan of nuclear self-determination and defiance might have struck a chord with his devout minority fan base, but to the youth of Tehran, the phrase was something to be mocked, an illogical rant that their elders had bought into but which should be viewed with disdain by their children. A second car passed slowly by us, this time containing a pair of heavily made up girls smiling ferociously. I smiled back and waved before they laughed and sped off. Finally, a lone patrol car glided up the strip. The cars disappeared down side roads as quickly as they had arrived, like in a scene from *The Truman Show*. The Jordan Game was over, for tonight at least. It was time to return to the Olympic. I said my goodbyes, climbed into my taxi and looked out of the back window as it pulled away. Behind me Arash and Pegah flirted openly whilst considering where to go next. Despite being in a country where pre-marital sex can still be punished by the flick of a whip, I got the feeling that out of everyone I'd seen that night, I was one of the few people going to bed alone.

The next morning's papers heralded Iran's performance in putting the mighty Costa Rica to the sword. It was proof they said that Team Melli was destined for great things. But, flicking through the *Iran News* and *Tehran Times*, it was clear that even a heavy defeat would have been spun as a glorious victory for the revolution. Every news story was loaded with small victories and yet another show of strength that would strike fear into the hearts of the 'Great Satan' (America). That day's big issue – other than the football – was Ahmadinejad's visit to Malaysia. Whilst his negotiators in Vienna vainly tried to convince the IAEA and the rest of the world that despite possessing the second biggest oil reserves in the world, it was completely logical for Iran to pursue nuclear fuel, Mahmoud had snubbed Austria and instead met with the Malaysian government in Kuala Lumpur to push his agenda with the non-aligned movement. Like the national football team, Ahmadinejad was clearly finding it difficult to arrange high-profile away trips. Still, the paper couldn't help heaping praise on the trip in its balanced front-page editorial in the *Tehran News*: 'Malaysia's clear stance on the issue of Iran's right to have a peaceful nuclear power programme . . . indicates that it is not affected by the imperialist powers,' wrote Hassan Hanizadeh. 'Due to its significant economic, political, and human resources, Iran – along with Malaysia – is able to play a key role in the great task of thwarting neo-colonialist countries' efforts to dominate the Middle East and East Asia through the use of the tools of power.'

It is perhaps no surprise that Iran ranks 162 out of 168 countries on the Reporters Without Borders Worldwide Press Freedom Index. After reading the morning's papers I found myself with a few hours to spare before my interview with Iran's captain, Ali Daei. Rather than kick my heels, I endeavoured to find out about one of Iran's fastest-growing sports: women's golf. Unfolding a large map of Tehran, a small splurge of green in the centre indicated Iran's only grass golf course. It was strange that arguably the most bourgeois of games had a foothold in a staunchly anti-Western Islamic republic so I had planned to visit and play a round. As the taxi pulled into the Englehab Golf Club car park, it was clear that Iran's best course wasn't quite up to international standards. To start with, the clubhouse was a dirty white Portakabin that listed heavily to one side. The course itself wasn't in much better shape. The scrubby brown and green fairways – with the Alborz Mountains and a dozen minarets in the background – were in bad condition. Not only that, there were only thirteen holes: the other five had been commandeered by the army twelve years ago to be used as parking space for their tanks. But for Tehran's eclectic breed of golfers, it was all they had. 'It's difficult to say what kind of people play here,' explained Joe, a twenty-six-year-old Afghan who plays off eight and was considered the course professional. 'But we see a lot of famous wrestlers, television actors, oil workers and ambassadors, these sort of people.' There were no beefcake wrestlers or Persian stars of the silver screen as I badly played a few holes. There were, however, lots of women. In fact, aside from me, Joe and a grizzly-looking tramp picking up balls nearby, the course was devoid of men. Puzzled, I asked Joe whether it was normal to see so many women playing at the Englehab. In Britain, I explained, it was not unheard of for female players to still be barred from setting foot in some clubhouses and the sign 'No Dogs, No Women' was a depressingly recent sight. Joe looked at me oddly. 'Yes, we have maybe 300 members, and over 50 per cent of those are women,' he said, before pointing over at the practice range. A line of covered women were practising their drives. I went over and stood next to the tramp. It turned out that he was the husband and coach of the woman who had just put one ball into the stratosphere. Dressed in a hip-length brown jacket, faded blue jeans and a Paisley *hijab*, Tala addressed the tee again, paused, and spanked another ball with the metronomic precision of a military drummer. 'She's going to go a long way,' beamed her husband. 'Tala's just joined the Iranian national team and we're practising for a big sand tournament in the south. She's got a really smooth swing.'

You wouldn't have expected golf to be a big hit in Iran, but for women, it's one of the few sports where the compulsory *hijab* doesn't have a detrimental affect on performance. Women footballers in Iran have to cover to play, a definite disadvantage against teams that don't have to cover, but in golf the *hijab* doesn't affect your swing. And whilst women's sport isn't actively encouraged in many Arab states – and especially not in Gulf states like Saudi Arabia – the Iranians had made the sport a priority. With financial help from the government, the club had gone about trying to get ordinary Tehranis onto the links by running mini-golf courses in the city's public parks and offering free tuition to beginners. 'We have three public classes on a Friday so both men and women come to play here,' said Joe as Tala exhausted her bucket of balls, smiled in our direction and walked off to talk tactics with the rest of her team-mates, who'd recently won bronze at the Women's Islamic Games. 'You won't find anywhere in any country where people teach golf for free.' He pointed at the Enghelab scorecard, which bore Imam Khomeini's opinion on the subject. It read: 'Sport activity is part of our Islamic teaching.' Iran may be an international pariah with an appalling human rights record, but compared to the likes of Royal St. Georges or St Andrews, Tehran's Enghelab Golf Club took the moral high ground.

As it turned out, I didn't have to go far to interview Ali Daei. Four doors along to be precise. Daei had stayed in Tehran after the Costa Rica game to meet up with his Saba Battery team-mates, an outfit owned by the Ministry of Defence. They were due to play a league match in the Azadi in what used to be called the Iranian Premier League. Now they called it the Persian Gulf Cup, to preserve, the Iranians say, the true name of the waterway that has been appropriated by Arab encroachment. The animus stems from the bi-yearly Arabian Gulf Cup, involving every Gulf nation from Iraq to Oman. Iran hadn't been invited to the party. Even Yemen, which is closer to Africa than the Gulf – be it Persian or Arabian – was allowed to play. For Ali Daei, the league match was a long way from his glory days in the late 1990s when he was considered one of the best strikers in Germany. After playing for Arminia Bielefeld and Bayern Munich, he went to Hertha Berlin and spearheaded their Champions League charge in 2000. Daei excelled and scored twice in Germany against Chelsea and once against AC Milan – the first Asian footballer to score in the Champions League. But even as age advanced and Daei went lower and lower to get a game (first Hertha Berlin, then to Dubai, then back to Iran) he continued to be first choice for the national team and had racked up an astonishing 109 goals, including his well-taken strike against Costa Rica. Sure, four of them came in a 7–0 drubbing of Laos, but a world record is still a world record. His exploits on the pitch in flying the Iranian flag abroad have made Daei phenomenally successful in his home country. He was the closest thing Iran had to a Persian David Beckham: he was handsome, owned a sprawling business empire (the Daei Sportswear company) and was good-naturedly mocked for his gentle, lisping voice. Even his wedding was broadcast on public television. Also like Beckham, some fans had begun to wonder whether Daei was now redundant at the national level. 'A lot of fans think he's past his best,' admitted Arash at the game. 'But the coach won't drop him, he's too important to the team.' Branko had admitted as much in our interview. 'There aren't many in the world like Ali Daei but he's more than a footballer,' he said admiringly of his captain. 'He is a leader, a national hero and a symbol of the country.' I'd had to get in contact with Amir to arrange an interview with Iran's favourite son, whose impeccable connections had come up trumps. A phone call, a 15-minute wait and it was all organised. Amir knocked on my door and escorted me the short distance to Daei's modest suite and pushed our way inside. Footballers tend to be a tough lot to interview. Cliché ridden and monochrome, most have been media massaged to within an inch of their lives and little is said that veers from a meticulously prepared script handed to them by their agent. You meet in fancy bars or cafés – usually somewhere of their choosing – and there's never a hair or button out of place. It was strange, then, to find Ali Daei on the floor of his hotel room, naked save for a pair of tight briefs that barely contained his modesty, being vigorously oiled up by his balding masseuse. Daei welcomed me in and offered me an oily hand before we were interrupted by a string of excitable children, with equally awestruck parents in tow and totally nonplussed by their host's almost-nakedness. He signed autographs, gave words of encouragement and posed for semi-naked pictures with the kids. What they will make of them in 20 years' time is another issue. I raised my camera and captured the moment. It was an instinctive move, one that owed more to pretensions of tabloid journalism rather than any feelings of spite or malice. But it was an action that nevertheless displeased Amir. 'You cannot do this,' he grimaced, letting his detached cool slip for the only time during the trip. 'He is Ali Daei.' As if his name was explanation enough, he grabbed my camera and quickly deleted the offending picture lest I smuggle the image out and sully his hero's reputation. He handed the camera back and shot me a displeased look. Daei didn't seem to have noticed at all as he waved goodbye to the last child and settled down on his front, directing the masseuse to his bulging calves.

Germany 2006 was Ali Daei's last chance at international glory. Having missed the 2002 tournament when he was at the height of his powers, France 1998 was his only World Cup appearance so far, but it brought Iranian football its greatest achievement. Early on the group fixture against the USA – who had reached the second round four years previously – was marked for its symbolism. It was the first contact the two nations had had in 19 years. Bill Clinton recorded a message before the match preaching reconciliation and Iran's European fans tried to smuggle opposition T-shirts against the Islamic regime into the ground. The world waited for the two countries' political antipathy to spill out onto the pitch. Instead the world watched as the Iranian players showered their American opponents with symbolic white flowers followed by warm, smiling embraces. It resembled a first date more than the opening salvos of a proxy political battle. Iran's goalkeeper – Ahmad Reza Abedzadeh – shook hands with his American counterpart Thomas Dooley and handed over a large silver shield bigger than a small child to show conciliation and friendship towards their American foes. Dooley sheepishly handed over a tiny pennant in reply, too embarrassed to make eye contact with his adversary. It was singularly one of the funniest moments in international football, and the Americans were visibly stunned. So much so they conspired to lose 2–1, provoking the biggest gathering on Tehran's streets since Imam Khomeini's funeral in 1989. Whilst the Americans gracefully took the defeat in the spirit of international fraternity, the Ayatollah back in Tehran was eager to make political capital. 'Tonight again,' he sternly extolled in an address to the national team on state television, 'the strong and arrogant opponent felt the bitter taste of defeat at your hands. Be happy that you have made the Iranian nation happy.' Daei smiled at the memory of that June night. 'All we cared about, our only goal [at France 1998] was to win against the USA,' he grinned. 'But we didn't take it seriously for the last match against Germany so that we could qualify for the second round. But this time around it will be different.' It wasn't just Daei who was convinced of Iran's impending footballing glory. If Team Melli's performance in France 1998 was all about showing the world that Iran could hold their own at the highest level, the team at Germany 2006 wanted to prove what many fans in Iran – and Branko – sincerely believed: that they could beat anybody in the world on their day and in Ali Karimi they had arguably one of the best players in the world. As the squad's spiritual leader the burden of expectation – from fans and politicians alike – had fallen on Daei's shoulders. After shaking hands with Branko, there was no question as to whom Ahmadinejad turned to next. 'The people of Iran, they're living with football so any good result has a big effect on the society and the country,' he explained as he started to get dressed. Ahmadinejad's words of encouragement and earlier meeting with the squad hadn't convinced him that the team was being used as a political pawn in the West or at home. 'No, politics and football are completely different, totally separate,' he retorted when I brought it up. 'We play football and that's what's important for us. We leave the politics to other people.' But Daei could, like the rest of the country, see that Iran's stock was at its lowest ebb for a quarter of a century. And even if the politicians wanted to hijack football for its own ends, he – as a proud Iranian – would do everything in his power to prove that Iran and Iranians were a world away from the cartoon baddies caricatured in the Western media. 'We'd like to go to Germany and prove that Iranians are completely different from the way the media show us. We have a high culture and our people work hard. The facts are totally different from the way the Western media are trying to show. It's very important for us to show the world exactly who we are.' The next day's papers proved just how hard that task would be. The IAEA's report was delivered and it wasn't good reading for Ahmadinejad. There was sufficient doubt that Iran was seeking to enrich uranium to make a nuclear bomb, giving the USA valuable ammunition in seeking sanctions, and possibly war, in the UN Security Council. Even winning the World Cup couldn't nullify that. Suddenly, Ali Daei and the rest of Team Melli had been handed the hardest PR job in the world.

THREE

Iran, Saudi Arabia And The World Cup

From a distance it looked like the Iranian Club was under siege. Dusk was falling on another asphyxiatingly humid July day in Dubai and the upmarket district through which Oud Metha Road ran was stationary. Irate drivers held their horns down in vain to try and clear the road, but it was no use. Streams of disparate people – groups of teenage girls; pensioners hobbling on sticks; young men wearing expensive suits with mobile phones pressed to their ears – were sprinting across the four-lane highway, creating a human river that turned the straight and true highway into a temporary crossroads. All were frantic to reach the heavily guarded compound on the other side. The ornate front gates were inundated with last-minute arrivals. Women argued with the guards whilst expertly fixing on headscarves, never breaking eye contact. The single guard tried to hold the crowd back but like King Cnut sitting on the beach and ordering the ocean to retreat, he was fighting a losing battle. The crowd just pushed past. Others scaled the tall metal fences that surrounded the compound, falling in a crumpled heap on the other side before getting up and half limping, half running towards the lights. The Iranian Club wasn't used to this many visitors. It was meant to be the conservative social club for Dubai's huge Iranian diaspora, but Iran's conservatism didn't travel well abroad. For a start they enacted Tehran rules. No booze, and women were expected to cover. Socially liberal Iranians preferred to let their hair down (literally) by drinking in the city's bars or dancing at the many Persian nightclubs instead. The only people the Iranian Club saw were devout families and ex-military types in retirement. But today was a national occasion and, like the BBC being the British comfort blanket in times of crisis or celebration, Iranians from all walks of life put their politics to one side and flocked to the only place they could be sure to be on the same side. For any self-respecting Iranian it was the only place in town to watch Iran versus Mexico, the country's first game in its controversial appearance at the 2006 World Cup in Germany.

'It has been like this for an hour,' our taxi driver sighed. The match kicked off in 15 minutes so Matt, Lee and I got out and joined the crowd. The guard was having another attempt at hauling the gate shut to stop the already bulging club – a 1970s style concrete monstrosity that looked like a run-down comprehensive school – from bursting at the seams. The three of us slipped in just as the gate closed, leaving hundreds locked out. One covered, middle-aged woman even tried to hitch her leg up on the sturdy fence to try and climb over, but gave up knowing that age would be the ultimate barrier to her entry. Hopes were rightly high inside. After visiting Tehran a few months previously I had witnessed a self-confidence that hadn't been translated by the world media, both in its football team and its youth. This World Cup, Iranians reasoned, was when Iran took a serious step to being one of the world's footballing powers. They had a good case too. The tournament had come with Iran's 'Golden Generation' at its peak: Mahdavikia, Zandi, Teymourian and the Asian Maradona, Ali Karimi. There was also, of course, the figure of Ali Daei to contend with. This would be the 38-year-old's second World Cup and a chance for him, if nothing else, to extend his world record for the most international goals. It was surely to be his last World Cup as a player. But as he had told me back in Tehran when he was sitting, semi-naked in his hotel room, this was a vitally important World Cup for Iran for different reasons. As the tournament drew closer, President Mahmoud Ahmadinejad's behaviour on the world stage had increasingly become more divisive. The country's nuclear programme was almost universally suspected of being for anything but peaceful purposes, the prospect of an American invasion was now being openly mooted by hawkish commentators on domestic news networks and the calls for the Iranian national team to be banned from the World Cup had become even more vociferous. The world's media had focused on the Iran versus Mexico fixture to see whether the president, as promised, would turn up to cheer on Team Melli. Protests had been arranged in Nuremberg by Jewish groups livid at Ahmadinejad's potential presence, pointing out that his views on the Holocaust meant that if these pronouncements had been uttered in Germany he would broken the country's strict Holocaust denial laws. If the protests didn't keep him away, then they had called for him to be arrested when – if – he landed in Germany. Even worse, neo-Nazi groups had planned on holding a counter demonstration in favour of the Iranian president. It wasn't exactly the kind of endorsement he or Iran needed. But I wanted to see the madness myself so I, along with two journalist friends, decided to book two weeks off work and follow the Iranian and Saudi Arabian fans as they negotiated Germany and tried to qualify for the second round. A Middle Eastern country had only managed it once before, the Saudis in USA 1994. But this was probably the best chance for Iran to at least match that, having gained a place in the FIFA top-15 rankings that year. History wasn't exactly on the region's side, though. In fact, most World Cup appearances by Middle Eastern countries had been best remembered for catastrophic failure or embarrassingly hilarious behaviour. Israel had acquitted themselves admirably when they qualified for Mexico in 1970, drawing twice and losing once. Iran, too, didn't do too badly in their first appearance in a World Cup finals, in Argentina in 1978, where the team famously drew against a Scottish team that had foolishly declared it would return home with winners' medals. The appearance of

Kuwait at Spain 1982, however, was remembered for all the wrong reasons. With a creditable draw against Czechoslovakia already in the bag, Kuwait took on France. The French were a bridge too far for the Kuwaitis, who went 4–1 down. Or so the French thought. By the time the fourth goal went in the Kuwaitis were standing stock still after hearing a shrill whistle. Assuming the referee had blown, they had stopped playing. The French played on and scored anyway. The Kuwaitis were livid but the referee had made his decision; it was a goal. The ball had even been placed back on the centre spot. But from the stands a man wearing traditional Gulf Arab dress waved towards the disgusted Kuwaiti players, urging them to leave the pitch in protest. Cue one of the strangest moments in World Cup history, as the white-robed figure of Sheikh Fahid Al-Ahmad Al-Sabah – brother of the emir and head of the Kuwaiti FA – strode onto the pitch with his red-and-white checked headscarf and black-and-gold cloak and calmly questioned the referee's wisdom. Amazingly, the referee backed down and called a drop ball. It was the last time he would referee an international match. The sheikh was fined a paltry $10,000.

Mexico 1986 saw the Iraqis turn up. They narrowly lost every game but it wasn't until afterwards that it emerged that the players had been subjected to beatings and forced head shavings as motivation to qualify for the tournament. In Italia 1990, the UAE and Egypt were making debut appearances. Whilst Egypt narrowly failed to qualify out of a tough group, the UAE's president Sheikh Zayed bin Sultan al Nahyan, knowing the limitations of his team, promised each player a brand new Rolls Royce, not if they won a game, but merely for scoring a goal. Sure enough, the UAE lost every game, conceding 11 goals. But two players, Khalid Ismail and Ali Thani, returned home to find a brand new Roller parked in the driveway. USA 1994 was perhaps the region's finest triumph, when Saudi Arabia reached the second round. En route they scored what was arguably one of the finest goals in World Cup history, Saeed Al Owairan picking the ball up near his own penalty box and,

aping Maradona's wonder goal against England in Mexico
1986, slaloming past the entire Belgium team before slotting
the ball home. France 1998 was less successful for the Saudis
but did throw up the match between the 'Great Satan' and Iran
in one of the tournament's most politically charged games,
which the Iranians ended up winning 2–1. After that it was
downhill. The 2002 World Cup saw Saudi Arabia humiliated
8–0 by Germany in their first game. It could have been worse,
the Germans having 26 shots on target. The Saudis went home
without scoring a goal. The Iranians, meanwhile, hadn't even
qualified. In total, the Middle East's record wasn't something
to boast about: played 30, won 3, drew 7, lost 20.

No one was thinking of Iran's failure to qualify for the last
World Cup any more, or even the disappointment of bowing
out early in 1998 after beating the Americans. Inside the packed
lobby children cried and parents remonstrated at the doors to
the club's huge cinema. They were too late. Inside, close to
700 people had already crammed into the two tiers of seating,
with another 400 left outside. Eventually extra televisions were
brought outside when the crowd refused to disperse. Dozens
more crammed the walkways or sat at the front. The vast
projected screen flickered into life, for a moment casting a
green glow over the cheering crowd as the equipment corrected
itself. The feed was from Iranian state television and as the
commentators pored over the team selection – Ali Daei and
Ali Karimi were both declared fit and were to start – the
club's manager stood in front of the crowd and urged them
to be respectful. Clearly he was confident of a good result
and didn't want a repeat of the last time Iran won a World
Cup match in 1998, when women threw off their *hijabs* and
danced in the streets of Tehran. Two young women walked
past draped in Iran's flag with smaller, smudgy versions painted
on their cheeks. 'We wore the flag and painted our faces to
show everyone that we really love our country,' Shahrzad and
Miadeh told a female reporter from a local paper standing next
to us. The noise was deafening when the game kicked off;
shouts of 'I . . . ran, I . . . ran,' rang out constantly. Across town,
one newspaper reported, several hundred Iranians watching

the game in a pub began chanting: 'Nuclear Energy is Our Right!' Although, given the ironic way it had been used in Tehran, it sounded like they might have been taking the piss. On the pitch, thousands of miles away in Nuremberg, all eyes were on the crowd. President Ahmadinejad had decided not to turn up, but instead decided to send one of his deputies, Mohammad Aliabadi, instead. Which hadn't gone down well either. 'Aliabadi's presence means we could have a repeat of the 1936 Olympics, when they were hijacked by Hitler for his own political purposes and presentation,' Rene Pollak, chair of the Zionist Federation of Frankfurt, told *The Observer* before the game. 'We should have denied him entry to the country. Western leaders should know by now that appeasing fascist regimes does not work.' Hundreds of people representing Jewish groups and exiled Iranians attended the protest in Nuremberg. A smaller protest by the far-right National Democratic Party was broken up when the police stopped a group of men marching towards Nuremberg's centre wearing Iranian jerseys and waving Iranian flags. I was considering packing my Iranian jersey for the trip, but seeing that the only European men wearing them in Germany during the World Cup were neo-Fascists, I made a mental note to leave it in the drawer. Not that anybody in the Iranian Club watching state television knew anything about the protests as the match kicked off in a sunny Germany and the lights dimmed. It was a tough start for Iran. Mexico was a team that had won three of their last four opening games at the World Cup, and they soon went ahead after some atrocious defending. But the crowd were soon back on their feet after the veteran central defender Yahya Golmohammadi fired into an open net. The Iranian Club erupted as high-pitched screams from the children present added to the roar. Iran pushed on and dominated the rest of the first half but missed a slew of chances. Ali Daei was dire. It looked like he was wading through treacle and had the first touch of a deep-sea diver. More worrying was the fitness of Iran's star man. Ali Karimi had been injured in the build up to the finals but the manager, Branko Ivankovic, knew that his team's bid for progress would be over without him. With

20 minutes to go he was shattered, having run the midfield superbly in the sweltering heat. Within minutes of his removal, however, Iran fell to pieces, Mexico scoring a second, before adding a third a few minutes later. The mood had changed at the Iranian Club. Before it was of hope, now it was ugly. Men would stand up and barrack Ali Daei, the person the crowd blamed for their defeat. People began trickling out even before the final whistle had blown. Outside I had hoped to catch victorious Iranian fans running into the streets to celebrate their victory. When the Iranian Club last hosted a victorious World Cup match involving the national team – that famous match in 1998 against the USA – a crowd had rushed outside and ritually slaughtered a goat. Now a trickle mooched out sullenly, unwilling to talk. 'Daei should not be anywhere near the team,' proclaimed one man, who wouldn't give me his name as he walked back out of the gates that had been the scene of such hysteria two hours previously. He wasn't angry, more upset that he had believed the hype. 'Why do Iran let me believe?' There was still hope though. Iran was to play Portugal. Win and they were back in with a chance, lose and their World Cup dream was over. We didn't have tickets, but we knew there would be protests, Iranian fans and neo-Nazis. It was a no brainer. Next stop, Frankfurt.

We stood next to the car as its hazard lights blinked as we gazed at the smashed glass lying all around us. We had been in Frankfurt for 40 minutes and hadn't even made it out of the airport, yet our transport was already prone. 'I told you I hadn't driven a car in ten years,' Matt said, finally breaking the silence. With just one driving licence between us, Lee and I had bullied Matt into taking the wheel of the hire car. 'You'll be fine,' we assured him on the flight from Abu Dhabi. 'It's like riding a bike, you never forget.' Within minutes of picking up the car he had shown us why we had good reason to worry, swinging out of the car park in reverse and careering towards the crash barrier. When it didn't open, he reversed at speed into the bollard. From ignition to implosion took all of four minutes. There was nothing else to do, we had to make do. No other cars were involved, so we kicked the yellow and clear glass into the gutter and sped off, the man in the ticket booth tutting as we handed him our exit pass. Matt drove towards the centre of Frankfurt terrified, hunched over the wheel like a myopic pensioner. 'The speed limit on Jersey is only 40 mph,' he explained as we crawled along in the slow lane.

Frankfurt is the most British of German cities, or so the Germans say – and not in a flattering way. It's the country's financial centre and is thus – so the stereotype goes – full of yuppies and rapacious, money-hungry capitalists. It was also going to be full of Iranians. The World Cup circus that was following Team Melli – the fans, the politicians and the protests – had left the heartbreak of Nuremberg behind and moved on to Frankfurt instead. The plan in Germany was to meet up with the Iranian team, go to the Iran–Portugal game itself, talk to the Iranian fans, attend the anti-Ahmadinejad protests and then head to Kaiserslautern, where we had tickets to watch Saudi Arabia's final group game against Spain. The Saudis had drawn against Tunisia 2–2 in their opening game and might still be in with a chance come the Spain game if they got anything against Ukraine, who had already themselves been beaten 4–0 by the Spanish. But I was more interested in who would be supporting Saudi Arabia – the Green Falcons. Would there be a large contingent of Saudi Wahabi Sunni Muslims descending on a city known for its huge American military base? If so then it could get heated. Both games also had an added touch of intrigue. The *Times* had reported that the two games had been listed, along with nineteen others, of being at high risk of terrorist attack. The stadiums where the games were taking place had all been ringed by three-mile no-fly zones and the Iranian team hotel was being protected by plain-clothes and uniformed police. FIFA had also hired a private security firm, just in case. The authorities were particularly worried about the large fan areas outdoors where tens of thousands of supporters were to gather to watch live feeds of the game. 'There will be hundreds of thousands of fans with rucksacks,' a policeman told the *Times*. It wouldn't have been the first time Islamist terrorists had targeted the World Cup. According to Adam

Robinson's book, *Terror on the Pitch*, an Al Qaeda-backed plot to murder a number of England players during their first match of France 1998, against Tunisia, was foiled at an advanced stage. Yet security seemed pretty lax when we waltzed into the lobby of Iran's team hotel. The plain-clothes beefcakes with wires running from their ears didn't seem to mind us poking about. Branko Ivankovic, Iran's manager who I'd met back in Tehran, was in the lobby. 'We were very unlucky,' he said, when I asked about the defeat to Mexico. 'The heat was a factor but we will come back stronger for the next game against Portugal.' The previous day's papers had also made an issue out of some of Branko's comments regarding how his players would be happy to meet Ahmadinejad if he came to Germany. 'It would be no different from Jacques Chirac meeting the French team,' he had been quoted as saying. Probably wisely, he failed to mention that he and the players had already met the President before the Costa Rica game back in February. All the political intrigue was getting to him and he wasn't sure whether, come the end of the World Cup, he still wanted to be the Iranian manager after his five-year stint. For a region where a new manager annually was the norm, five years was akin to Sir Alex Ferguson's tenure at Manchester United. But if Branko lost against Portugal, he would have no choice. 'We don't talk about politics,' he said, getting up to leave when I asked him about the controversy that had surrounded his team. 'I am only concerned about football.' It was a sentiment echoed by the fans staying at the hotel. A mixed group of a dozen Iranian fans lounged on nearby sofas. They had flown here from Tehran. The women chose to remain covered throughout. I asked one fan whether the controversy over the President's possible appearance had been reported back home. 'I, err, no. I don't want to talk about politics,' she replied shakily. 'I am here just for the football.' Her brother-in-law jumped in instantly. 'There are maybe five, six thousand of us who have flown from Tehran, I think, but we are here for football only.' Nobody, it seemed, wanted to be seen to be going off message. The players marched through the lobby towards the team bus that was waiting to take them training. The fans had been hanging around to catch a glimpse of them and rushed to take pictures on their mobile phones. For Branko and Team Melli, tomorrow was make or break.

That evening every country was represented at the International Village, a compound where the fans of every nation could mingle, eat each other's food and drink each other's hooch. The Iranians, however, weren't there. Whilst the centre of Frankfurt was full of second-generation Germans of Iranian descent drinking the city's bars dry, the Iranian FA decided against having their stand anywhere near the alcoholic excess of the other nations. So they were allowed to have their celebration of all things Iranian on the other side of the river, hidden away from the debauched revelry. It was early evening and the sun was still warm as a troupe of singers and dancers performed traditional songs in *Farsi*, only stopping when a prominent member of the FA would stand and give a short speech about 'the need for peace in the world'. Several hundred were clustered around the singers in a circle when a commotion began to break out. A phalanx of European bodyguards had formed a circle around a tiny, bearded man wearing a Nehru shirt and brown jacket. The bodyguards looked around shiftily as he waved goodbye to the Iranians watching the show. One man barged past me as he ran to get a closer look. 'I'm sorry,' he apologised breathlessly. 'Who is that?' I asked, expecting to hear that he was maybe a diplomat, or a famous singer. A popular ex-player, even? 'That's the vice president.'

Vice President Mohammad Aliabadi – President Ahmadinejad's man in Germany and the man whose presence had sparked angry protests in Nuremberg – had turned up the night before the game to be around friends and have a little taste of home. It must have been a tough job, travelling from city to city, having abuse thrown at you for something someone else said. So it was time to ask him about his boss directly. A few dozen well wishers had crowded around him as he walked, making his security detail look even jumpier. 'Mr Vice President,' I called out, not being sure what the protocol was for addressing a vice president. I was sure I had heard something similar on *The West Wing*. He remained passive; his eyes met mine. He had seen me, but ignored my shouts. Instead he looked in the opposite direction, waving at a group of confused German tourists who had stopped to see what the fuss was about. The question had also alerted his meatheads to the presence of the possible hostile entities. 'Mr Vice President?' I shouted again, holding up a camcorder that we had brought with us on the trip. 'Do you share President Ahmadinejad's view on the Holocausssss . . .' I felt a blow to my neck as one of his guards dived in the way of the camera, jumping up and down and waving his arms to make himself as big as possible to try and obscure the shot. Suddenly his security went into overdrive, as if they'd just heard the crack of a bullet emanating from a nearby book depository. The guards nervously looked left and right, ushering the vice president up a nearby stone staircase out of the park and onto the main street. Ironically, he found himself standing in front of Frankfurt's Jewish Museum, which was holding a night of Jewish folk music. 'Mr Vice President?!' I shouted for a third time, his still smiling figure now moving up the staircase and almost out of view. The security guard was still in front of me, stepping left when I stepped left, moving right when I moved to the right. 'Will you be taking in this evening's Jewish folk recital?' The last thing I saw was a wave of his hand as he disappeared behind a stone wall. It could have been him answering in the affirmative, but I doubted it.

The walk from the train station to Frankfurt's futuristic Commerzbank-Arena offered a contrasting view on the Iranian government. Whilst anyone that would have to get back onto a plane to Tehran was scared to mention anything about Ahmadinejad, Israel or whether he might turn up in Germany or not, the Iranians that had lived in Germany since fleeing the country after the fall of the shah in 1979, and their children, followed a different line. In fact, Germany held the third largest Iranian-born population in the world, after Canada and the USA. The stream of fans walking the short distance from the station all flew the Iranian green, white and red. But it wasn't the flag of the revolution they carried, it was a flag from the past. It bore the golden lion, the pre-1979 symbol of the shah. The flag itself was a protest against the post-revolution regime. 'I'm Iranian, I was born there, I love Iran but the way they treat women there, I can't believe it,' one Iranian-British woman, holding the shah's flag, told me outside the stadium. 'One day I'll go back, but not with a headscarf.'

She was also in the same predicament as us. 'Have you got any tickets to sell?' she asked. 'No, I was going to ask you if you had any. How much are they?' '800 euros.' That was that. Between the three of us it would have cost 2400 euros to get into the stadium. Rather more worrying was the absence of any protesters. We had hoped to see the anti-Ahmadinejad protests, but there didn't seem to be a Star of David in sight. 'No, it is not here,' a policeman on a horse replied in perfect English. 'You have to go back to the city, it is after the game at the Opera House.' As we had no money, and no protest to invest in, we decided to head to the fan zone next to the Maine River, where an approximate crowd of 50,000 who couldn't get a ticket would be watching the game – near where we had heckled the vice president the previous night. We walked back past the convoy of Iranian fans with their pre-1979 Iranian flags. Only the periodic flash of Portuguese maroon broke the ubiquity. It would be as close to a home match for Iran as it was possible to get without holding it in Tehran.

We rushed back downtown, back on the train and then the long walk along the river in searing heat towards the big screen where we should have watched the game. It was due to start any minute but already, half a mile from the screen, there was a pedestrian traffic jam. Tens of thousands of Iranian fans had turned up to see their team. So many, in fact, that by the time we arrived at the purpose-built stands with the match well under way, they were full. Not everyone wanted to be inside though. A gaggle of protesters stood under the shade of a line of trees, each one peddling a different dissident political platform: equal rights for Iranian women; an end to racism for non-Persians in Iran. At the end of the line stood Mansoor, a young student, with a pack of leaflets eagerly giving them out to anybody that passed. He was an Iranian marxist, campaigning for a socialist revolution in Iran. 'In Iran now, you don't know what it's like, it's hopeless. The theocrats have taken away hope.' Just as he said that a distant, worrying silence emerged from behind the trees. Portugal had scored with 20 minutes left. All hope that Iran would qualify was lost. For Team Melli the World Cup was effectively over. We decided to walk to the Opera House and see the protest when Ronaldo stuck the nail in the coffin with Portugal's second goal. But as we approached, another silence greeted us. The square on which the Opera House resided was empty. A stage sat empty to the side, as security guards quickly cleared away the crash barriers. The floor was a mat of blue and white. Stars of David fluttered along the floor. Whatever protest had taken place here, we'd missed it. A single, lone protester stood in the middle of the square, an Israeli flag on his back and a cardboard hat with a Star of David on it. Stars of David seemed to cover every single piece of his body. 'You can't trust the Arabs, you can't trust the Arabs,' he repeated. 'You mean the Persians?' I corrected. 'You can't trust them,' he continued.

Close to a thousand protesters had been standing in the spot we were in a few hours previously, waving placards that said: 'Israel has a Right to Exist' and 'Support Israel Now'. A former Holocaust survivor and renowned academic, Arno Lustiger, the Associated Press reported, took to the stage and, to rapturous applause, told the rally that Ahmadinejad's presence would be a 'provocation to all German Jews'. They didn't have to worry about that any more. Protests were planned for the final group game in Leipzig against Angola: a 1–1 draw that added insult to injury – but Ahmadinejad wouldn't be there. The national team had been there to serve a purpose. Previously football had been a crucible to ferment dissent. Ahmadinejad wanted to co-opt it for his own nationalistic ends, to prove Iran's strength in the face of adversity. But the campaign had been a PR disaster. On the pitch the glittering array of Iranian footballing talent had failed to live up to the hype. Off the pitch, Iran's position as the world's number one pariah state had been confirmed by the protests and vitriol that had spilled out in every city. Iran's reputation had, if anything, been denigrated even further. Even the team couldn't escape that. Ali Daei was the chief scapegoat for many fans, and he quickly retired from the game along with a slew of other Iranian footballers, only to emerge, 18 months later, as the surprise choice as Iranian national team coach. Branko quit too, his legacy in rebuilding Iran's footballing reputation tarnished by his team's failure to jump properly at the last hurdle. He would later emerge as manager of Dynamo Zagreb where he would win the double. The three of us left the Opera House and the scraps of blue-and-white paper swirling around the square. The protester remained, standing stock still, awaiting the next battle.

By the time we were ready to travel south Saudi Arabia's World Cup arithmetic was much, much simpler. After Iran's capitulation in Frankfurt, we drove our broken car to Cologne, where we slept in tents by the autobahn in between wading through the broken glass and piss left in the streets by the English fans that had watched the draw against Sweden. In a filthy pool hall near the centre of town a flickering television screen played Ukraine versus Saudi Arabia. No one paid any attention to it except us. Saudi Arabia were losing 4–0, meaning they were effectively out of the running. They could still qualify for the second round if Tunisia drew with Ukraine 0–0, but they'd have to hit six with no reply against Spain. We headed south along the Rhine to the industrial town of Kaiserslautern and began the hunt for Saudi Arabia's fans. We started by setting up camp in the specially constructed site that had seen waves of fans come and go as their teams breezed through the city. Thankful not to be sleeping by the autobahn any more, we paid up for a few nights in advance. The camp was empty, recently evacuated by the Australians who had been there, along with the Brazilians. 'Are there any other Saudi fans?' I asked the warden. 'Other?' he replied, confused. 'We're here to support Saudi.' He choked into his can of coke. 'No,' he laughed, 'you're the first.' It was just the Spanish and ourselves then.

The short walk into town might have provided some answers. The fan zone, which was heaving with a multinational crowd, might have seen some Saudis pass through it, but the security guard was equally confused. 'Saudis?' he repeated. 'No, I haven't seen any here. They must all be staying in the rich hotels outside of town.' Maybe the market stall selling Saudi flags and scarves could shed some light. 'Have you sold many of these?' I asked hopefully. 'Yes, they have been quite popular. But not to any Saudis.' There appeared not to be a single Saudi fan in Kaiserslautern for the game. According to a story before the tournament in *Al Watan*, a liberal Saudi newspaper, hardly anyone had applied for visas at the German embassy and the Saudi FA had resorted to giving away free tickets in the hope of enticing European-based Saudi students to the games. Still there were no takers, which was odd. In Saudi, the local football league was hugely popular with Al Hilal, the team from Riyadh and the Saudi Premier League's most successful team with 11 championships, and Al Ittihad, a seven times championship-winning team from Jeddah, attracting crowds of up to 80,000. Foreign stars had graced the league too, with Al Ittihad almost pulling off arguably the transfer coup of the century when they announced the signature of Luis Figo for one season on a bumper pay deal. A few weeks later David Beckham announced his huge transfer to LA Galaxy, and the deal lost its lustre somewhat. Figo, perhaps not fancying the 50-degree heat and conservative social restrictions compared to Beckham's plush LA lifestyle, pulled out of the deal on a technicality. It was probably just as well. There would have been the tricky issue of what to do with Figo during an away game at fellow Premiership side Al Wahda FC, or to give them their nickname, the Knights of Mecca. Non-Muslims were barred from entering the city. It was one away day he would have had to, by Sharia law, sit out.

No, the main problem appeared to be that large numbers of fans couldn't afford to travel to the games. In a country awash with oil money, as many as 20 per cent of under-30s were unemployed, with huge disparities between the rich and poor. Only the very wealthy could afford to travel which, if they had, probably meant they wouldn't be sharing a campsite with us any time soon. The stadium was nowhere near full when the Spanish and Saudi teams were led onto the pitch. A few dozen Saudis waved flags from the corner of the stadium and sang the name of Sami Al Jaber. Al Jaber was a Saudi football legend, having played in four World Cup finals, from USA 1994 to Germany 2006. He became Saudi's first (and only) player to have turned out for a European side, after a brief but unsuccessful spell at Wolves. Unsurprisingly, the six goals never materialised. Spain won in what was commonly regarded as one of the worst matches of the 2006 World Cup: Spain putting out a reserve side that could barely string two passes together, Saudi Arabia gamely trying to break through Spain's solid back line but to no avail. We walked back down the main street in town with the thousands of Spain fans. A single Saudi fan sauntered down the main road out of the stadium wearing a white kandoora with a huge, stiff collar, sunglasses and red-and-white headscarf. German families would stop him and ask for photos as their children climbed over him, such was the strangeness of his dress. We weren't the only people struggling to locate the Saudis, either. Amongst the crowd two Americans, one in his 50s, the other in his early 20s, kept a keen eye out for any Muslims. 'My uncle is so good at this,' explained John. 'So good at what?' I asked. John handed me his book. It was a textbook on the benefits of Christianity. John and his uncle had turned up to try and convert as many Muslim fans as possible.

'How many people has he converted today?' 'Well, it doesn't work like that. We give them the book, plant the seed and then they go away and embrace Christ. Look, he's talking to a few now.'

John's uncle had done better than us and had located two Saudi fans, sporting green headscarves with Saudi flags printed on the front, leaving the stadium. John's uncle was deep in conversation, but being so obtuse that they didn't really understand what he was getting at. 'Here,' he said finally. He passed them a copy of the textbook that had been translated into Arabic. The Saudi fans looked at him, looked at the book, read the first line and handed it back. 'No, thank you,' the Saudi fan said, smiling politely, walking away as quickly as possible. And who would blame him? Back in Saudi being tarred with the apostate brush meant death. 'I was close there, John,' the uncle said in a disappointed southern drawl, watching his two potential sales walk away. The preachers disappeared off into the Spanish crowd, hoping to find the rest of Saudi Arabia's fans. They had gone before we could tell him that he'd probably already met all of them.

FOUR

Israel

There's something perplexing about having a young girl point a gun at you. Usually, having any kind of firearm prodded in your direction would immediately send the kind of panicked neurological signals that bypass the rational part of the brain and head straight for the bowel, but the child-like soldiers patrolling the Israeli border between the West Bank and Jordan seem to intimidate with a bit of panache. The Allenby Bridge crossing is one of only two corridors afforded to the Palestinians to escape from, and back into, the West Bank. Getting through in and out is hard enough on a good day but it was just 11 days after Israel stopped shelling Lebanon and Hezbollah ceased firing back its shoddy supply of Katyusha rockets into the north of the country and security was tight. Although far from the blanket patrols of intimidating soldiers favoured by most countries, Israel has chosen to staff its border exclusively with teenagers. If Russ Meyer were still alive today, the script would write itself.

I had become one of an increasingly irate mass of travellers trying to squeeze through the two small desks at the Israeli reception terminal, an innocuous concrete slab that – if it weren't for the huge, grainy black-and-white posters of young Israeli soldiers who had been kidnapped during the country's last incursion into Lebanon during the Eighties – could be a provincial bus station anywhere in the home counties. Hundreds of Palestinian families had been at Israel's border post for hours in the harsh midday sun of late summer after visiting family in Jordan, attending weddings in Iraq or kissing goodbye to sick relatives in Syria. The young Israeli border guards, fearing queue rage, encouraged us to move along the line by vigorously shaking their machine guns. We inched along as our bags and possessions were torn apart, prodded, scanned and squeezed before stepping through metal detectors, pairs of probing hands and then finally the Allenby Border's jewel in the crown: a machine that blows air to see if you have any explosive dust on your clothing. For a brief second it crossed my mind that I might once have let off a firecracker in the T-shirt. I started to play out nightmare scenarios: me being hauled out of the queue and worked on by Mossad agents, presumably under the impression that I was in fact some kind of blond, possibly Chechen Islamic terrorist disguising myself as a journalist. The guard waited and stared at me sternly. I stared back from the large, plastic box, sweating slightly and running the past week over in my mind to discount the possibility I might have accidentally brushed against high-grade munitions. The green light goes, the girl smiles, I walk through. 'Passport,' barked the curly-haired teenager behind the Perspex glass counter, rudely pulling me out of my train of thought. 'What is your business in Israel?'

'Well,' I stuttered, 'I'm a British journalist writing a story about the start of the Israeli football season so I'm heading for . . .'

'A journalist? Football?' she interrupted, as if this was the worst lie she had ever heard. Then she clocked the Iranian stamp on my passport. This, I began to think as she ushered over colleagues to see the alien stamp from a country whose president has made it his number one objective to push their country and its people into the sea, was the end of the road. It had only dawned on me as I was waiting for the bus to take me over the Jordan River – once a raging torrent that moulded the huge, flat Jordan Valley but now a grungy green trickle thanks to over damming – that visiting Israel's sworn enemy six months previously wasn't the best idea. But border stamp politics were rife in this region. The land route from Jordan was the only way I could get into the country as the UAE, like all other Middle Eastern states bar Egypt and Jordan, didn't recognise Israel's existence. With no direct flights, I had to fly to Amman, take a bus to the outskirts and take a separate Allenby taxi – for which I was handsomely fleeced – to the border before climbing aboard a special Allenby bus whose only journey was the 500 metres between Jordan and Israel. In a different, parallel universe, the 45-mile drive from Amman to Jerusalem would take under an hour. Today, with check points, crossings, borders and searches, it takes four hours, two buses, two taxis and three separate pieces of paper that would avoid the Israeli passport stamp – a kiss of death for anyone wanting to visit anywhere else in the Middle East. I hadn't really worried about the stamp until I sat next to Simon on the short bus ride from Jordan to Israel. Simon was Swedish, had a shaven head and was intimidatingly reading a book entitled *Advanced Arabic* in preparation for his autumn term at Hebron University, where he was studying. This was his third attempt at getting into the country and he had become something of an expert on failure in this area. 'You have to watch out, never tell the Israelis you are going into the West Bank or that you are visiting any Palestinian territories,' he said, taking sharp intakes of breath as he flipped through my passport. 'Iran, that might be a problem. I mean, last time they wouldn't let me through and didn't tell me why.' If the Swedes had a problem getting in anywhere, it's safe to say that no one is safe. Everybody likes the Swedes. They've even managed, unlike the Swiss, to avoid the stigma of their Second World War neutrality. But the Israelis tended to have a schizophrenic relationship with the British: on the one hand, giving them grudging recognition for the 1917 Balfour Declaration – a letter penned by then Foreign Secretary Arthur Balfour that sowed the seeds for the creation of Israel – on the other, feeling that the British had betrayed the Jewish people in the way it policed the struggle between Arab forces and the fledgling Haganah between the end of World War Two and the creation of Israel in 1948. Such moves like violently suppressing Israel's armed militias, amongst them the Irgun and the Stern Gang, and preventing boatloads of shattered European Jewish Holocaust survivors from landing in British mandated Palestine – one ship, the *Exodus*, was even sent back to Hamburg – didn't help. Simon shrugged knowingly as I turned around at the desk and the crowd of female Israeli border guards grew around my passport.

'So tell me again, what is your business in Israel?' she repeated after conferring in Hebrew with her fellow guards.

'I'm a football journalist, I'm going to see Maccabi Haifa's first match against Maccabi Netanya in . . . ' I didn't get a chance to finish.

'Maccabi Haifa, they're my home team!' the guard replied excitedly, cracking a smile and giving her age away for the first time, before composing herself and looking at me doubtfully. She had devised a foolproof test.

'Who is your favourite player then?' Much like the blinded contestant on Eighties kids' fantasy game show *Knightmare*, one step left would see me plummet into oblivion, one step right and I was home and dry, avoiding the end of level boss who was impeding my progress.

'Well, I like Yaniv Katan but Yossi Benayoun is my favourite,' I proffered unconvincingly.

This was a shot in the dark. Being a West Ham fan, I knew that Alan Pardew's most astute bit of business was to sign Israel's mercurial midfielder, who was also the captain of the national team. But for all I knew, jumping ship for England might have made him as popular on Haifa's terraces as Hassan Nasrallah. Thankfully Yossi Benayoun was more popular than Moses. 'Yossi Benayoun,' she sighed nostalgically. 'The best player Israel has ever produced.' He may never know it, but I owe Yossi Benayoun a debt I can scarcely begin to pay. And it wouldn't be the last time that the mere mention of the cultured, bowl-haired midfielder – an unlikely sex symbol in Israel – would get me out of a pickle. I picked up my bags and headed

the Western Wall for the Jews and the Church of the Holy Sepulchre for Christians. On the surface, the city could almost pass as a model for Middle Eastern multiculturalism: packs of fedora-wearing Orthodox Jews brush past crowds of abaya-clad Muslim women without either party being too bothered by the other's existence. The heavily armed police on every street corner tell a different story. Guns are everywhere, carried by seemingly pre-pubescent kids. But this is the demographic reality of Israel. With a population of just seven million, five and a half million of it Jewish and falling, and with constant threats at all of its borders, Israel needs a steady stream of conscripts to make up the numbers. Every Israeli man, woman and, from the look of it, child has to do their bit: three years of military service. And knowing the high probability of Israel getting into some kind of scrap with its unfriendly neighbours, they're likely to see front line action too. It was hard to imagine transporting the packs of olive green khaki-wearing soldiers, all of whom were entrusted with a machine gun and commanded the utmost respect from passers-by as they checked everyone's ID, to the ASBO-riddled estates of England.

With Haifa experiencing collective hysteria after being on the front line for the past month, and with Jerusalem long used to tension for straddling both Israel and the West Bank – the Jewish western half with its foot in the former, the Muslim eastern half seized from the Jordanians in 1967 in the latter – Tel Aviv gives a good impression of a city that doesn't really care that a war is going on. The locals semi-affectionately know the place as 'the bubble', a reference to the fact that Hamas, Hezbollah, Islamic Jihad – in fact any militant Palestinian organisation that has attempted to attack major cities in Israel – still haven't been able to devise a rocket that can reach the country's capital. Thus, Tel Aviv has remained relatively untouched and is famed for its 'life goes on as normal' detachment, its abundance of drugs and for being the party capital of the Middle East. Not to mention its vibrant gay community, a state of affairs that no doubt angers Israel's Orthodox Jewish burghers as much as the militant Islamists coveting their ancestral lands from afar. The party bubble didn't seem to stretch to the Tel Aviv Youth Hostel, my home for the next five nights, thanks to a combination of poverty and stinginess. The dorm was dark and heavily stained, with a smell that managed to mix bleach and human refuse. My bed was tiny and had a large, crusty red stain splattered in messy concentric circles from a bald epicentre on the wall, as if matter had struck it at speed and smeared itself outwards. Perhaps it was the remnants of a tomato, or a pomegranate, being thrown at the wall. The room also had Victor. Victor had stumbled up to the front desk with a rifle, stinking of booze, after driving up from the Negev desert. In her wisdom, the woman at the front desk had decided that Victor and I should share the room. Just the two of us. The fear didn't really kick in until Victor had sunk his second beer and taken off his shirt to show me his bullet wounds. The stain above my head suddenly had a viable explanation – the detritus from a rifle-induced suicide. Fifty-seven years old, with scraggy grey hair and an unkempt beard, Victor was an army man, three months away from his pension, who was on his way north to shore up Israel's Lebanese border. He'd seen three wars now, and taken hits in all of them. Unsurprisingly he didn't have much time for the Arabs. 'You can't trust them, they hate us,' he said whilst cramming in alternate mouthfuls of bread and tinned tuna on a plastic bag. 'Why can't they just leave us alone?' Victor seemed lost in the memories of a long-forgotten battlefield, and I took it as my cue to leave and see what Tel Aviv had to offer. I'd arranged to meet Amir, the editor of weekly listings magazine *Time Out Tel Aviv*. He had achieved a little notoriety in recent weeks after being interviewed by various American television networks along with his counterpart at *Time Out Beirut*. Amir, however, still had a job to go to whilst his opposite number was cowering in a basement under his office. Amir was in his late 30s, with salt and pepper hair and an embarrassing musical past (he used to be the guitarist in Prototype, Israel's early Nineties answer to REM). He was a self-confessed liberal and had been troubled by the war, yet was annoyed by the lack of understanding internationally for Israel's position. 'I feel bad for what is happening in Lebanon, I really do,' he agreed whilst expertly rolling a joint in his modern, minimalist flat. 'But few people seem to be concerned by how we feel here, the fear of attack, the lives lost. Civilians have been killed on both sides.' In keeping with his liberal beliefs Amir supported one of Israel's left-wing clubs, Hapoel Haifa. Israeli football can be split roughly into three prefixes: Hapoel (which translates as 'the club of the workers', who represent the left), Maccabi (as in Maccabi Tel Aviv, which denotes that the club is traditionally of the liberal middle classes) and Beitar (as in Beitar Jerusalem, which represents the religious right). For years the political and religious divisions created hated, sometimes vicious rivalries that mirrored the deep schisms in Israeli society. In recent years, however, football had begun to become big business in Israel. Television deals were signed, stadiums spruced up and Israeli football experienced a new phenomenon: billionaire Jewish sugar daddies willing to pump their fortunes into their hometown clubs. Some were more welcome than others. Arcadi Gaydamak was one to make the headlines after buying Beitar Jerusalem. The controversial tycoon might be beloved by his club's fans but his rivals are loath to forget his more fruity business dealings: arms smuggling out of Angola, an international arrest warrant outstanding in France and shady oil deals out of his homeland, it's alleged. Daniel Jammer is another, a German billionaire who bought Maccabi Netanya and straight away enquired of Real Madrid as to whether David Beckham would consider moving to the club (he wouldn't, unsurprisingly). But not every infusion of foreign cash had been successful. Amir's Hapoel Haifa had a brush with infamy when Rubi Shapira, a lifelong Hapoel fan whose dad used to be the club's kit man and who had made a fortune in African fishing concessions, bought the club and promised to bring the fans their first championship, which he duly delivered in 1999. The problem was that Rubi was so hell-bent on his dream he bankrupted himself in the process. One month later he flew to Africa and shot himself in the head. They've been stuck in the second division ever since.

Nobody seems to go out before 2 a.m. in Tel Aviv. It's even harder to handle when you have high levels of THC coursing through your veins, making you want to do little more than gibber on the floor and sleep. Amir seemed fine. Clearly he'd been weaned on the stuff. Somehow I managed to hold it together long enough to get past the bouncers of one of Tel Aviv's best clubs – a grimy courtyard surrounding a split-level shed with a sunken dance floor. Its warehouse chic was more affected than it perhaps realised. But the city's nickname becomes abundantly clear the moment you get inside. Despite being a few days after the end of hostilities, and with a relapse still very much a possibility, hundreds of people packed the bar, danced on the tables and kissed in corners. Perhaps this was what it was like during the Blitz in 1940s London: people throwing caution to the wind, shagging, taking copious amounts of drugs and generally acting as if the world would end tomorrow. But Amir was too preoccupied with something far more serious than thoughts of my grandparents' sexual peccadilloes. The war had exposed Israel to a greater threat than Lebanon or even Hezbollah: Iran. 'If they get the nuclear bomb,' he sighed through a bottle of beer, 'where do you think they'll hit? Here.' As if on cue, behind him two beautiful skinhead boys kissed without inhibition. 'This is everything they hate. Tel Aviv has a big red cross on it.' The bubble's unshakeable party atmosphere hadn't been rocked by the war against Lebanon, or even a decade's worth of suicide bus-bombings, but ordinary Israelis had been stung by the bellicose pronouncements of its Persian neighbour. Whilst the outside world saw the war as a simple conflict between a state and an armed militia within a state, Israelis viewed it very differently: as an opportunity to prove its military strength to its wider Arab and Persian foes whilst vanquishing Iran's Shia ally on its northern border. She failed on both counts. The press was having a field day against Ehud Olmert's government: the right was apoplectic with rage for not destroying Hassan Nasrallah's guerrilla army, Hezbollah, failing to force the return of the two captured soldiers and giving succour to its soon to be nuclear enemy. The left was unhappy at the huge civilian toll that Lebanon had endured.

The possibility that Iran might one day destroy everything we could see in nuclear fire was enough to lower the mood, and we retired to a popular café for a nightcap. I had to get an early night. Tomorrow was the first day of the Israeli football season. 'That, over there,' pointed Amir animatedly, 'that is Dana International's manager.' He continued, nodding in the direction of well-known Hebrew singers, middle-aged record producers and an overweight transvestite who was wearing a woman's top so small it sat on top of his rotund belly. 'He is a famous soap star,' Amir gave by way of an explanation. As war raged across the region, it was comforting to know that somewhere in the Middle East, life went on as normal. Or as normal as a bar full of Israel's transgender glitterati can be.

In the shadow of Maccabi Netanya's crumbling stadium, with the low, late-afternoon sun shining harshly, Oren hadn't seen business like it in years. Wearing his obligatory Maccabi Haifa green-and-white strip and clutching a large, flat wooden suitcase of football merchandise, his pitch for cheap, polyester scarves and fake gold Star of David necklaces bearing his beloved team's name was being met with an unusually positive reaction. The fans – usually indifferent to Oren's mercantile overtures – crowded around, laughing, before putting their hands in their pockets and dropping a few shekels in his palm. The source of this new-found wealth wasn't early-season optimism or an upsurge in sympathy for a team whose hometown had been the focal point of Hezbollah's bombardment. Instead, Oren thrust the key to his success into my hand – a small, green sticker. On it a cheeky cartoon Haifa fan is urinating onto the hastily Photoshopped face of Hezbollah leader Hassan Nasrallah. Crude it may be, but for only five shekels apiece, it was a bargain and the Haifa fans couldn't get enough of them. 'It says "Nasrallah you are garbage",' grinned Oren as he shifted another to a still-chuckling fan. 'He's no good, he shoots rockets where there are civilians. They fire deliberately on civilians and when we retaliate they say we are bad. We have a chant for him today: "Yallah, yallah, Nasrallah, I kill you, I kill you, Inshallah".' Shlomi, his fellow merchandise seller, was a little more sanguine. 'If it was up to me I'd bomb every house in southern Lebanon,' he spat through a mouthful of semi-digested sunflower seeds. 'Give my regards to Nasrallah if you see him.'

After awaking on Friday morning to a pulsating headache in my dormitory room and discovering that I had been joined in the night by a group of heavily armed conscripts on their way north to the front line, I tiptoed through the pockmarked piles of army regulation rucksacks and rifles – trying not to wake Victor who was snoring in the wake of his previous night's bender: several empty bottles of wine and a beer can with fag butts pushed haphazardly around it. I travelled the short journey north to Netanya with Ahikam, a photographer who wanted to capture the opening-season fervour. Handsome and in his early 30s, Ahikam seemed relaxed to the point of narcolepsy, although this was unsurprising given that he carried a large block of hash with him everywhere he went. In fact, everyone in Israel seemed to have a regulation amount of cannabis on them, although given the daily threats of war, suicide bombings or impending nuclear attack, it's probably a wise move. It might also have something to do with the proximity of the finest hash production line in the world: Lebanon's Bekaa Valley. It was one trade that hadn't been in the remotest way affected by years of war. Israel's huge consumption of soft drugs had even reached the outside of Netanya's stadium, or 'The Box' as it's referred to due to its small size and enclosed atmosphere, where teenagers smoked constantly to prove their manliness. The crumbling walls and lack of an east stand gave the place a neutered, dilapidated air of a 1970s third-division ground on the brink of liquidation, like the Old Den, or Ayresome Park. There was little intimidating about The Box, despite the profusion of barbed wire. The inscription on the front gates in Hebrew – 'Welcome to Hell' – seemed to be steeped in irony. The war against Lebanon was fresh in the minds of the hundreds of Maccabi Haifa and Maccabi Netanya fans milling around trying to buy tickets for the Ligat Hal'al curtain raiser. Haifa's season had started earlier but not quite as they expected. With the city under siege and rockets getting worryingly close to the pitch, UEFA ordered that Haifa's Champions League qualifying home match against Liverpool be moved to a neutral location. After scoring first but succumbing to a highly respectable 2–1 defeat at Anfield, Haifa drew in a sub-zero Kiev, ending their hopes of Champions League glory. Then the first game of the season, a home tie against Ashdod, was cancelled and instead the fans had to trudge south to the decrepit charms of Netanya, a shabby coastal town known for its high crime rate and moderate beaches.

The ghost of Nasrallah was everywhere. The fans angrily chanted his name and his image was desecrated and corrupted on hundreds of placards, posters and T-shirts. Which isn't to say that Haifa's fans are virulently anti-Arab – far from it. Whilst teams like Beitar Jerusalem refuse to sign Arab players for fear of upsetting their right-wing fans, Maccabi Haifa can boast current Israeli international and the country's most famous Arab player, Abbas Suan. 'The fascists, like Lazio, they are Beitar Jerusalem,' explained Kornel, a 20-year-old soldier who fought in Lebanon and who was also a member of the Green Apes – the closest Haifa got to a hooligan brigade. 'We are less political like that because we have no problems with Arabs. The war hasn't caused any problems between us. We are from Israel, they are all Israelis too.' The Green Apes were here en masse. Hanging around in the shadow of their crumbling host, drinking cans of Becks and singing 'I'm Forever Blowing Bubbles' in mockney accents – a hangover from the movie *Green Street*, which every hooligan group in Israel seemed to have watched to get tips on how to be a proper 'firm' like the notorious ICF. The fact that their most recent export, Yossi Benayoun, had moved to West Ham was a reason to be doubly proud of their famous son. They all seemed a bit too nice to be considered hooligans, though – one part liberal integrationists; one part ultras; one part youth club – as they crowded around to show off their initiation tattoos: either a large green ape on the shoulder blade or the letters ACAB, an acronym for All Cops Are Bastards, printed prominently on the forearm. They even had a huge ACAB poster – illustrated by a mean, American-looking cop – to hang on the hoardings during the match. Proudly liberal, the Green Apes differentiated between 'their Arabs' and 'Nasrallah's Arabs' and insisted that war has only brought Haifa's Jewish and Arab fans closer together. Except for Hezbollah, the only other organisation that united Haifa's Jewish and Arab Muslim fans was Liverpool – or 'Chicken Pool' as they were known. Liverpool's refusal to play their Champions League qualifier in Israel had made them public enemy number two. 'Rafa Benitez is a chicken. Sissoko is Nasrallah's cousin. He fights for Hezbollah!' shouted Tamar, a middle-aged woman escorting her son to the match. She scarily tapped at my notebook just to get the point across. 'Haifa is a safe place. Not even in England is it safe. What about your airports? And games were played after the bombs in London and Madrid, weren't they? You should write it in bold: Israel is safe.' With their Jewish brethren under attack and the opening game being something of a symbolic moment for the city of Haifa – a chance to show the world that it was bruised but unbowed – you would have thought that Israel's footballing fraternity would come together in a show of national unification. Netanya's fans, jealous from Haifa's near domination of Israeli football over the past half-decade, had a different plan: almost every fan wore Liverpool's yellow away kit. 'It's because we play in yellow as well, but it's to annoy Haifa,' explained Hagai, a 25-year-old fan who lived by the ground. 'We are glad they were kicked out. We hate Haifa because they think they're the best team in the world and take all our best players.'

Inside the stadium one stand was packed with thousands of Haifa fans wearing green and letting off luminous red flares. Having started to watch football in England just before the dawn of the Premiership, when crowd violence could rear its head at any moment and the prospect of electrified fences to keep fleet-footed fans off the pitch was an all too real threat, it was still a shock to see armed Israeli police patrol the perimeter fence through the badly observed minute's silence. The favourites quickly go one down, then two, then three. Netanya's fans go crazy, scarcely able to believe that they were there to witness one of the great shocks of modern Israeli football. The game finished 3–1, the Green Apes rolled up their cop-baiting banner and left in silence without apportioning blame on players or management. They knew that the only person to blame for their team's poor preparations was a bearded ideologue, hidden in a bunker hundreds of miles away somewhere near the Syrian border.

The Israeli landscape undergoes a subtle change as you drive north from Tel Aviv towards the Lebanese border. The industrial suburbs of the big cities gradually morph into plush, green olive groves, expansive valleys and signposts for flat, sand-yellow towns with names familiar from numerous past newsflashes: Afula, Jenin, Hebron. As the road north skirted the walled enclave of the West Bank an abundance of minarets gave away that more than just the terrain had changed. The majority of Israel's Arab – mainly Muslim – community can be found on the fertile planes in the north of the country, although this wealth of natural resources hadn't translated into any economic or social parity. This was also Katyusha country, the southernmost point where Hezbollah's most advanced rockets landed. After watching Maccabi Haifa's capitulation the previous night, albeit an understandable one given the team's preparations, Ahikam and I were headed for the small Arab town of Sakhnin to interview its most famous son, Maccabi Haifa's recent big-money signing and Israel's most prominent Arab footballer Abbas Suan. His transfer to the country's most successful team was almost inevitable after his Herculean efforts of the past two years. Abbas came to the nation's attention after leading his hometown club Bnei Sakhnin to the Israeli cup in 2004, a success that shone a light on a community viewed suspiciously both by their Jewish countrymen (for being pro-Palestinian fifth columnists) and by the wider Arab world (for being Zionist collaborators). His status as a poster boy for Israel's Arabs and the liberal left was cemented when he came on late and scored a last-minute equaliser in a World Cup qualifier against Ireland in 2005. For now, though, we were lost and, in a leftfield attempt at getting us back on track, Ahikam asked a child wearing Bnei Sakhnin's red kit whether he knew where Abbas Suan's house was. The child scrunched up his face in confusion before looking back incredulously, pointing up the road, to the left, as if the answer was so obvious it didn't merit a reply. Everybody, it seemed, knew where Abbas Suan lived.

We pulled up at Abbas' modest stone town house and negotiated the large courtyard bustling with life: brothers, cousins, uncles – the entire Suan clan had decamped within his modest four walls. His father, whose face wore the deep creases of a man who had worked the land for half-a-century, shuttled back and forth to the kitchen, fetching tea, fruit and plates of dates for his guests, before sitting down and regaling us with stories from his childhood memories: his grandfather had bought land for farming from the Turks and moved to Sakhnin as a child before finally having all but a tiny plot seized during the *nakba* – or 'The Catastrophe' as it is known – when the Palestinians were expelled or fled in 1948 when the state of Israel was created. As Abbas arrived, his father tidied the empty plates and disappeared into the kitchen. It was all but the briefest of glimpses into a past that was still fresh in living memory. 'The Haifa fans accepted me very quickly,' yawned Abbas as he sat down, still rubbing his eyes after being awoken from a lie-in on his only day off. 'I know that in the beginning some kids wrote some slogans against me because I was an Arab but the club stamped down on this because they have so many Arab fans and they've had Arab stars playing for Haifa in the past.' The Haifa fans might have greeted his signing positively, but it has been harder to convince the fans of other teams of the merits of playing an Arab in a largely Jewish team. 'Generally speaking, Israeli fans are wonderful, one of the best in the world. At the same time there are a few that behave shamefully and we're all shamed by them,' he said, referring to one team in particular. 'I'm speaking about the fans of Beitar Jerusalem which behave beneath an accepted conduct.' Abbas has had a somewhat fractured relationship with the Beitar fans. After scoring his historic goal against Ireland, his next game was an away tie at Jerusalem's notorious Teddy Stadium. The home fans welcomed his achievement by unfurling a banner. It read: 'Abbas, You Are Not One of Us.' After one game, a group of fans managed to break into the stadium whilst he was giving a post-match interview and attacked him. Perhaps

most surprising of all, Abbas very nearly became Beitar's first
ever Arab player. The club's billionaire owner Arcadi Gaydamak
has close links with Bnei Sakhnin and has donated millions of
shekels to keep the club afloat. Then one day, on a visit to the
club, he decided he wanted to sign their star player for himself.
'I said I was ready, I could do it,' he said with an unexpected
hint of disappointment. 'I believe he was trying to break the
image of Beitar and say Arab players can play for them. But
he got into trouble in Jerusalem. In the end he apologised and
said he couldn't sign me.'

The past three months hadn't gone well for Bnei Sakhnin.
The club were relegated from the Israeli top division, lost their
captain and almost went bankrupt before Gaydamak came to
the rescue. Then the war came and the age old suspicions levied
against Israel's Arabs were once again raised. It was only a matter
of time, given that Abbas refuses to sing the national anthem
('I don't take the Hatikvah, but I stand and respect it. It's the
anthem of the Jewish people. So what can I do? I am Arab
and Muslim') but was proud to fly the flag of the state, before
the country's media came to him when the war started. 'When
the war broke, everybody asked me what I thought. A drop of
blood from a Jewish or Arab child is the same, and the missiles
don't distinguish between Jews and Arabs. So I was against the
war, but I was worried for my family as rockets fell in Sakhnin.
It was a big failure but politicians stick to their chairs. I wish
politicians would enter Lebanon in a tank. Maybe then they
wouldn't be so ready for a war.' After we had finished talking,
he agreed to drive us to his old home, Bnei Sakhnin's Doha
Stadium – so called because the Qatari government stumped
up the cash to have the place renovated, a remarkable gesture
given that Qatar doesn't officially recognise Israel's existence. As
he stood on the pitch and surveyed his alma mater, the parallels
between the club's descent and the plight of his people during
and after the war weren't lost on him. If anything, the role that
has been foisted on him – of spokesman and role model for
a whole community – had never been as important as now.
'When we won the national cup I was proud for the Arabs in
Israel and the fact that we were narrowing the gaps between

communities through football,' he said nostalgically. 'Now there are many symbols attached to me and many see me as an Arab symbol in Israel. I will always accept it.' Whilst most players, in response to any kind of articulation of feeling or emotion, offer that most inane of clichés – of 'doing my talking on the pitch' – Abbas had decided that more was needed to show just how segregated Israel's '20', as the country's Arabs refer to themselves, are. But the size of the task of accepting Israel's Arabs is brought into sharp focus when you consider Israeli Jews' widely held views on their fellow Arab citizens. On the eve of Israel's 60th birthday, the *New York Times* reported that a majority of Israeli Jews now favoured the expulsion of some Israeli Arabs as part of a two-state solution. On the journey home we again passed the distant minarets of the West Bank, an area of extreme poverty ringed by the new Berlin wall, as it has been dubbed by campaigners, adjacent to an affluent Western democracy. Anywhere else in the world, such a juxtaposition of wealth and extreme privation would be considered vulgar. But for most Israelis, even Ahikam who agitated throughout his military service and was eventually given a dishonourable discharge, it's the price that the Palestinians have paid for years of terrorism and duplicity. 'I just can't understand these people like the International Solidarity Movement protesting here, what has it got to do with them?' he spat when I asked him about the wall. Even calling it a wall causes offence. 'It's not even a wall in most places, just a fence. You don't see them [the ISM] protesting in China at human rights abuses.' I pointed out that several activists and journalists, including Rachel Corrie, had died in the West Bank protesting against the wall. 'Yes, but look at the reality. Since the fence we have had no attacks from suicide bombings. I was against it at first, too, but we feel safer because of it. If the Palestinians want their own state, fine. But it's crazy. How will they live? They could have been part of Israel and had a better quality of life and, if they were smart, they would have outnumbered Jews.' You can see his point. The fence has created a problem for Israeli liberals, who despised what it represented but were forced to admit that their country was safer because of it. That, plus the seeming failure of Israel's unilateral withdrawal from southern Lebanon in 2000 – a move which the Israeli right blamed for allowing Hezbollah to rearm – and Sharon's disengagement plan from the Gaza Strip had forced everyone to reassess their opinions rightwards, even the most trenchantly left-wing Israelis who would have thought those views to be the preserve of right-wing extremists a decade ago.

Wearing a red T-shirt and admitting I was a journalist was looking like a bad idea. It was 24 hours after Haifa's capitulation and the Israeli football circus had moved to the Bloomfield Stadium in Tel Aviv for one of the biggest matches of the season: former greats Maccabi Tel Aviv versus the moneyed passion of Beitar Jerusalem. You couldn't guess it was a Tel Aviv home game, though. Outside the futuristic ground all you could see was the gold and black of Beitar. But some fans had taken exception to my choice of top. Red is the colour of arch rivals Hapoel Tel Aviv, the capital's other club known for their passionate socialist views and the polar opposite of Beitar's right-wing terrace racism. 'We hate Arabs and Muslims!' screamed 19-year-old Eliran as I tried to explain that I was not a Hapoel agitator. 'If an Arab played for Beitar we'd burn their ass and burn the club. They are our enemy.' Eliran was a member of La Familia, Beitar's infamous hooligan group renowned for being the most violent and uncompromising in the land. 'Ten supporters went to meet Sakhnin and make peace with the Arabs,' he explained. 'But Beitar found out. They were beaten up and banned.' They also don't have much time for journalists. 'Beitar have the best hooligans, we'd fuck the ICF,' boasted Itzick, a bare-chested fan who seemed a lot more intimidating than his 15 years should allow and who had clearly watched *Green Street* and *The Football Factory* on repeat. 'And we hate journalists.' Now seemed to be a good time to play my Yossi Benayoun trump card. 'Yossi Benayoun!' yelped Itzick excitedly when I told him my allegiance. 'He should come and play for us. You seem OK for a journalist. The rest can go fuck themselves.' And with that he ran into his crew of bare-chested boys, who were all screaming in unison, in perfect accented English:

I'm West Ham till I die.
I'm West Ham till I die.
I know I am.
I'm sure I am.
I'm West Ham till I die.

I was safe, for the meantime at least.

Beitar Jerusalem is not unique for sporting a fan base that holds some uncomfortable views. But what is unusual is the phenomenal amount of power the fans wielded both within the club and within the Israeli political system. Outside of its core activities of organising fights and making racist flags, La Familia also liaised with club officials on the issues that affected the fans, like high ticket prices and whether the management were planning to sign any Arab players. It was their virulent protests that eventually persuaded Gaydamak to abandon signing Abbas Suan. But Beitar is also the team of government. The club has long-standing links with the Likud party and if a politician has any chance of getting elected, he must first parade himself in front of the Beitar faithful. Ehud Olmert is a massive fan, something that makes the average supporter overlook more than they perhaps should, even a disastrous military campaign against Lebanon. 'Olmert used to be here every game. But now he doesn't turn up any more, the police don't allow him to turn up as he's a security problem,' shrugged Nadav, one of Beitar's few self-styled liberal fans, whilst hanging around in a nearby park waiting for the gates to open. 'But he's popular because he introduced Gaydamak to the club. In Israel there are a lot of people who want to come to the government and they come to Beitar Jerusalem, they take pictures with the fans because there are lots of right-wing fans here, especially those that support Likud.' Rumours abound that Gaydamak's acquisition of Beitar had more to do with his political ambitions than any great love for the club. By the sound of the fans who were singing 'I believe the Messiah is here, Arkadi, Arkadi' before the game started, he already had a few votes in the bag. The Bloomfield Stadium was full two hours before kick-off and the 7,000-strong army of gold-and-black Beitar fans were deafening. With a false sense of security garnered by my Yossi Benayoun get-out-of-jail card, I had decided to climb the large north terrace and join the Beitar faithful, red T-shirt and all. But the fans were friendly, offering me cigarettes and sunflower seeds. This, I thought as another chant grew and filled the stadium, wasn't as bad as I thought it would be. Sure, the minority might have some dodgy views but they seemed good, stand up fans really. It was only then I realised what they were singing. 'I know this one,' translated the only other English speaker in the ground, Jeremy, a British journalist working for the *Jerusalem Post*. 'They are singing: "We Hate Nazareth, We Hate Sakhnin, I Swear On The Menorah There Will Be No Arabs Here."' Others followed, each more sanguine than the last: 'War, War, War'; 'The Empire Will Return'; and 'Tel Aviv Will Be Sacrificed By Fire'. Beitar thought they had taken the lead, but the goal was ruled offside. The fans were incandescent with rage and hurled missiles at the referee and linesman. A yellow smoke bomb, red flares and a volley of half-eaten pretzels rained down. The decision stood although it made no difference to the final result: Beitar won 2–1 and the players were on their knees in front of their ecstatic fans as if they'd won the championship already. Unable to escape the heaving mass, I was carried along with the throng of Beitar fans that streamed out into Tel Aviv's southern suburbs and what began as a good-natured celebration started to degenerate into a riot. We ran along the main road as fans let off red flares and climbed atop parked cars to get a better view. The police waded in to try and control the melee by charging the crowd, firstly with police horses and then by driving a *Chips*-style motorbike at them, and at us – at speed. One fan in front of me was punched flush in the face whilst another policeman took a swing at me with his baton, but missed. The jubilant Beitar fans danced in the street, partially lit by the smoky glow of flares and firecrackers. For a brief moment it seemed that the fans' earlier promises to turn Tel Aviv to fire were coming true. Even the police admitted defeat by falling back to defend a main junction whilst the party continued in the shops and car parks around them. Rarely do you get a chance to sit back and watch a bona fide riot. There was something frightening but exhilaratingly anarchic about it. For a fleeting few minutes, there were no rules, no government, only the pack and an internal dynamic being held together by a common passion. The downside of this was, as two skinheads grabbed me and tried to rip my T-shirt off, that if you appear to be off kilter with that internal dynamic, you're fucked. 'Take off your Hapoel top, you fuck, it's disrespectful,' screamed one, mistaking me for a Hapoel fan. Maybe it was the pure, blind terror in my eyes, my stuttering assurance that I was an English journalist or the desperate begging for them not to hit me in the face that convinced them. Although the fleeting joy of victory, which no doubt briefly outweighed the latent hatred for someone who — for a Beitar fan — represented two of the greatest evils that walk the earth, probably had more to do with it. They looked at each other, smiled and ceased molesting me — convinced that I was a friendly journalist and not the local scum who were out to sully Beitar's good name. 'I wear this every day, to every game,' the smaller man said apologetically. 'It's special, and I give it to you. I'm sorry.' He patted me on the head and ran, leaving me panting, confused but slightly warmer thanks to the thick cotton Beitar scarf — embossed with the Star of David and a menorah — that now coiled across my shoulders. I can only imagine what would have happened if Beitar had lost.

Uri had something to show me. After escaping the hordes of rioting Beitar fans by the skin of my teeth, I had decided to opt for a more cerebral experience the following day — an interview with the sports editor of *Ha'aretz*, Israel's foremost liberal daily. At least, that was what I thought I was getting until I met Uri outside his plush, modern offices in Tel Aviv. Within seconds of shaking my hand he had unbuttoned his shirt and was baring me his shoulder blade. Tattooed on it was a red hammer and sickle with the words 'Hapoel Tel Aviv' etched around it. 'If I ever get into any trouble with the Ultras, I just show them my tattoo. That soon shuts them up,' he said, grinning. With his school geek glasses and sensible shoes, Uri didn't look like the type of guy who'd flirt with the darker side of terrace politics, but passions run a little deeper in Israeli football. 'Even before the state of Israel was founded, everything was very political and football was no different from that,' he explained after putting his shirt back on and taking me to his favourite restaurant – a spit and sawdust curry house run by two Israeli hippies that stank of Nag Champa incense. 'Every big political group had its own team: Hapoel teams represented the big unions that were running the country – the workers and labourers; the teams of Maccabi represented the middle class; and the teams of Beitar were representing the right-wing nationalist minority.' Hapoel Tel Aviv was Israel's most famous socialist club, a team that had until the mid-1980s been owned by a union and who had welcomed Arab players and fans with open arms. They were the team of the kibbutz settlements – from Eilat on the Red Sea to Haifa on the Mediterranean coast. To their political and footballing opponents, they were simply and disparagingly known as 'The Communists'. But despite their strong political identity, things had slowly been changing at Hapoel Tel Aviv. 'We had a cup final against Beitar in 1999 which was three days after the elections. Labour won and we took a huge banner to the game that read: "We fucked you in the elections, now we'll fuck you on the pitch,"' Uri recalled. 'But now the political identity of the clubs has faded. The one thing left is the name. All the teams now have private ownerships, have a very vague connection with the Labour party or the union and what are left are basically the fans.' Money – in the form of billion-shekel takeovers from the likes of Gaydamak at Beitar and lucrative pay-per-view television contracts – has begun to flood the game in Israel. But Israeli society still had a long way to go before dealing with its deeply held racism and political divisions. 'The only thing that stays the same is hatred – the level of hatred,' said a resigned Uri. 'You have 20 teams hating the other side and maybe two or three teams supporting their own side. Israeli society is so tense, there are so many conflicts: religious, political, economic, social. It can get really ugly. In Israel it's not a culture of supporting, it's a culture of hating.'

Everything that Uri said about the deep internal divisions within Israeli society had resonated with what I had seen outside the grounds, on the terraces and on the streets. But back at the Bloomfield, 24 hours after Beitar Jerusalem fans were threatening to burn Tel Aviv to the ground and wishing death to the Arabs, the atmosphere was one, if not of conciliation, then certainly of tolerance: Hapoel's fans were singing the name of Walid Badir, an Arab player famous in Israel for playing for the national team and, more importantly, for a brief stint in the Premiership; his single season in the top flight coming with the now defunct Wimbledon FC. It was a Monday night and this was the final game of the season's opening weekend, a tricky tie against Tel Aviv's smallest but most right-wing team, Bnei Yehuda. The crowd was smaller than the previous evening, but given that the game was on television and it was a school night, it was understandable. The north stand was awash with red-and-black and socialist imagery: flags of Che Guevara, hammer and sickles, the large red banner of Hapoel's Ultras – the team's hardcore fan group whose reputation had forced Uri into having his back branded, just in case – and placards adorned with a bottle-green marijuana leaf. It was more reminiscent of student protest from the early Seventies, almost anachronistic compared to the prescient hatred of Beitar's travelling support. At the front a bald man surveyed the scene with a mixture of pride and apprehension. 'There is less politics than there used to be, the parties are less important,' lamented Ronin, a wealthy architect who moved from Argentina 15 years ago but quickly adopted Hapoel after being attracted to the club's left-wing roots. 'Most fans now come from the south of Tel Aviv, like Jaffa. They are poorer so they are a different type of fan, more right-wing. Usually you say that the left wing are poor people but not in Israel, it's the other way around. Rich people are on the left.' He introduced me to Faud, the leader of Hapoel's Ultra group, a young skinhead in his early 20s. Faud was one of the new breed, a fan from the southern suburbs of Jaffa who still clung to Hapoel's left-wing imagery despite voting for Likud. 'The union may have been left-wing, but the workers have always been right-wing,' he announced. Despite the shifting allegiances within the club, he denied there were any tensions between the fans that represented its past and those that represented its future, especially when it came to the issue that has divided Israeli football most in recent years. 'My deputy is Arab. We have two Arab players. Most have one but we have two. If we don't like [Bnei] Sakhnin it's because they beat us, not because they're Arabs. We love Hapoel, he is left, I am right, but we are all Hapoel.' The match ended 1–1 and the fans trudged out into the balmy Tel Aviv night. As I walked through the stadium's main gate someone familiar was standing by the lamppost wearing a red Hapoel shirt and selling the club's merchandise from a large, flat wooden suitcase. It was Oren, who only three days previously had been insisting he was a passionate Maccabi Haifa fan whilst selling green-and-white scarves and his popular Nasrallah stickers. Tonight, everything he sold was red and black. He saw me, cracked into a big smile and began laughing hysterically. He had been caught red-handed.

'I thought you were supposed to be a Haifa fan?' I asked.

'I sell everything to everyone,' he replied, unable to contain the hilarity of his duplicitous allegiances. 'Wherever the money is, that's where I am.' For one Israeli at least loyalty, religion and politics didn't mean a thing. Oren was a microcosm of one future that awaited Israeli football – a thoroughly apolitical animal who went where the money and the success were. You could imagine him equally standing in front of the Doha Stadium selling red-and-white scarves to Sakhnin fans. That's not to say that money can totally dilute the game, and society, of long-respected schisms – especially in Israel. After all, more than a century of Zionism had thrown together groups of Jews from across the world with wildly different cultural and political beliefs – from Yemen to post-war Poland. Antagonisms were to be expected. The one hatred that seemed to remain was the century's old enmity between Jews and Arabs. Although even this nettle had begun to be grasped. Around the side of the Bloomfield, Bnei Yehuda's hardcore fans waited by the side entrance reserved for officials, ready to harangue their players and the referee, before convening their weekly 'Parliament' to discuss the team's performance. All of them were Arab Jews, otherwise known collectively in Israel as the Mizrahim, which means 'from the East'. The Mizrahim fled persecution in Iraq, Yemen, Morocco or anywhere else in the near-East, the majority arriving after being expelled by Arab governments in the wake of Israel's creation in 1948, and had proved more willing to accept a hard-line approach to dealing with Israel's Arab neighbours than their white, socialist countrymen. It was the Mizrahim that swept Likud to power in the 1977 election – a huge political shift that ended the post-1948 hegemony of the Labour government, dominated by white European settlers known as the Ashkenazim. The clash between the two – the white, socialist Ashkenazim of Hapoel Tel Aviv, versus the religious, right-wing and nationalistic Mizrahim represented by Bnei Yehuda and Beitar Jerusalem – was not just a clash between competing teams or ideologies but a fundamental struggle between two competing visions for Israel. 'We are Arab Jews,' explained Avi, a member of the 'Parliament', just as the referee appeared and the 40 or so other fans started hurling abuse at him. 'We understand the Arab culture, we speak their language, grew up in their countries. But the others, who came from Germany and Europe [the Ashkenazim] don't. We know the mentality which is why we are what we are.' Uncompromising as this 'know your enemy' maxim was, even Bnei Yehuda had taken the plunge and signed a Muslim Arab player. 'We didn't have any Arabs play for us until four years ago and he wasn't very good,' explained Avi, although it hadn't dissuaded the 'Parliament' from considering another Arab player for playing for Bnei Yehuda. 'As long as he's good we don't care now. Beitar hate the Arabs but we're a little bit more realistic,' he said as the 'Parliament' walked to a nearby falafel stand to continue dissecting the match long into the night. 'After all, if someone comes and fucks me in the ass, it hurts, sure. But the second time he does it, it doesn't hurt so much. We've had an Arab [Muslim] player once, next time won't be too painful. It'll hurt just a little bit less.'

It was time to leave Tel Aviv and its disconnected aura. I'd packed my bags, said goodbye to Victor – who had installed himself as the dorm drunk and still hadn't got around to leaving for Lebanon – and travelled back to Jerusalem. I had one last

thing to do. After speaking to fans, players and journalists, I
wanted to speak to an outsider, someone who was equally new
to the hatreds and passions of Israeli football as me. Osvaldo
Ardiles had an impeccable sense of timing. He was appointed
manager of Beitar Jerusalem to much fanfare by Arcadi
Gaydamak as proof that Israel could attract a football figure
of international calibre. His managerial record may have been
mixed, to be polite, but he had given the club something – an
air that it was going places. The problem, he found, was that
it was difficult to attract players to a country that was firstly
under attack from Hezbollah, and secondly the site of more
terrorist attacks per capita than any country in the world, bar
Iraq. As a result he started the season with virtually the same
squad he'd inherited, unable to spend Gaydamak's billions. I
was interested to see what he made of the country whilst it
was at war, not to mention Beitar's rather negative reputation.
The problem was that he didn't seem particularly keen to
speak to me. 'You have to understand,' explained Beitar's press
officer as I phoned for the fourth time to arrange a time to
meet Ossie. 'Mr Ardiles is under a lot of pressure.' Eventually
it became clear why he didn't want to speak to me. 'I'm sorry,
he just won't speak to you. He found out you were an English
journalist and he refuses to speak to English journalists. There's
nothing I can do.' Maybe it's not that surprising. Ossie, after all,
had experienced the worst of the British tabloid media twice,
the first when he was hounded out of the English league as a
player for having the temerity to be an Argentinian during the
Falklands War, the second for being hounded out of his job as
manager of Tottenham for not being very good. In the end, his
fretting did him no good. After just a few months – and after
losing just one game – he was unceremoniously booted out
after disagreeing with the owner over team selection. But I
didn't know that as I sat on the roof of my hostel with the sun
going down, wondering what the hell I was going to do to fill
the gaping hole in my article. Then I heard something unusual,
a distant rhythmic coupling distorted through a speaker. Was
that someone screaming? I ran out of the hostel and followed
the noise across main roads and a park before coming to a

huge bank of people clustered around a stage. In the midst of war and just a few miles from the extreme privation and jealousies of the West Bank, the city's teenagers had gathered to watch an impromptu rock festival, held in honour of those who had lost their homes in the war. It was, as it turned out, a gift to the nation from Israel's most generous benefactor: Arcadi Gaydamak. With September just a few hours away, the concertgoers streamed to the bright lights – giggling female soldiers in fatigues, students wearing skull caps, young women with black-and-white Palestinian-style keffiyehs tied around their necks. With the light fading, the Prince wannabe on stage gyrated and yelped as the crowd danced and roared its approval. It was the last moments of summer and, for a fleeting moment, Israel felt safe, alive and united.

FIVE

Iraq At The Gulf Cup

It took a few seconds to register that I was staring at the world's most famous moustache, seconds before its owner expired for good. I had taken a few minutes to consider the ethical ramifications of watching Saddam Hussein's execution video. After all, he may have been a genocidal maniac, but is it ever right to watch a man die – on video? It was early January, England, and the afterglow of Christmas had long been snuffed out by six-hour days and perpetual freezing rain. Boredom had driven me to the internet where I had come across an article on Slate.com by Christopher Hitchens. He was in Iraq, reporting on the mood in Baghdad during the dictator's final hours. Crazy, I thought, who the hell would take that job? Iraq, as always, was on the verge of collapse and this markedly insensitive triumphant act had further driven a wedge between Iraq's three competing communities: the Shia, Sunni and Kurd. It was halfway down the article that I saw it. At first I was taken back by the insensitivity of it. 'Watch the Saddam execution now!' screamed the brightly coloured advert. He may have been a shit, but there was something distasteful about being so, well, bald about it all. Yet there was a sick fascination to the link. Looking around to make sure none of my fiancée's family would walk in on me, I clicked on it to sate my macabre curiosity.

It was immediately clear that the video was filmed on a camera phone. The picture was shaky and grainy. The screaming voices of the crowd pierced and popped through inadequate speakers as Saddam suddenly focused into view. He stood, bolt straight, in what looked like a filthy abattoir shed. Around him the crowd bayed and hollered in high-pitched whines, giving proceedings the air of a 1970s wrestling-match watched by overexcited, hysterical pensioners. You could see other people taking photos and filming the action, capturing a slice of bona fide history, possibly to show the wife when they got home after a long, hard day of goading. The Americans had been so proud of the capture, and so sure of the healing effect that Saddam's death would have on his newly fractured country, that they hadn't thought to properly police the execution. The resulting video only went to further incense and strengthen his Sunni brethren. It would take a lot to make any man feel sorry for Saddam, but as he stood there, unmoved, silent, making peace with whatever god he truly believed in, he looked almost dignified. When Saddam dropped it caught the surreptitious cameraman by surprise, taking him a few seconds to focus back on the action. The picture swayed, catching the odd blur, possibly of a man on a rope, possibly not. Everything was dark, before an image loomed into view: Saddam on his back, neck broken, tongue lolled to one side, eyes closed. Dead. I turned the monitor off and immediately felt ashamed. It was hard to imagine how anyone would think that the tawdry spectacle of Saddam's demise could hope to bring any kind of closure. To start with, Saddam was executed on Eid, the Muslim festival that marks Abraham's willingness to sacrifice his son to God. But there are two Eids, a Shia Eid and a Sunni Eid one day before. Saddam was a Sunni, and had used his power to enrich and empower Iraq's Sunni minority whilst putting a glass ceiling in place for the country's Shia majority. Saddam was executed on the Sunni Eid. The Kurds too had reason to complain. Saddam was executed, officially, for ordering the execution of prominent Shia clerics after a failed assassination attempt in the 1980s. But the execution happened before Saddam's long-winded court case could consider the evidence relating to the

Anfal Programme, a genocidal policy that aimed to wipe out Kurdish identity by destroying Kurdish villages, banning the language and gassing thousands of its people. The programme saw 4,500 out of 5,000 Kurdish villages destroyed, killing some 182,000 people. Saddam feared the Kurds' long-standing desire for independence and was scared they might defect to the Iranians during the bloody Iran-Iraq war. The Kurds wanted blood, and it was snatched away from them prematurely. It looked like bloodshed would follow, the Sunnis angry that their now marginalised minority had been further defamed – they might have hated Saddam in the main but he was one of theirs – the Kurds desperate for some kind of revenge, and the Shia empowered by the sight of their great enemy vanquished. I was thinking about the bleak future that faced Iraq when the phone call came. It was a cheery voice with a slight Teutonic twinge to it. 'James, hello, just to let you know that we have had an opening on a press trip we are organising to Iraq. Will you be free to join us?'

With Iraq about to blow, Austrian Airways was planning a press trip to the northern Iraqi city of Erbil, the Kurdish capital. Erbil, the Austrian PR told me very matter-of-factly, was safe. So safe in fact that the airline had started twice-weekly flights from Vienna with one eye on a potential tourist boom. As the rest of Iraq burned, the northern Kurdish region was experiencing stability, peace, a property boom and an unusually high number of requests for holiday villas. Since the first Gulf War, the Americans had imposed a no-fly zone over the northern part of the country. Saddam, rather than fighting the troublesome minority any longer, chose to wash his hands of them, leaving them to their own devices. Throughout the Nineties, the Kurds started building the infrastructure of devolution. They initiated their own government, the Kurdish Regional Government, and formalised the Peshmerga guerrillas into a semi-official Kurdish army. When the Americans came a second time, they were ready. Almost straight away, life got better for the Kurds. Their oil was no longer taken from them without compensation and an electricity grid could now be built. But most importantly, the Peshmerga kept the peace, which is why, when Baghdad started to erupt, thousands – Shia, Christian and Sunni – fled north to the safety of Iraqi Kurdistan, to its new malls, high-rise flats and burgeoning tourist industry. Now they even had their own border, border stamp and passport.

It sounded like a crazy idea, but it also solved a problem for me. Ever since I had returned home from Israel I had scratched my head about how I would write a chapter about Iraqi football. The game's history in Iraq had been tragically unsuccessful but characteristically macabre. Iraq's 'golden generation' emerged in the early 1980s and the national team qualified for its first and only World Cup in Mexico 1986. But behind closed doors the players were subjected to a reign of terror. Saddam's bloodthirsty son Uday, who used his penchant for torture and sexual violence to motivate his players, ran the Olympic Committee, which was in charge of footballing affairs. If the team played badly, he'd threaten to chop off the striker's legs. If training didn't go well, he'd lock them in a cage. When the team failed to reach USA 1994, he made the players train with a concrete football. When they failed to qualify in 2002, Uday had a new idea: whip the soles of his players' feet. Stories began to trickle out from the few sportsmen who managed to defect, but the true horror of Uday's rule only came to light when the USA stormed Iraq's Olympic HQ in 2003. In the basement they found Uday's motivational arsenal, which included a rack and a medieval torture device used to rip open a man's anus. Post-Saddam, the game continued to suffer. In the instability that followed the American invasion in 2003, the league's fixtures in Iraq were rarely fulfilled. Games in Baghdad frequently ended with the death of a spectator, if not a player, and matches between teams from rival sects were all but impossible to play without sparking off some form of localised civil war. Worse, players were targets for criminal gangs who would be kidnapped for ransom. The best players fled the carnage and were now gracing the leagues of other Middle Eastern countries like Qatar, Bahrain and Saudi Arabia. But most importantly the Lions of Mesopotamia, as they are known, had been targeted by insurgents for political reasons. The national team had become a rare beacon of unity, mixing players from each of the big groups in Iraq, Shia, Sunni and Kurd. And they play totally unimpeded by their supposed intractable differences. In fact, the team was arguably the last symbol of national unity left in Iraq. Which is what the insurgents hated. Almost all the players, coaches and staff of the Iraqi national football team had received death threats making it impossible for them to meet, train or play matches in Iraq. Instead, they had to relocate to Amman, Jordan or Erbil to train in safety. In fact, the relative safety of the Kurdish north saw the best players who couldn't secure moves abroad sign for Erbil FC. The war may have been bad news for most Iraqis, but for Erbil FC, previously a mid-table outfit of little significance, the war had brought them unprecedented success on the pitch, including their first Iraqi Super League title. But there would be no games in Erbil whilst I was there. There were far more important matters to attend to. The national team was due to compete in the Middle East's most prestigious football tournament: the Gulf Cup. The biannual competition, being in the UAE capital of Abu Dhabi, featured those Middle Eastern countries blessed with a coastline on the Persian Gulf. Iraq qualified by dint of its 20 kilometre-wide beach frontage although Yemen, strangely, was also able to compete. Iraq, Saudi Arabia and Kuwait had dominated the tournament since its inception in 1970, winning 15 out of 18 championships. But that might have had something to do with the fact that the region's other big team, Iran, was conspicuous by its absence. The Iranians had refused to participate because of the age-old problem of whether the Gulf was the Arabian Gulf or the Persian Gulf. The Arab states wouldn't budge and Iran declined to enter. For the rest it gave a rare opportunity to obtain international silverware. Iraq had been drawn against Oman, Bahrain and Saudi Arabia and was in with a good shout of finishing second and making the semi-finals. The trip coincided with Iraq's second group game against the Bahrainis and I'd have enough time to then fly to Abu Dhabi to meet the players, talk to them about their traumatic conditions and watch the crunch game with the Saudis. Perhaps a little quicker than the woman from Austrian Airlines might have expected, she got her answer. 'When do I leave?'

Iraq looked peaceful from 10,000 feet. The Austrian Airlines plane glided through the cloudless sky, across Turkey and then south, over the Zagros Mountains – a long-coveted hiding ground for the Kurdish Peshmerga guerrillas and their wilder cousins the PKK, who used to organise sorties into southern Turkey to help their Kurdish brothers' fight for independence – before the wide, flat, scrubby gold plains of northern Iraq opened up. The plains stretch south all the way to Iraq's minuscule coastline. Iraq historically had to pay a high price for this misfortune of geography. With little in the way of natural defences in the face of invasion, conquerors from Alexander the Great, to Darius III, to the Mongols had swept through here leaving behind the obelisks and monuments of their conquest. Erbil was even the place where two of these dynasties collided, Alexander vanquishing Darius, his Persian foe, outside the city's gates. Yet for all of Erbil's history, from the air it resembles Milton Keynes. Not that there are any concrete cows to be found, rather that it was meticulously and beautifully planned 3,000 years previously. The city is made up of a series of expanding, perfectly formed concentric circles, all emanating from the ancient citadel, which the Kurds claim is the oldest continuously inhabited site in the world. Within ten minutes we would be in Iraq, but first there was the matter of landing. Unlike normal landings, where a slow gradual descent leads you softly to earth, flying into an Iraqi airport means braving the corkscrew. The corkscrew is a way of avoiding any surface-to-air missiles that insurgents might choose to let off in your direction and involved the plane plunging earthwards in a steep corkscrew motion before pulling out at the end before we hit the dirt. The planeload of dignitaries, anonymous businessmen dressed like something out of a Graham Greene novel, journalists, the American ambassador to Austria and various Kurdish politicians, gritted their teeth as the plane nose-dived before landing, minutes later, surprisingly smoothly. The airport had a bloody history. The same runway we had landed on had facilitated the worst excesses of the Anfal Programme, launching the planes that dropped bombs and nerve agent on terrified villagers, including the 1988 'Halabja Massacre'. Then it was Saddam's key military airport in the north, now it was the Kurds' gateway to the rest of the world. In the excitement of realising that I'd be able to spend a bit of time with Iraqi football fans, in Iraq, I hadn't actually considered the ramifications of coming on holiday to the world's most dangerous country. It only dawned on me that it wasn't perhaps the safest idea whilst standing outside Erbil International Airport. I naively, almost stupidly, waited for my ride to the hotel, as if getting off a plane on Iraqi soil was no different from arriving at Heathrow, impatiently checking my watch and looking for a taxi rank all lined up and ready to transport all the other tourists who made the trip to northern Iraq to see the sights. But there was no rank of shabby local taxis or, in fact, anything resembling anonymous local transport. Instead, out of the distance, a rumble of noise approached. A screaming motorcade fit for minor royalty screeched into view, sirens blaring: two vans, four SUVs with black-suited Kurdish special service officers and a pickup truck full of heavily armed troops. Someone somewhere had told me northern Iraq was safe and open for business. There hadn't been a suicide bombing in two years, they told me, and anyway, the Kurds loved the British and Americans, the only group in Iraqi society who actually believed the West's pronouncements that they were liberators. The abundance of roof-mounted machine guns, Peshmerga guerrilla fighters and black-suited men wearing dark glasses and jaw lines that could cut glass detailed to take us on what was a seemingly straightforward journey told me otherwise.

The screaming motorcade flew through red lights, police helpfully holding the traffic of bemused Kurdish drivers at bay as we progressed to our hotel unimpeded. Almost every patch of spare ground seemed to be in the middle of being built into something grand, a sign of the building boom that the Kurds were enjoying. Every other patch of land seemed to be in the midst of hosting impromptu football matches between rusted goalposts. The only distinguishing markings I could make out as we sped past in a blur was the goalkeeper's white England shirt – number seven – David Beckham. The cavalcade pulled into the Sheraton Hotel. It wasn't really a Sheraton. It had been once, but now it was the Erbil International Hotel. All the taxi drivers still knew it as the Sheraton. There was plenty to offer the tourist in Erbil, our guide Rawand, who with his luxuriant, side-parted dark hair and moustache looked like an Indian prince rather than a media officer for the Kurdish Regional Government, had assured us. In pride of place was the ancient citadel. It sat 300 metres above sea-level, dominating the surrounding city. When we arrived it was a ghost-town of tightly packed stone huts that had stood there for 3,000 years. It had been cleared of the 850 residents who still lived there to spruce it up in anticipation of the forthcoming tourist boom. Yet Saddam's presence could still be felt, even amongst the ancient architecture. The southern gate had been demolished and rebuilt in the Babylonian style, an attempt by Saddam to 'Arab-ise' the Kurds' most treasured landmark. The only sign of life was at the nearby Kurdish Textile Museum. Outside fluttered the green, white, red and gold of the Kurdish flag. The Iraqi flag was nowhere to be seen. In fact, I wouldn't see it once for the duration of my stay. Inside hung a collection of maps that told the true story of Kurdish ambition. Rather than showing a region constrained by the northern borders of Iraq, they depicted a greater Kurdistan stretching from Kirkuk in the south, extending well into Turkey and encroaching on Iran. There was even a small strip of Mediterranean coastline. 'It's mainly nationalists who believe in that,' Rawand explained as we travelled to our next tourist spot – the broken 800-year-old minaret in Minaret Park, the dark-suited minders following in a car behind. 'But you have to remember how different we are. The younger generation, born after 1991, don't know what Iraq is. They don't even speak Arabic.' Rawand had highlighted the dichotomy at the heart of Kurdish society. On the one hand, being part of Iraq had been a boon since 1991. They have been able to build autonomy, if not independence, that would have been unthinkable under any other political conditions. Yet statehood was an invisible dream, something that was inevitable and for the first time in living memory a real possibility. Like China, the Kurds seemed to live by the motto: 'One country, two systems.' But for how much longer? The two conflicting desires were equally evident with the national football team. After returning to the hotel, I went about trying to shake off my black-suited shadow. In the confusion caused by jumpy-looking US plain-clothed security officers protecting the US ambassador to Austria, I managed to sneak out of the front gate and into the cool, darkening evening. Erbil by night was pitch black and noisy. The city had few street lights and hummed to the sound of a thousand generators, necessary since Saddam never bothered to attach the Kurds to the national grid. The dark street was alive with shoppers picking up groceries after their day's work. Every few minutes, someone would approach me and grab my hand, shaking it wildly and uttering the only piece of English they knew: 'Thank you Tony Blair, thank you George Bush.' Each of the many cafés that lined its pavements had a television flickering in the corner showing that night's game: Oman versus Kuwait. The only one that didn't, ironically, was the Real Madrid Café. Its sign bore the faces of famous Real players, Beckham, Ronaldo, Roberto Carlos, all with chef's hats superimposed on them. Inside, all the staff wore identical white replica Real shirts. I sat in a small kebab house and ordered a tea to watch the end of the match. Kuwait were losing and Hawar and Massoud, who were avidly watching it too, couldn't have been happier. 'Good, I hope the Kuwaitis lose,' Massoud offered as Kuwait slipped closer to defeat. 'Why?' I asked, expecting some fraternity to a place, like the Kurdish north, that had tasted occupation at the hands of Saddam's troops. 'It was part of Iraq,' Hawar jumped in. 'But the tribe left because of the oil.' It was another example of the schizophrenia that surrounded Kurdish attitudes to Iraq's territorial integrity: Kurds essentially agreeing with Saddam's rationale for the first Gulf War. The Iraqi football team too was universally loved but so too was the Kurdish national team, even though one undermined the other. The Kurds harboured ambitions of FIFA recognition, a state of affairs that would blow Iraqi football wide open and could effectively destroy the national team. After the fall of Saddam Kurds were, once again, allowed to play in the national team after an unofficial ban. Now the squad for the Gulf Cup featured more players from Erbil FC than any other team and included Hawar Mullah Mohammad, one of Iraq's most talented strikers. 'He is Iraq's best player,' agreed Massoud. 'And as Kurds we are very proud.' FIFA affiliation for the Kurdish team would force Iraq's Kurdish players to make a decision one way or the other. It had already split some families. Whilst Hawar Mullah Mohammad played for Iraq, his younger brother Halkurd currently turned out for Iraqi Kurdistan. I left the café, vowing to watch the Iraq versus Bahrain game with Hawar and Massoud, and walked back along the street receiving more plaudits for my nationality along the way. I couldn't work out why I needed a full-time bodyguard, given everyone's friendliness and the fact that there hadn't been an attack in Erbil since 2005. At the hotel, the black-suited guard was still in the lobby, reading his paper.

The road north out of Erbil got colder, whiter and more barren the higher we climbed. The pretence of spring that had fooled blossom from the trees on Iraq's northern plains gave way, very quickly, to a bitter winter. Snow lay on the floor and the stumps of hewn trees gave the vast panorama a nakedness, a vulnerability that almost spoke directly of Iraqi Kurdistan's brutal recent history. 'You noticed there are no trees, haven't you?' Rawand's face loomed in front, breaking my concentration out of the minibus window. 'That's because Saddam stopped the import of kerosene after the 1991 uprising so we had to cut down all the trees for warmth.' Almost every blight on Iraqi Kurdistan was attributable to him – poverty, soil erosion, birth defects, power outages. 'Saddam didn't build any infrastructure,' he continued, finding his seat again. 'No oil refineries, nothing. He just took all the goods and gave us nothing in return, just bombs and executions.' We were headed towards the most fortified building in northern Iraq, the residence of the KRG's president Massoud Barzani. Barzani was one of the great figures of Iraqi politics, a survivor who had lived through assassination attempts and taken up arms against Saddam's regime as well as his Kurdish political rivals. As leader of the Kurdish Democratic Party, he had been locked in an internal struggle for dominance with the Patriotic Union of Kurdistan and their leader Jalal Talabani in the 1990s. Once their bitter enmity saw the KDP ask for support from Saddam to quell their political opponents. Now the two rivals held arguably the most important presidencies in Iraq: Barzani in charge of the north, Talabani as president of the new Iraq.

Our bus approached the first checkpoint. The troops, wearing green army fatigues and the distinctive red-and-white checked headscarf – worn in the Kurdish style, curled around in a short, tight bob – were expected to be thorough. Every item on the bus was checked, every page of my notepad swept, every camera tested. Dogs were brought forward to sniff each of us individually. Even Rawand was being frisked. 'Everyone has to be searched,' he said as he was being patted down. 'I have personally met with George W. Bush and even he had to be searched like you.' But in Iraqi Kurdistan it pays to be careful. The Kurdish leadership had long been a target for Ba'athists and now insurgents. Barzani's own father narrowly avoided assassination when a suicide bomber exploded just feet from where he was standing. His tea boy took the brunt of the explosion.

'What happened to the tea boy?' I asked. 'He died, of course,' Rawand replied. 'But his son was rewarded and he is now very important in the government.'

With the guards satisfied that the busload of mainly middle-aged, mild-mannered Austrian aviation journalists was not a threat to Kurdish security, the bus trundled on to Barzani's vast palace in the hills. We were led inside, through huge wooden doors, before being sat behind an overly large, circular conference table that wouldn't have looked out of place in the lair of a James Bond baddie. Barzani, with his tightly trimmed moustache and green army uniform stretched over his paunch, entered and sat down in front of us. 'Our aim has always been for democratic rights for Iraq first, national rights for the Kurds second within a federal democratic and pluralistic Iraq,' he relayed to us eloquently, before saying something not often heard in the Middle East. 'I want to say thank you to the

USA and the American people for helping us throw out this dictatorial regime.' Earnest Austrian political journalists lined up to ask questions about troop movements, the status of the oil-rich, ethnically Kurdish city of Kirkuk and independence. The mantra was the same. Autonomy in Iraq now, independence as the final goal. But I had far more lowbrow considerations.

'Mr President, do you support the Kurdish national football team's attempts to gain FIFA membership, will you be watching Iraq play Bahrain later this afternoon and if so what do you think the score will be?'

The room tittered collectively but Barzani, it turned out, used to be a handy player back in his youth. The Iraqi ambassador to Austria had vouched for his goal-scoring prowess earlier in the day. 'He was a great striker,' he told me. 'And I should know, I always played behind him.'

'Being a footballer myself and having played football in the past, I strongly support the Kurdish attempts to join FIFA,' Barzani replied forcefully, giving his most bellicose answer. 'Even during the times when Saddam was in power, I supported the Iraqi team. Now that he has gone, of course I still support them.' He refused to give a prediction on the result, but he had articulated perfectly the Kurdish position. One country; two governments. One country; two football teams. The president shook each of our hands as we left the palace and descended back on Erbil. The next few hours were crucial if I was to catch the game with a crowd of Kurdish fans. The match was due to start at 4 p.m., giving me a couple of hours to get the rest of the trip out of the way before I could disappear into a café somewhere. It didn't exactly go to plan. A trip to a local church to meet Erbil's Christian bishop overran. I tapped my feet and counted the minutes down on my watch, even managing to flee to a nearby bar in the Christian quarter to check what television channel the game was on. With 30 minutes to go I had a dilemma. Part of the trip was to meet the KRG's Prime Minister Nechirvan Barzani, the president's young nephew. I had a choice, shun the prime minister and damage British-Kurdish relations or hot foot it back to the city centre and watch the football. I decided to stay, do the interview and then catch the last half-hour, which was the most important part of the match anyway. I regretted it the moment the bus pulled away leaving us at the White House, the PM's residency on the outskirts of town. No expense had been spared for the White House: marble floors, ornate mosaics, expensive carpets, antique furniture. We waited in a press conference room. And waited. And waited. The first half was coming to a close and he still hadn't shown up. Bahrain had gone 1–0 up in the fourth minute, a header in front of a huge Iraqi flag that had been unfurled across the stand. Eventually the other, younger Barzani came out with the US ambassador to Austria, talking about co-operation and something else I didn't follow. I had moved to the back of the room, kicking the floor like a sullen schoolboy in detention. I had written one sentence during the whole affair: 'I bet he was watching the first half, the swine.' As soon as the last clap died down, we were outside, in the police convoy, tearing towards the hotel. Before I had been concerned about anonymity. Now I could have kissed the police driver on the face for his reckless speeding. We screeched through Erbil's outlying districts. The streets were empty. Outside the window I could make out shops and cafés as we whizzed by, full of punters crowded around blinking television sets watching the game's crucial dénouement. The convoy pulled into the hotel just as the final whistle went. The game had finished 1–1, a late equaliser by none other than Hawar Mullah Mohammed, the Kurdish local hero. I'd missed everything. That night celebratory gunfire was seen in the sky above Erbil. I continued to curse the prime minister's tardiness as I tried, and failed, to fall asleep.

It was time to leave Iraqi Kurdistan and begin the long journey to Abu Dhabi. But there was one last thing I wanted to see before I left. A short taxi ride from the hotel stood the Franso Hariri Stadium, Iraq's second biggest football stadium and home to the fledgling Kurdish national football team. It was renamed in 2001 after the death of Franso Hariri, a prominent Christian Kurd who had been assassinated by Islamists. The ramshackle ring of concrete had seen better days, and was covered in graffiti on the outside. Someone had scrawled the words 'Del Piero' on a wall next to one of the exits. Walking around the perimeter the peeling posters charted Iraqi Kurdistan's struggles. Old posters advertised the Erbil Olympic Committee in Arabic. A sign welcomed the visitor to Erbil in English and Korean – recognition that South Korea's coalition contingent was here to keep an already amiable peace. Another advertised the Hewler ping-pong team, the ancient Kurdish name for Mesopotamia preferred by nationalists. A small, open door guarded by a squat, bald man called Mohammed was the only sign of life. Mohammed led me to the pitch, a sea of yellow potted with indiscriminate slashes of dying green. On the far side a huge, Lenin-esque bust of Hariri loomed over the half-way line. The tunnel was covered in portraits and pictures from Iraqi Kurdistan's bygone footballing past, from the founding of Erbil club in 1968, through to the league championships of the Seventies watched by multicoloured crowds, to the tight shorts and figure-hugging shirts of the Eighties, through to the boom of the Nineties. The crowds in all the shots had one thing in common. All flew flags coloured white, red, green and gold. There wasn't a single Iraqi standard among them. Outside on a small patch of sandy wasteland, a group of schoolchildren had scratched out a football pitch in front of a handball goal. They stopped and stared as I walked past. One kid plucked up the courage to ask: 'Why are you here?' The group of 12 year olds weren't all Kurdish. 'I am Arab, but we all play together,' announced Ibrahim proudly. A Kurdish boy hugged him. 'We are like brothers.' The others started heckling. 'He's a terrorist! He loves Saddam!' The group broke down into hysterics before inviting me to play with them. Penalties, with me in goal. I didn't do so bad, saving the first six, before one of the kids, older than the rest, got me with a classic. 'Look!' he shouted, pointing at the sky. Stupidly, I followed the line of his finger upwards. He poked the ball home and the boys celebrated with arms outstretched like Italian professionals. I was furious, until I realised that my body had taken up two thirds of the goal, and that they were all playing barefoot. I left them to their celebrations and headed back to the hotel and back to the convoy. The screaming motorcade heralded our departure as noisily as it had our arrival. At Erbil International

Airport we were walked through security and sat in the lounge designed for visiting diplomats. CNN blared in one corner. The contrast between Iraqi Kurdistan and the rest of Iraq couldn't have been starker. In Baghdad 75 people had been killed in simultaneous bombings. Twenty-five American troops had been killed when a helicopter was blown out of the sky. Five other American troops were killed when insurgents, dressed in military uniforms, managed to sneak into a secure compound. Scores of others were murdered, maimed and raped in brutal acts of violence so small and attritional that the press didn't even bother mentioning them any more. Whilst the Kurds thrived and I had walked Iraq's northern streets unmolested, even being patted on the back for an accident of birth, Baghdad – just 200 miles away – was experiencing its bloodiest weekend since the start of the war. Whatever weak glue the Iraqi national football team exerted over this fractured and broken nation, it was now more important than ever.

It was only a few hours after arriving in Dubai that my master plan had fallen to pieces. After my flight had taken off from Erbil, corkscrewed back into the sky, touched down in Vienna, taken off for Heathrow, changed for a flight to Bahrain and then, finally, twenty-four exhausting hours later, landed in Dubai I had to quickly take the one-hour taxi drive west to the UAE's capital Abu Dhabi to meet the Iraqi team. I had come a long way and I didn't want to miss it. The taxi driver chatted amiably about cricket as I furiously scribbled pertinent questions in my notebook. Training was going to be at 4 p.m., but I was late. So late in fact that I had missed it. At the entrance to the village where all the players were staying, the twitchy security guards wouldn't let me through the gate. I picked up the phone and called Akram Salman, the veteran Iraqi coach who was in his third spell in charge of the national team. Actually, it was technically his fourth. After being threatened by insurgents five months previously he quit his post and fled to the Kurdish north. The FA refused to accept his resignation and he was talked into coming back. 'My players are very tired now so we can do this another time,' he told me. It was understandable, but it still left me sitting on the edge of a desert highway, with the meter ticking and absolutely nothing to show for creating a carbon footprint bigger than Texas. 'But there are some people staying in Le Meriden hotel,' he added, sensing that I might start crying. 'They will talk to you.' All wasn't lost. With four points from their first two games, a win against Oman and a draw against Bahrain, it would take a miracle for Iraq not to qualify for the semi-finals, even if they lost heavily to Saudi Arabia. I could, I reasoned as the taxi pulled into Le Meridien Abu Dhabi, simply interview them once they had made safe passage through to the semi-finals. In the lobby the Gulf Cup organisers had set out a stall manned by two miserable men wearing white dish dashas and headscarves. A sign was draped over it: 'Welcome Brothers!' Hussein Saed Mohammed was finishing off some business in the lobby when he agreed to speak to me. Hussein was arguably Iraq's most famous footballer. He held Iraq's international goal-scoring record – scoring 63 times in 131 appearances – and was the team's talismanic captain, leading Iraq from 1975 to 1990 and scoring the goals that marked Iraq's high-water mark: World Cup qualification in 1986. His goal-scoring prowess had alerted the world's best clubs but he never got a sniff at playing for any of them. 'I had many teams that wanted me to play for them. Real Madrid wanted to know about me,' he told me as we sat down in a café. But his dream move was scuppered. 'The government refused and wouldn't let me go and be professional.' The Iraqi regime's pathological hatred of foreign, Western influences was one reason for it. The other was Uday Hussein. Saddam's sadistic son had a habit of asking for a huge cut from any contracts players signed to ply their trade abroad. Former Iraqi captain Habib Jaffar – who told *The Guardian* how he was regularly beaten with cables and forced to jump into vats of raw sewage – had to hand over 40 per cent of his earnings to Uday when he signed a contract with a Qatari club. Hussein would have been expected to do the same. Now he was in charge of building Iraq's footballing future as the president of the Iraqi FA. But despite the hardships he had faced, he didn't want to talk about his time under Uday. 'We don't want to speak about the past,' he replied tetchily when I asked about the influence

Uday had over the dressing room. 'I am the President for three years and we have had many difficulties now. No players have suffered like Iraqi players have suffered. All our teams qualify for all the tournaments. And we are proud that we have united our people under the umbrella of sport. You will see tomorrow in the stadium, all the people will be there in the stadium to support us, many Shia, many Sunni, even some Kurdish. And also no violence is in Iraq when our team is playing. Everyone is watching television.' It was a foolproof plan: engender Iraqi unity through a sporting example whilst keeping the insurgents off the street with a steady stream of matches and tournaments. Yet sportsmen and women had increasingly paid a high price for their visibility post-Saddam, along with the fans. 'They have kidnapped my driver and my bodyguard. For what reason? What do they need? Last year we had a match in Baghdad, a semi-final, 50,000 people were in the stadium and they fired many rockets at them. Why kill people who want to come and watch football?' he asked incredulously. 'The cycling coach was killed; the wrestling coach was killed; the captain of the volleyball team was killed; many killings. But we don't stop because sportsmen are part of the people in Iraq. When the people suffer, we suffer with them.' The list he left out was even bigger: the taekwondo team that was kidnapped and never heard of again; Iraq's head tennis coach murdered along with two players; the majority of the Olympic committee, plus thirty staff, seized in one raid by kidnappers wearing army uniforms. To literally survive in his post for three years was an achievement in itself for Hussein. His aim was to get back to the glory years, to the team that excelled in the 1980s even with the constant fear of mutilation and imprisonment. 'I am proud of our players and our coach. We put it here on our logo, on our jersey.' He pointed at the breast of his brown sports jacket – 'I am Iraqi.' 'In the future we will be a great team again.'

It was dark now, but as my taxi pulled out onto the main highway back to Dubai it became clear that something big had happened. At first it sounded like a low growl, like feedback from a malfunctioning bass amp. Then you could make out the whistles, and then the screams. We had just reached the

Al Jazira Mohammed Bin Zayed Stadium at the wrong time. Kuwait and the UAE had played each other in a winner takes all clash to see who reached the semi-finals. The game was finely poised from the 35th minute at 2–2; a goal either way would have sent either team through. But Ismail Matar, the UAE's golden boy striker, popped up in injury-time and all hell broke loose. UAE football fans don't celebrate their victories like everyone else, with songs, fights or parades. Instead, everyone piles into expensive 4x4s and careers around, spinning doughnuts, or hanging ten or so mates out of the side window. The police knew what was coming and had closed off all the side roads, creating an anarchic death march of teenagers, packed a dozen to each car and swerving at high speed whilst the driver waved the green, white, red and black flag of the UAE out of his window. Like something from the 1970s cartoon *Wacky Races*, comically crunched cars littered the highway as the revelry took its toll. I hung out of the taxi window to take some photos. One man, on his own in his saloon hatchback, took both hands off the wheel, waved at me and subsequently crashed into the car in front. I sat back in my seat, fastened my seat belt and watched the crazy kids hanging out of their unfeasibly expensive cars blaring their horns, faces covered in red-and-white keffiyehs to hide their identities. The hosts were now in the semi-finals. Tomorrow I hoped Iraq would join them.

Even from the main road it was obvious that the Al Nahyan stadium wasn't fit for its purpose. My bus had trundled slowly down the desert highway between the UAE's biggest Emirates and deposited me right outside the ground. It was an hour before Iraq was to take on Saudi Arabia but the gates on the 12,000-capacity stadium were locked. An Indian street seller standing on the pavement told you which country the crowd crushing at the main fence were supporting. He was covered in Iraqi flags, selling them for ten dirhams at a time, possibly the first time in years that selling the Iraqi flag had been a profitable business. Every available gate was unapproachable as angry groups of fans tried to remonstrate with the confused-looking policemen behind the barriers: young families; groups of teenage girls with their faces coloured red, white and black; a pack of young men; a solitary old man wearing a deep-lined face and a well-worn blazer. These were Iraq's well-heeled diaspora, the lucky ones, the affluent middle class who had managed to flee to the UAE with its good jobs and promise of stability. 'As you can see many Iraqis support the team more than anything so we can't get any seats, we are just walking around at the moment trying to get in,' lamented Mohammed, a 19-year-old student who had arrived two hours previously with his classmates to try and get a ticket. I was here to speak to as many fans from as many different parts of Iraq as possible for a short news story for the BBC's *Radio One Newsbeat*. It was a bizarre commission: to interview the team and the fans for a one-minute production on how football was uniting Iraq's warring factions. Presumably it would have been wedged between stories on the Arctic Monkeys and Lily Allen. In London they had given me a microphone emblazoned with the letters BBC on the side and instructions to speak to the fans. 'Make sure you ask them their name and whether they are Sunni or Shia,' the production assistant told me. The problem was, everyone seemed to be a little offended that I wanted to know. 'I don't care if I am Sunni or Shia, I want to be from Iraq,' Mohammed replied coolly. 'I have been here the last two years although most of my family are still in Iraq. We want to get them out. We are just trying to support Iraq and get to the finals. There is no difference and we don't care about this racism. We are Iraqis. We are all Iraqis. That's all that matters.' Another fan was equally put out. 'I will not say whether I am Sunni or Shia. Because we are all the same: Muslim,' was how Zaid, an 18-year-old Iraqi woman wearing a dark headscarf and an Iraqi flag painted on each cheek, put it. 'We want to support our country in any way. The only thing we can do is come and support the national team. They [the insurgents] are targeting everything that has a symbol of peace. For now, this is it.'

Zaid had only been in the UAE for two years, fleeing Baghdad not when the American bombs fell, but when the anarchy that followed gripped her home city. 'It's like hell, our families are still there,' she said, inching along the large queue and peering hopefully around the two hundred or so people in front of her holding exactly the same hope of a ticket. 'I was there during the war but have been here for two years. It is actually destroying every single beautiful thing in our lives. The city, the neighbourhood, everything. We just want it to end.' Who was to blame, I asked. 'Actually, I don't know who to blame.' She shrugged. 'All the blame goes to the outside forces because they made us different from the inside so all the Iraqi people are suffering now.' I took it as a sign that I should stop asking people's sectarian leanings. In future I vowed not to ask again. Most editors demanded some kind of sectarian dynamic to the stories that you filed. Even if it was a story of unity, the divisions still had to be clarified, which was something Iraqis were, understandably, weary of talking about. The most common lament I heard from Iraqis living in exile was that nobody cared who was Sunni or Shia or Kurd before the war. Even that distinction was flawed as most Kurds were Sunni Muslims too. Now it was the only prism through which outsiders viewed their country. Journalists were guiltier of that than most. Certainly a nearby plain-clothes policeman with a walkie talkie – a rare occurrence where plain-clothes, in this case the pristine white flowing dish dasha and head scarf, was far more elaborate than the police's junta-style uniform – was keen that I stopped asking questions too. 'You need to watch out, you have money in your pocket,' the policeman informed me, patting me on my back and walking me away from the supporters. I was confused by his advice. The crowd appeared to be made up of mild-mannered doctors, teachers and students. As soon as we were out of earshot I found out his true intentions. 'Don't ask anything about politics,' he said sternly underneath his bushy moustache. 'They are coming here only for sport.'

'So I can't ask anything about politics?' I asked. 'No, no, no. Sports is good, yanni, speaking about sport is different.' Still, at least my BBC-branded microphone could be put to some use. I had a far bigger problem. I hadn't anticipated the huge Iraqi turnout and was, like the 500 people still milling all around

NETANYA HOOLIGANS
Vocal supporters of Maccabi Netanya arrive for the start of the season clash with Maccabi Haifa. The match took place a week after the end of the Israel-Lebanon war and had to be switched from Haifa to the coastal town of Netanya after a rocket fired by Hezbollah narrowly missed Haifa's stadium.

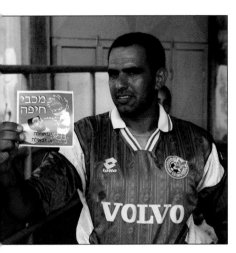

PISSING IN NASRALLAH'S MOUTH
A merchandise seller holds up his fastest selling product outside before Maccabi Netanya's game with Maccabi Haifa: a cartoon of a Haifa fan urinating into Hezbollah leader Hassan Nasrallah's mouth.

NO GUNS, NO STICKS, NO HAWKS, NO CATS
A sign, erected by the Abu Dhabi police, instructing supporters what they couldn't bring into the stadium if they wanted to watch Oman take on Bahrain in the semi-final of the 2007 Gulf Cup. The list included hawks, machine guns, cats, swords and newspapers.

SAUDI FANS MAKE SOME NOISE
Saudi fans make their voices heard during the first half of Saudi Arabia versus UAE at the 2007 Gulf Cup.

ALLAHU AKHBAR
Fans of Saudi Arabia and the UAE police pray together at half time during their semi-final clash in the 2007 Gulf Cup.

DEVASTATED SAUDI FANS
Saudi fans looked stunned seconds after Ismail Matar scores a 90th minute winner for archrivals UAE in the 2007 Gulf Cup semi-finals.

SANA'A OLD CITY
A sand storm blowing through Yemen's capital.

CHEWING *KHAT*
A young Yemeni soldier holding a machine gun guards Sana'a's national stadium. The bulge in his left cheek is the *khat* he is chewing, a drug that is taken by virtually every single man – and most women – in the country.

TAUNTING THE OPPOSITION
Young fans of Yemen's Yarmouk sing in honour of their team as they take on Al Ahli, traditionally considered the government's team. Yarmouk is known to be Yemen's most religious football club and insists that all their players pray five times a day and have modest, non-Western haircuts, or they are dropped from the team.

PALESTINIAN MAN PRAYING
A lone football fan prays before Wad El Nes take on Tulkarem in a Palestinian cup match at Jericho International Stadium. It was one of the few matches to take place in the West Bank: The presence of Israeli checkpoints meant that the Palestinian league in the West Bank had been in hiatus for years.

AFTER THE MATCH, THE KNIVES
Fans of Yarmouk and Al Ahli collect their jambiyas, which are carried by virtually all men in Yemen, from the police after a league game. Fans had been banned from taking the knives, and guns, into the ground after an upsurge in crowd violence.

IT'S A GAME OF TWO HALVES BOYS
Tulkarem coach Mohammed Sabah gives last minute instruction to his players before his team take on Wad El Nes in the quarter-finals of the Palestinian cup. Sabah also coached the Palestinian national team.

GOING TO PENALTIES
Players and coaching staff from Tulkarem watch on as a tense quarter-final against Wad El Nes nears its conclusion. The game finished 1–1 but Wad El Nes went through on penalties.

GETTING READY FOR THE GAME OF THE SEASON
A young Al Ahly fan takes a drag on a cigarette before his team play hated city rivals Zamalek in Africa's biggest football match. On his left cheek is painted a heart, on the right the number 8, both in homage to Al Ahly midfielder Mohamed Barakat.

KEEPING A TIGHT LID ON THINGS
Riot police form a ring of steel around Cairo International Stadium in anticipation of Al Ahly versus Zamalek. Crowd violence had been so bad that all games between the two sides are now played at a neutral venue.

TRAINING DAY
Players from Palestine's women's national football team take a breather after training. There is no women's league, grass pitches or any chance of the team playing at home.

A PRAYER BEFORE TRAINING
Jordan's national team pray in their changing rooms before training at the West Asian Championship. The team, like most in the Middle East, pray together before every game too.

PLAYING FOR EACH OTHER
Iraq's national team train before their crunch group game with Palestine in the West Asian Championship.

IRANIAN WAGS
Wives and (possibly) girlfriends of the Iranian FA watch their team at the West Asian Championship. It was a rare treat for them: in Iran female spectators are banned from attending football matches.

IT'S A GOAL!
A rare moment of celebration for young Iraqi refugees watching Iraq score against Palestine in the West Asian Championship. Iraq would get to the final, only to be beaten by Iran.

GUARDING THE DOPE TESTERS
Police guard the doping room at Amman's International Stadium after Iraq beat Palestine 1–0 in the West Asian Championship.

THE DEJECTION OF LOSING
Members of the Palestinian national football team reflect on being knocked out by Iraq in the West Asian Championship. Many of the players were unable to return home after violence broke out between Hamas and Fatah supporters in Gaza.

HAIL TO THE HERO
Iraqi midfielder Hawar Mullah Mohammad is swamped by fans after scoring in Iraq's 1–0 victory over Palestine. Hawar, a Kurd, is one of Iraq's most popular players.

A PRAYER BEFORE PLAYING
Officials and fans pray to Mecca before Jordan take on Syria at the West Asian Championship. Supporters on the terrace (top right) join in.

WE COULDN'T DO IT WITHOUT YOU!
Iraqi captain Younis Mahmoud thanks the fans after Iraq
reach the semi-finals of the West Asian Championship.
The following month he would unexpectedly be picking
up the Asian Cup after Iraq beat Saudi Arabia 1–0 in
the final after he scored the winning goal. He was later
short-listed for FIFA's World Player of the Year award.

WARNING: SYRIAN MILITARY ZONE
Outside the training ground of Al Jaish, a
Syrian Premier League club that represents
the army. This was the picture that got me frog
marched to see the army's top brass.

GIVE US VICTORY
Two Wihdat fans pray before the end-of-season clash with rivals Faisaly. Wihdat is a team from Amman's
Wihdat Palestinian refugee camp whilst Faisaly is seen as the team of 'pure' Jordanians. The Wihdat
versus Faisaly game is one of the few arenas where the enmity between Palestinian and Hashemite
Jordanians is seen. Sure enough, riots broke out after the game.

the stadium, without a ticket. At one gate I spotted a gap. Stiffening my back and trying to look as confident as possible I walked up to the security guard, waving the mic as if I had just walked outside. 'Where is your pass?'

'Oh, I left it inside.' Nothing. 'You can't come in without a pass.'

I was screwed, standing at the gate with a useless BBC microphone and no story. Until I was saved by an incredible act of kindness by an Iraqi man walking through the gate. 'Here,' he said, passing me a shiny piece of paper. It was a VIP ticket. 'Please let me give you some money,' I begged. 'No, I insist. It's a gift for the BBC.' He was pointing at the microphone, as if having an extremely tenuous connection to the BBC was a good enough excuse. Even if I didn't work for them, I paid my licence fee, I rationalised tenuously, so in a way it was above board. I thanked him and walked into a wall of police. The authorities weren't taking any chances. Hundreds of club-carrying officers milled around looking intimidated and scared. At first they wouldn't let me in the stand. I raised the microphone. They let me through. Then they wouldn't let me by the pitch. I put up the microphone. A British woman organising the tournament saw it and waved me past. 'They're very strict with security,' she apologised. 'They have to keep the Saudis and the Iraqis separate or there would be trouble.' The stadium was buzzing, the telltale cacophony of beats, whistles and the repetitive chant of 'Iraq!' Huge flags hung down from the stands, under the watchful gaze of Sheikh Zayed. A massive portrait of the man revered by Emiratis for being the father of the nation bore down. I had gone as far as I could go. The police would not let me take any pictures pitch side of the fans. Eventually we came to a compromise. A policeman would escort me around the pitch once. I had five minutes to document the one small quarter, half-filled with the green of Saudi Arabia's travelling fans, the other side overflowing with Iraqi pride. We only paused when the policeman put his hand over my lens and held me still so that we could respect the two national anthems.

I took my seat in the anodyne surroundings of the empty

VIP section. From the very first skewed kick Iraq were in trouble. The Saudis were slick and running rings around their opponents. Eventually, their dominance told. Goalkeeper Noor Sabri gave away a blatant penalty but somehow stayed on the pitch. Captain Yasser Al-Qahtani blasted the Saudis ahead 1–0. Then things went from bad to worse. Iraq had a man sent off and, apart from Hawar Mullah Mohammad – who had scored in each of the previous games – Iraq looked devoid of any attacking verve whatsoever. It shouldn't have mattered though. Even when the final whistle blew, 1–0 was enough for both to go through. The players hung around the centre circle waiting for news of the Qatar versus Bahrain game. I didn't have a radio, nor any access to the internet. But when the players started falling to their knees in the centre circle, holding their crowns as they pressed their foreheads against the grass, I knew it wasn't good news. Bahrain had scored an injury-time winner and had gone through, level on points, level on goal difference, level on head to heads, but, crucially, ahead on goals scored. There wasn't any anger amongst Iraq's fans as they left the stadium in silence. Simply resignation. But, then again, if there was one thing that Iraqis had had to come to terms with in recent years, it was high hopes being dashed by damnable luck. After following the team half-way across the world, I still hadn't spoken to the players. My story was in pieces. The next day, I phoned Akram Salman, Iraq's manager. He wasn't happy.

'No, I am sorry. We won't talk to you. We can't talk to you. We go home soon because of what happened last night. Did you hear about last night?' he asked, still shocked by the result. He didn't know it yet but it was to be his last game in charge. After a forensic investigation of the Gulf Cup he was fired four months later without taking charge of another game, proving that, even after you put your life on the line for your country, there's no sentimentality in football.

I offered my condolences and begged for an audience. 'We are too depressed to talk,' he continued. 'The players are very, very depressed. Very depressed. Very . . .' His voice trailed off croakily before he hung up.

Given that their homeland was in flames, their families under curfew and their lives under threat, that had to be very depressed indeed.

My time in the UAE was nearly up. With the Iraqi football coach refusing to see me I was left with nothing but a few quotes, a BBC microphone (which I had to return) and a branded note pad from the Erbil International Hotel that I'd swiped before I left the Kurdish north. But there was one last reason to stick around. Gulf Cup fever had hit the UAE. The hosts' victory over Kuwait had set up a semi-final clash against Saudi Arabia and the nation waited with bated breath. It wasn't often that football hysteria gripped the UAE, a country that had only existed since 1971 when seven emirates that had made up the Trucial Coast of the British Empire won independence: Abu Dhabi, the capital, Dubai, Sharjah, Fujairah, Ajman, Umm al Qwain and Ras Al Khaimah. But it was Abu Dhabi and Dubai who shared the power and hogged the limelight. Dubai in particular, under the leadership of Sheikh Mohammed bin Rashid al Maktoum, had seared itself onto the world's consciousness with a string of high-profile sporting events and increasingly ridiculous building projects. While Dubai got all the press, Abu Dhabi was quietly building one of the world's largest sovereign investment funds from the huge oil revenues it enjoyed (ten per cent of the world's oil sits under the UAE, almost all of it in Abu Dhabi). Yet Dubai was so good at marketing itself abroad – Dubai's airline Emirates sponsored Chelsea and PSG, and part sponsored the 2006 World Cup whilst the company gave Arsenal $200 million for naming rights over their new stadium – that most foreigners assumed it, and not Abu Dhabi, was the UAE's capital. Dubai had even gone a step further by dipping its toe into ownership of a foreign football club. Sheikh Mohammed's sovereign investment fund, DIC, had been aggressively pursuing Liverpool FC and had got close to securing a deal before the board plumped for an offer tabled by American businessmen Tom Hicks and George Gillett. At the time of writing, DIC was still sniffing around. There was even talk of Dubai having a crack at bidding for the 2018 World Cup, even though it would be held in Dubai in the middle of summer, at a time when the outside air temperature regularly nudges 50 degrees. They were nothing if not ambitious.

Dubai and Abu Dhabi had a history of low-level antagonism, a state of affairs exacerbated by Dubai's current turn in the limelight. But with the UAE's media forbidden from discussing anything controversial about the intrigues of the UAE's royal families one of the few times this enmity was exhibited was when teams from the two emirates played each other in the local league. The first I knew of this was, when watching the local news on television in Dubai, I saw the unedifying sight of two stands full of men wearing the traditional *dish dasha* fighting. The two sets of indistinguishable fans were from Abu Dhabi's Al Wahda, whose president was none other than the UAE's president Shaikh Khalifa bin Zayed Al Nahyan and Dubai's Al Wasl, whose chairman was the youngest brother of Sheikh Mohammed. Yet for all the money and all the glitzy, eye-catching projects, the local league was in a relatively poor state with low wages and an antiquated transfer structure that meant it was the clubs, and the powerful ruling families, that held the power. No UAE player had ever played in Europe, although there wasn't any shortage of talent. The country's best player was Ismail Matar, a diminutive, pacey striker who burst onto the world stage at the FIFA World Youth Championships, which was held in the UAE in 2003. Matar won the Golden Boot, only the second Asian player to win the award at an official FIFA tournament. Previous winners tended to have a big impact on the world stage – Maradona, Prosinecki and, most recently, Messi had all had the honour bestowed on them. The interest of big European clubs was pricked and Inter Milan were reportedly sniffing around. Yet, oddly, Matar chose to stay in the closeted confines of the UAE first division with Abu Dhabi's Al Wahda rather than seek fame and fortune abroad. The answer may be found in the bizarre case of his international strike partner Faisal Khalil. Faisal had attracted the attentions of second division French club Chateauroux, who he signed for from Dubai's Al Ahli in early 2006. 'I am very happy with this first step towards a professional career with Chateauroux and I hope it will be successful,' Faisal happily told Dubai television once he'd made it to France. 'I know Chateauroux are a second division side. But I hope I can contribute with my team-mates to win promotion to the first division. I will do my best.' Chateauroux's manager was equally happy with the signing. 'I had visited the UAE and watched Faisal play against Al Wahda in the league and also with the UAE national team against Brazil,' he confessed to *Gulf News*, even though the friendly match between the UAE and Brazil had resulted in a humiliating 8–0 thumping. 'He is a talented player and we are sure he will succeed with us.' Everyone was happy. Everyone, that was, except his old club Al Ahli who were livid they had lost a key player midway through the season. Instead of getting mad, they got even. The UAE FA mysteriously refused to issue the proper documentation to allow him to play in France. Even though Ahli were playing hardball, Faisal was still confident of fulfilling his dream. 'I think two weeks is a good time to get all these formalities out of the way and I should be in a position to play for Chateauroux after I get back to France in the first week of March,' he said. Al Ahli was demanding an apology from the striker and his immediate return. But higher powers had got involved, Dubai's crown prince no less. Twenty-five-year-old Sheikh Hamdan bin Mohammad Al Maktoum also happened to be Al Ahli's president and intervened to solve the crisis. Whatever he said did the trick. Within days of the royal family's intervention Faisal was back to the UAE and ready to turn out for Ahli. Again. 'It's sad that players are so gullible and they have fallen prey to the empty promises,' Jassem Al Sayed, who represented Faisal, told *Gulf News* when his player had returned home. 'Faisal Khalil was lucky as his club has stood by him.'

The one area where foreign influence was tolerated was when recruiting the manager. The impressively toned figure of Bruno Metsu, who had memorably taken Senegal to the 2002 World Cup quarter-finals after beating world champions France in the first game, was now prowling the touchline for the UAE. He hadn't, however, initially been the first choice. With much fanfare Dick Advocaat had been unveiled as the man to take the UAE on to great heights, and maybe even

World Cup qualification in 2010. At the time I was working on *Time Out Dubai* and had planned to interview Dick until a better opportunity came about. Gordon Ramsay, who had opened a restaurant in the emirate, was guest editing the magazine for a day. Gordon and Dick had some form: Gordon was a young player for Glasgow Rangers before injury caused him to retire and seek alternative employment in the catering industry; Dick had successfully managed Glasgow Rangers, famously winning the treble in his first season. Both still held a deep affection for the club, so they jumped at the chance to meet and talk Scottish football. Dick was pretty happy to see us. He had been living out of a hotel since his arrival a month previously and didn't have much to do as the UAE hadn't qualified for the 2006 World Cup. His next competitive tournament was the 2007 Gulf Cup 18 months or so away. Every time the Old Firm was mentioned, he lit up, reeling off anecdotes about how he once throttled Fernando Ricksen and called him a 'fucking fucker' after getting sent off in an Old Firm game. It was, Dick maintained, the finest derby in the world. It was also a long way away from the more sedate environs of international management. His whole demeanour dropped when asked about the World Cup. 'We can't qualify for the World Cup,' he said, looking deep into his plate. 'But we're getting ready for the next Gulf Cup.' It was added so half-heartedly you felt he was about to cry. Dick poked around his salad niçoise as he tried to summon up a modicum of excitement regarding the UAE's next friendly, against Benin. He seemed pretty unhappy to be stuck in the desert. But lunch was good and his spirits seemed lifted as Gordon shook his hand and we said goodbye. 'He won't stick around long,' whispered Gordon as Dick descended the futuristic staircase. I didn't realise just how soon he would be proved right. A week later we had gone to print with the interview and, on the way home from work, I picked up a copy of the *Gulf News*.

Advocaat's Sudden Departure Shocks UAE

The sudden departure of Dutch coach Dick Advocaat from the UAE to sign with the Korean FA has made the UAE football officials, media and supporters furious for many reasons.

The first was the way Advocaat left UAE [sic]. He secretly went to Dubai Airport. He left the car keys with the reception of the hotel where he was staying after he arrived last month to start his job with the FA.

Advocaat did not inform any FA officials about his departure. When the FA board members read about his signing with the KFA in a local newspaper, they tried to call him but his mobile was switched off.

Equally galling for the UAE FA, there was no clause to penalise Advocaat if he walked out. Although Yousuf Al Sarkal, the chairman of the UAE FA, seemed more upset he hadn't had the chance to fire Dick himself.

'Never in the past did any coach terminate his contract with the UAE FA. It was always the FA that had sacked coaches.'

It was too late to retract the interview. The magazine had already gone to print. The next day I sat at my desk wondering whether this was a sacking offence when the phone rang.

'Hello?'

'Hello James, it's Dick.'

'Dick, where are you?'

'I'm, ahh, in Holland.'

The lunch, it turned out, was the turning point. Dick had to get out and get out quick and with the South Korean FA offering the chance to guide the 2002 semi-finalists to Germany it was a no brainer. A few phone calls later and he had hurriedly packed and fled the country. He'd lasted less than six weeks. 'I'm sorry,' he said as I tried to work out whether to feel angry or guilty. 'It was too good a chance to miss.' At least he had the good manners to call. The man the FA turned to next had no problems adapting to the job. Metsu was a footballing chameleon, a consensus seeker who soaked up his players' advice and acted accordingly. More importantly, he arrived in the UAE a Muslim after converting during his time in Senegal. With a semi-final to show for his efforts, the UAE FA must have counted their blessings that Metsu was on hand to take the reins.

If the nervous looking Saudi men sitting at the bar in the Madinat Jumeirah in Dubai, wearing their team's green football kit and sipping on large glasses of lager, were to be believed, victory for the Green Falcons was a foregone conclusion. 'We will win 2–0, for sure,' boasted one as he ordered a double whisky. '[Yasser Al] Qahtani is the best.' The game was due to start at 8.15 p.m., but the Saudis were planning on getting there at 1 p.m., such was the expected rush for tickets. Clearly tickets would be at a premium. I took a taxi down to Abu Dhabi's Jaziera Stadium a few hours before kick-off. I should have taken the Saudis' advice. Already, two-and-a-half hours before the match was due to start, every seat was taken. Thousands milled around outside whilst the police, arguably never having seen so many of their countrymen in one place before, struggled to control the mob. Groups of Emirati teenagers in traditional outfits stormed one fence, half a dozen making it over the sharp metal prongs before the police could beat the rest back with their batons. I doubted I would ever make it over in time before getting a beating. I had to find another way. One stand seemed remarkably quieter than the others. With strict segregation between the fans being enforced, the only seats left were with the Saudis. I picked a green Saudi flag off the floor, waved it at the policeman guarding the gate and he let me in. Inside, the stadium was deafening. Three stands in front of me were blanketed in the white of the UAE's national dress. Only patches of green from the many UAE flags and two small slivers of black broke the monotony – the women's section. Despite being outnumbered the Saudis were louder, banging drums and singing religious songs, the UAE fans' weak replies only audible during the occasional lulls. The match was tense and tetchy, neither team making any clear-cut chances. At half-time some Saudi fans, along with the policemen charged with looking after them, sought divine inspiration in a quiet corner, deep inside the bowels of the stadium, by praying together. The second half wasn't much better and, with the game heading for extra time, the Saudi crowd relaxed slightly, allowing their gaze to be distracted from the tense stalemate. Their complacency was to be exploited. The referee gave the UAE a ridiculous free-kick in a dangerous position. 'The referee!' exclaimed Mohammad, a young Saudi in traditional dress standing next to me. He rubbed his fingers together in an accusatory manner. 'Money.' With the game deep in injury-time Ismail Matar smashed the ball into the left-hand corner with virtually the last kick of the game. The stadium exploded in white and black from its torpor. Robed sheikhs ran onto the pitch towards the mound of bodies that had covered the tiny striker. The UAE bench joined them, as did the disabled section. One man in a wheelchair was determined to reach the pack, wheeling himself heavily over the grass towards his hero as fast as his arms could take him. Matar emerged from the melee and sank to his knees as the stadium continued its apoplectic celebratory rage. The Saudi section felt like the eye of a tornado: the barometric pressure of quiet violence bearing down around us. There was stillness and silence. Mohammad brushed past me whilst furiously shaking his head. Others simply sat, stunned, robed heads in hands. There were still people on the pitch when the match continued its last few pointless moments. Seconds later, it was over, Metsu and Matar were national heroes and the Emiratis resumed their crazy 4x4 dance on the nation's highways to celebrate. It wasn't the end of the UAE's journey either. They went on to beat Oman in the final, Matar again proving the difference, scoring his fifth goal to lift the country's first ever piece of silverware in front of 60,000 fans at the Zayed Sports City Stadium. He never did get the move abroad his talents merited. But for his efforts one prominent local awarded him two prized camels worth $109,000 each. Even Inter Milan couldn't match that.

SIX

Yemen

The young, machine gun-wielding soldier was the only man – well, boy – standing outside Sana'a's national football stadium. The imposing concrete bowl – ringed by faded walls of the red, black and white of Yemen's flag – was supposed to be filled with the voices of 20,000 angry Yemeni football fans, cheering on the country's biggest team, Al Ahli Sana'a. But the stadium was silent, and the vast car park was empty, save for the young boy rhythmically chewing on the bulge in his left cheek as he gripped tightly onto his weapon.

'Is there not a football match on?' I asked, whirling around trying to catch sight of someone. Anyone. I had just travelled for two days, from Spain to London to Qatar and then, finally, Yemen on money that wasn't my own. I'd borrowed the cost of a ticket off a friend on the flimsiest of reasons; so that I could be here, to find out more about football in Yemen. It made sense at the time, but with the grinning boy soldier and his AK47 the only witness to my weeks of planning, it suddenly felt like madness. Silently he lifted his barrel and pointed it to his left, gesturing me to follow its line. In the distance, in the corner of the car park, stood the headquarters of the Yemeni Football Association, an orphaned breezeblock box adorned with an unnecessarily large sculpture of a football. The soldier grunted and I followed his cue to leave. The nerve centre of Yemeni football was equally devoid of life, except for a caretaker who had been roused from his afternoon slumber after hearing me bang on the locked doors of the FA's entrance. 'OK,' he told me after I explained my predicament as he sat in his room, on the floor, with two friends and half a dozen half-full bags of what looked like spinach. All he men had the same bulge in their cheeks. He pointed to his mobile: 'Hamid.' Hamid Shaibani was the only man he knew who might know what was going on. He was also the man in charge of Yemeni football, the FA's general secretary. The caretaker pressed the phone to his non-bulbous right cheek, rattled off an apology in Arabic and handed me his phone. 'The match was cancelled!' Hamid sang back enthusiastically. 'We had an Olympic qualifier to play in Sharjah, against the UAE, so we cancelled the match.' This, I later discovered, was not unusual in Yemen, where the fixture list for the First Division was often treated with the same amount of respect as a stray dog. The fans didn't know when, where or against whom a match would kick off until the day before the game.

When people think of Yemen, football isn't at the forefront of their minds. Usually it's just anarchy, terrorism and guns. Lots of guns. This, after all, is a country that is only second behind Saudi Arabia in providing the men who wage *jihad* on foreign battlefields in Iraq and Afghanistan. It also happens to be the ancestral home of Osama Bin Laden. The American military also received one of its pre-11 September bloodiest noses here after the USS *Cole* was hit by a suicide bomber whilst moored in the southern Yemeni port of Aden killing 17 sailors. In the Western press Yemen is usually a pretext for a story of an attack, kidnapping or beheading meted out to a Westerner. But I had come across a story, a football story, that pricked my interest. Being ranked as one of the worst teams, not just in the Middle East, but in the world, meant that few people outside of Yemen cared for its football leagues, cups and invariably disappointing qualification campaigns for the big international tournaments, but one story had reached the radar of the international press.

Yemen Withdrew Following Doping Concerns:

AFC Yemen pulled out of the Asian Games soccer tournament because of a lack of cash to drug test their squad following reports that players were addicted to a banned substance, the Asian Football Confederation (AFC) said. Yemeni soccer chiefs withdrew the team on Thursday, citing insufficient funds to carry out dope tests ordered by the Yemen Olympic Council (YOC), the AFC said on its Web site. The YOC had advised the YFA to consider pulling out following media reports that a number of players were using the banned drug *khat*, a leaf which has a stimulant effect when chewed. (Reuters)

A whole squad of players being banned for drug use was interesting enough, but the fact that the drug of choice was *khat* made it even more intriguing. *Khat* is the curse of the horn of Africa, a drug that is only grown at high altitudes from Kenya all the way to Oman and which has, legally, weaved its way into the Yemeni psyche. It's a small, innocuous-looking leaf that, when chewed over time, produces a mild euphoria and a heightened sense of awakening followed by lethargy. Depending on who you talked to it was either a mild stimulant that had the same giggle-inducing properties as weed or an aggressive cocaine-type high. Just ten minutes at the ground had shown me that every adult – and marginally post-pubescent adolescent – exhibited the telltale signs of *khat* abuse – the distended cheek, watery eyes and thousand-yard stare – from the soldier to the caretaker to the youth-team players from local club Shaab Sana'a who had earlier arrived at the stadium and were milling around outside. 'We all know what would happen if the coach caught me chewing *khat*,' replied Ali, a 16-year-old goalkeeper, whilst running his finger across his throat. 'I'd be cut, cut from the team. If he found out he would carry me out of the stadium himself.' The other four kicked gravel around in a circle and avoided eye contact when I asked whether any of them still took the risk. The Asian Games debacle had been something of an eye opener for Yemen's sportsmen, and the young players were glad the team had been kicked out. 'It was embarrassing, yes,' admitted Naif, a 20-year-old striker. 'Because, if they had played and were on *khat*, they wouldn't have been very good. They were lucky because it would have been more embarrassing if they had gone on the pitch.' Keeping the kids off the stuff long enough to play football was a big problem – even the Shaab youth team said there was pressure from family to chew at big events like weddings. Hamid was the new general secretary of the FA, and had been drafted in to get tough on *khat* and wean his charges off the green stuff. 'There will be another game, we are not sure what game, but there will be one,' Hamid finally admitted, putting my mind and racing heart at rest. 'I'll pick you up where you are standing now, on Thursday and we'll talk.' Hamid hung up, and I walked back to the front gate, past the soldier, and waved goodbye. He was too stoned to lift his arm in reply.

I wasn't that surprised to find Abdul, the manager of Sana'a's venerable Taj Talha hotel, totally fucked. After landing at Sana'a International Airport I took a taxi to the old city with Jeff, a blond-haired American in his early 20s who 'used to work for the state department'. I was convinced he was a spy. Still, it was cheaper to share the cab, even if the cash came from the CIA. I had been warned a few days previously by a friend from Dubai to try and get to the towering, ancient hostel deep in the Yemeni capital's old city before 1 p.m., otherwise 'the man behind the desk won't know what's going on'. Sure enough, by 2 p.m., Abdul was half-cut. Tall, with a receded hairline, beak-like nose and a thin Nasser-esque moustache, Abdul's glassy, unfocused eyes scoured his small manager's booth looking for my keys. His right cheek was bulging with matter, a thick green paste that could only be seen in cycles, when a periodic chew revealed his dusted and blackened teeth. After falling over twice, bursting into a fit of hysterical laughter and giving me the keys to someone else's room, he finally, and with shaky hands, found the right set. 'Thank you, what are you doing here?' he asked with a half grin on his face, unable to look straight. 'I'm a journalist,' I replied. 'Ah, *khat* is very good for journalists,' he shouted, finding a common ground and pointing at his bulbous cheek. 'You chew and then you write. Later we go to the market and chew together.' I thanked Abdul for his offer, before he stumbled into a backroom and collapsed onto a filthy low-rise mattress for his fitful afternoon sleep.

Your first half-hour in Yemen reveals four odd but essential facts. The first, and most important, is that this is a nation addicted. No one is quite sure when Yemenis started chewing *khat*. One study discovered that Yemenis had been chewing it before the discovery of coffee. But by all independent verification, *khat* has been a catastrophe for Yemen and the other states where it can be grown, being blamed for the anarchic situation in Somalia and Sudan and massive unemployment in Kenya. For Yemen, the consequences have meant flatlining productivity, stubbornly unresponsive economic growth and extreme poverty, not to mention poor performances on the football pitch. Poor Yemenis sometimes fund their habit to the detriment of food for their family, and the whole economy is based around its consumption. From sunrise until 1 p.m., life continues as normal. Then an estimated 80 per cent of the nation downs tools and heads to the *khat* market to buy a fresh plastic bag of the stuff. Midday is when the *khat* comes down from the mountain and most believe that it has to be chewed within a few hours or the active ingredient that gets you high is lost. The rest of the day is spent chewing and lying around. President Ali Abdullah Saleh, the country's first democratically elected leader since the unification of north and south in 1990, had tried to lead by example by stating that he would not chew *khat*, nor would his armed forces. But he dared not ban it. There would be riots in the streets, as there were in Aden in the mid-1950s when one political party in South Yemen banned the drug. The issue destroyed the party and *khat* was back on the streets a year later. Even Islam is powerless to outlaw it. Whilst the devout and the intelligentsia frown on its consumption, and *khat* is banned in every Middle Eastern country bar Israel (and only then because of its large Yemenite population), it is not considered 'haram' (forbidden under Islam) as it wasn't mentioned in the Koran.

The second thing you notice, after realising that everyone is addled, is that Yemen is awash with knives and guns. Every man, when he comes of age, is given a jambiya, a curved knife that sits in the front of his belt. The knife serves notice on your position in life: the more expensive the jambiya, the wealthier the man. But that's not all. Guns are everywhere, a hangover from the days before reunification when tribal loyalties and deep mistrust of central government meant that few threw down their Kalashnikovs. According to the 2007 Small Arms Survey, Yemen had nearly 60 million guns in circulation, or 61 small arms for every 100 people. Add the knives to the party and you have the world's most highly armed population.

The third is that Saddam Hussein is a god. On nearly every street corner, wall, car and shop window, a picture of the moustachioed madman comes staring back at you. You can even buy 4x4 spare wheel covers bearing images of him in his pomp. He was always revered for being a symbol of Arab nationalism, for his financial support to the families of Palestinian suicide bombers and for his opposition to 'Zionist imperialism' during the first Gulf War. But Yemenis have another reason. Yemen had backed an Arab solution to the Gulf War, a stance which angered the Saudi royal family so much, fearful that Saddam's Middle Eastern tour would visit Riyadh after Kuwait, that they banished all of the kingdom's Yemeni remittance workers. In 1991 Yemenis made up the largest proportion of foreign labour in Saudi yet 850,000 were forced home, almost strangling the newly united country at birth. His death a few months earlier had only deepened his status as a martyr, in a way Sunni ex-Ba'athists in Iraq could only dream of.

The fourth, rather ironically given the third point, is that the second most common fixture after Saddam on Sana'a's walls is the Star of David. The ancient Jewish symbol is carved on every other building in Sana'a's UNESCO-listed old city, a legacy from the days when tens of thousands of Jews lived here. A small community still existed in the north, but most were expelled by Yemen after the creation of Israel in 1948.

Leaving Abdul to his rest, I traipsed up the seven flights to my room which overlooked the old city. Whilst the rest of Sana'a is littered with half-built concrete buildings and debris, as if an occupation force had recently left in a hurry, the walled, old city is a fragile, beautiful reminder of Yemen's wealthy past, when its abundance of natural resources – coffee and incense – made it one of the richest countries in the world. Yemen's ancient architects had been credited with inventing the first form of skyscraper and this small section of Sana'a was packed with crooked, ten-storey, mud-built proto-high rises, all jostling for air and ringed with plaster to make the whole district look like it was carved from gingerbread. You suspected that one strong gust was all it would take to turn the city to dust, yet it had stood defiant since the second century AD and had seen Christianity, Judaism and Islam pass through. The large key opened the door to my sparse room, its plain white walls only enlivened by the coloured light streaming through the stained-glass windows depicting two interlocking Stars of David. On the roof a sand storm blew through the old city's warren-like passageways, coating everything in dust and turning the air sepia, it had done since the time of Christ.

To help me get my bearings I had been trying to arrange an interview with Adel, a sports reporter at the English-language *Yemeni Times*, but our increasingly heated conversations over a crackly international line ended when it became clear that only a bribe would purloin any time with him. Still, his boss was more forthcoming and agreed to meet me at his offices near Hamdan Street, the Oxford Street of Sana'a. Outside their dreary offices every parked car had a picture of Saddam prominently displayed. Adel greeted me like I was a long-lost friend, forgetting our disagreement on the merits of bribery, and kissed me twice on both cheeks before leading me up to the *Times'* modest office. Banks of old PCs were manned by silent journalists tapping out the next day's edition. Adel ushered me into the office of Raidan Abdulaziz Al Saqqaf, the newspaper's managing editor. Rotund but with the face of an adolescent, Raidan had been working at the *Times*, which his sister edited, since he returned from studying in Nottingham and had spent most of his life outside of Yemen. He wasn't impressed with what he had come back to. 'Yes, he is quite popular,' he sighed when I asked why so many people carried pictures of Saddam around with them. 'You see, we believe in the conspiracy theory here. It is deeply rooted in our culture here. We ...' he emphasised sarcastically, exonerating himself from the same view, '... think that what happened to Saddam is part of a conspiracy and he is a hero. He fought against America.' The perception in the West is that Yemen, and her imposing President, is an ally of the West capable of making and changing policy in his homeland that follows the Western-approved model of economic liberalisation and moderate Islam. The problem, Raidan explained, was that no one was telling the kids that. 'Yemeni children are taught a subject called nationalism. It blames all the poverty and backwardness of Yemen on occupation and colonialism and the influence of foreign powers. So you grow up thinking that Israel has been taken away from the Arabs by America. If you see the news, you will see that they don't mention the most important news. It's a systematic brainwashing of our culture. If they say Israel, they say "Israeli enemy". If they say America, they say "the occupation forces in Iraq".' Our conversation was halted when his phone rang. 'One minute,' he apologised, listening to the anonymous caller's tip, before holding his hand over the receiver. 'Four Ethiopian prisoners have died in Sana'a prison.'

How did they die, I asked, expecting to hear about a riot or torture. 'Starvation,' he replied coolly, as if this was quite a normal phenomenon. 'The guards didn't even know they were on hunger strike. We only found out when the embassy was called to pick up the bodies.'

After the next day's splash had been secured and a reporter dispatched, we continued talking, this time about *khat*. Raidan didn't chew, but he recognised how important the drug was for Yemeni society. 'In order to understand this problem, look at the Yemeni people. About 70 per cent are dependent on agriculture. We've had droughts, diseases and no subsidies. Ninety-two per cent of our wheat is imported. If you produce agri-products you can't compete so there's mass migration from rural to urban areas. Sana'a is expanding with 250,000 people a year, that's 3.5 per cent a year, the second highest in the world.' Which is how *khat* has gained its foothold. The only way people can survive is by planting a quickly grown, valuable crop. '*Khat* is a plus and a minus. It's bad because of the damage to your health and people spend almost all their wages on it. But there is a benefit. Crop prices are down across the board. Except *khat*, so many people stop growing vegetables and grow *khat*. It's a cash crop, the same as poppy seeds in Afghanistan. There have been negative effects and anyone of sound mind would ban it as it's addictive. It's cheap, makes people money and it is sociable. That is why it is so popular in Yemen.' The drug was essential to the social fabric of Yemen. Like, Raidan told me, 'meeting friends in a pub in England'. Every house had its own majlis, a room designed for long *khat* chewing bouts. Some had two, one for the men, one for the women. Female chewers, like Asian teenage smokers targeted by Western tobacco firms, were the *khat* industry's big growth area, the next big market to get hooked and to exploit. Even a rival newspaper had its own majlis for editors and journalists to chew and discuss stories. I left the offices of the *Yemeni Times* and took a taxi back to the Talha. It was time to find out what all the fuss was about.

Abdul was waiting for me impatiently outside the hotel. It was early afternoon, just when the sweet leaves had been brought fresh from the mountains to market, and he didn't want to miss out on the good stuff. He took my hand and led me through the warren-like alleyways of Bab Al Yemen, the walled ancient quarter. Shopkeepers sharpened their curved knives, or sold spices in huge, overpowering sacks that spilled out on to the tightly woven cobbled streets. Another polished picture frames in a shop that dealt with only one extremely popular visage: Saddam Hussein. The impersonal bustle of market day gave way to a crush. There was no laid-out permanent stall or signs that directed you towards Bab Al Yemen's *khat* market. Instead, men streamed blindly towards a pre-programmed, long-ago understood point, like pigeons returning to a coop. Abdul picked up the pace as others joined us, a half-run every six steps belying a hint of desperation. The market was an unmarked arch guarding an alleyway full of *khat* sellers. They sat calmly, cross legged, with their produce laid out in front of them on blankets, their steely demeanours contrasting with the frenzied bidding that was going on above and around them. Clearly they had understood the golden rule of drug dealing: never dip into your own stash.

I didn't have a clue what I was looking for. One bushel, which cost 5,000 rials (about £13), looked exactly the same as another that cost 8,000 rials. Buyers barged past as more men packed into the tiny alleyway. 'This is no good,' Abdul finally said after looking at a third, identical bag, with the squinting half-eye of a jeweller examining the veracity of a newly discovered diamond. Finally, Abdul was satisfied we had a good deal, and I handed over 1,000 rials for a bag. For the money, I would be getting some moderately swanky stuff, the kind of *khat* that a low-income Yemeni would take to a wedding. For their daily hit a 500-rial bag of *khat* would do. Even then that represented half of Yemen's average daily wage of $6. The trick, Abdul said, noticeably more relaxed on the walk back to the hotel now that his daily fix had been secured, was to 'look for the red leaves. The more of them, the better it is.' Back at the hotel Abdul collapsed back on his mattress and began to unravel the thin plastic doggie bag that held that afternoon's hit. I had read romantic descriptions about the rituals of Yemeni *khat*-chewing: the drinks, the conversation, the friends all gathered to catch up, as intricate and dainty as Victorian afternoon tea. I watched Abdul, on his haunches, greedily stuff leaves into his cheek in the dark corner of his office, the bright spring sunshine blotted out in the Talha's cool, medieval interior. It wasn't exactly what I had in mind. I said my goodbyes, went to my room and packed the *khat* into my bag for another day.

A feral cranial thump woke me the next day. It was 11.30 in the morning and I had the worst hangover of my life. Something was wrong, a deep foreboding that you only get when you know the previous night you did something very bad. You just can't remember what it was yet. I was due to meet Hamid in 30 minutes. I threw on some clothes and ran out of my room and hailed a cab. Then it started to come back. With *khat* off the menu for the time being, I had decided to try and find a beer somewhere in Yemen. Being a strict Islamic county, this was a tough task but I had heard that the Movenpick, Sana'a's only five-star hotel, had a bar. Luckily, I'd managed to blag a free night on the proviso I wrote a travel article about the place. Jeff, the blond American possibly in the employ of the American secret service, was waiting for me at the Horseshoe, Sana'a's number one nightclub. It was also Sana'a's number one whorehouse. Streams of Adenese hookers filed in past oblivious security guards and national policemen that guarded the Movenpick's entrance. Inside was like walking into a provincial British nightclub circa 1988: neon piping, hairspray haircuts and a DJ committing the unforgivable crime of badly mixing together Kylie Minogue into Jason Donovan. The buying clientele was mainly Arab businessmen and before long all had several girls on each arm. Packs of girls still looking for business danced together, casting furtive looks. We got a drink and Jeff started speaking to a girl I assumed was a prostitute, as she had long dark hair and was wearing a long black abaya like the other girls. 'Oh this?' she said, pointing to her outfit in a Californian drawl. 'Men don't hassle you as much if you wear it.' It turned out that Jane was a 26-year-old American of Saudi parentage from California. Her ex-boyfriend, a Californian solar panel salesman, had traded her in for a '21-year-old fuck toy' and she decided to get as far away from him as possible and ended up teaching English in Yemen. She was clearly bored out of her mind with having to shoo away men trying to solicit her and was glad of the company. After a few hours, it seemed perfectly normal for the three of us to get a room to drink more and talk politics but it wasn't a credible excuse for the five national policemen who knocked on the door and insisted that unmarried couples weren't allowed in the room. 'But you have a bar downstairs full of prostitutes. What's wrong with us talking?' I asked, incredulously.

One of the officers, wearing a threadbare blazer and sporting a huge moustache, grabbed my arm and tried to drag me out of the room. 'ID,' he barked. 'No, where's your ID?' I barked back, fuelled by drunken bravado.

'Who is this man, asking me for ID?' he spat. A stand-off ensued, me not showing my passport, him refusing to show me his. In the end, a passing bell boy brokered a truce to ensure I wasn't arrested. We could finish our drinks but then we had to leave. It turned out that the national police not only protected the place from possible terrorist attack, but also spied on the guests using a network of cameras in the hotel, making sure that nothing un-Islamic was going on. Or rather, nothing un-Islamic that they couldn't command a cut from. 'You should always go up separately,' advised the hotel's Lebanese manager the next day, admonishing my rookie mistake. My protestations that it was an entirely innocent encounter were met with a knowing nod.

I ended up passing out on my bed as the sun rose, a foolhardy decision that I now regretted as the taxi slalomed through Sana'a's potholed streets back to the national stadium. I was late and again no one was there. Even the *khat*-chewing boy soldier who had been patrolling the grounds had deserted his post. In the distance, a Honda Civic approached. It was Hamid, who hadn't forgotten about me after all. With dark hair and dressed in chinos and a jacket stretched over a large paunch, he ushered me upstairs into his large office. The walls were adorned with pictures of great Yemeni teams of the past, whilst the trophy cabinet was, understandably, given that Yemen ranked 137th in the world, rather bare. Hamid eased himself behind his large desk, a Yemeni flag in one corner and a portrait of President Saleh hanging ominously above him. As it turned out, the Yemeni FA had only really existed in its current form for the past year. FIFA suspended them in 2006 after the sports minister tried to install one of his cronies in the job, breaching FIFA's rule on political interference. Hamid was drafted in to bring a fresh approach to Yemen's seemingly intractable sporting malaise. He was one of the new breed, a liberal technocrat who had lived in New York, China and the Netherlands working for the UN. Now he was charged with modernising football in Yemen. His first job was dealing with the fall out from the Asian Games debacle and trying to kick *khat* out of the game. Even if the modernist had to resort to draconian methods to achieve it. 'We only started looking at this [the issue of *khat* abuse] last October,' he explained. 'We asked every player to sign a contract to say he won't chew *khat* and if any test result shows he chews *khat* he will go to jail.' Jail might be a tough option, given what I'd heard at the *Yemen Times*' office, but for Hamid it was a necessary deterrent. 'Footballers earn $1,000 a month, even middle-class people here only earn $200, so they must look after themselves. We spend $50 a day on national team players, so imagine over six months. If we find he chews *khat*, he must compensate the association.' The problem was that, with the drug so ingrained in Yemen's culture, it was a hard, almost impossible sell. 'They [Yemen's footballers] were all using [*khat* for] a long time. We tried to educate them as *khat* destroys their energy. The next day you are dead [but] when you are chewing the *khat* you feel like a big man.'

It wasn't just the players whom Hamid was trying to forcibly wean off *khat*. The fans too had been banned from bringing the drug into the grounds, along with their knives and guns. 'We have security in the stadium to stop that, they cannot bring their knives in,' he added, walking to a window and absentmindedly looking at a woman wearing an all-enveloping abaya as she slowly walked across the car park to the women's gymnasium opposite. 'We have tight security. Some people smuggle it in, but it's not like it was. Did you hear about last week? At a match the fans started throwing stones at the referee. The problem is that everyone in Yemen has weapons, Kalashnikovs mainly. We have to take them off them before they go into the grounds. Then they come out, get their weapons and fight. That happened twice here.' The last time was in 2006, when the Yemeni national team unexpectedly lost 3–0 to Thailand at the same stadium. The crowd responded to the insipid display by rioting outside, smashing up windows, setting fire to cars and shooting up the stadium as the victorious Thai team cowered inside. 'Unfortunately, it's a tradition,' Hamid sighed, grabbing his keys and ushering me out of the door to meet the national team doctor. 'No one trusts the government. The new generation, though, they don't chew *khat* or carry weapons. I don't carry weapons, I never have. But they expect to beat teams like Indonesia and Thailand. We played India recently and it was 1–1. I was really worried. But we scored a second and there was no trouble, even if we didn't play well.'

The team doctor Mosleh Saleh Ali Salman was waiting for us at Hamid's local, a grimy restaurant near downtown Sana'a. Outside, groups of smiling men slung themselves over the back of their Toyota pickups clutching that all important Yemeni fashion accessory: the Kalashnikov. We settled down on a bench laden with what looked like 18 different varieties of lamb, before the doctor made a startling admission: *khat* wasn't that bad for you after all. 'We haven't done a study on this [but] there is some British study, I hear about it, about *khat* and they recommended that you should chew *khat*,' he shrugged, ignoring the well-researched evidence that *khat* can cause mouth cancer. 'We have prohibited players from chewing it. They can chew far away from the team but chewing *khat* reduces the training. They can't perform in the stadium to their best so chewing *khat* will reduce their promise.' Hamid was making furious phone calls to find out which match was to be played tomorrow. Rumours were that Yarmouk would take on Al Ahli, a Sana'a derby that was given extra spice by the fact that the owners of Yarmouk were deeply Islamic and had incorporated their religious doctrine into the club's constitution. The club would only sign Muslim players and only pick a player for the first team if they had proved their religious credentials by praying five times a day. Missing prayer, or having a Western-style haircut, were two foolproof ways of getting dropped from the team. Al Ahli, on the other hand, were Yemen's most popular team. The name comes from the Egyptian team Al Ahly, arguably the Middle East's first popular Arab owned club. It means 'The National' and since its inception in the early 20th century, following the club has been seen as a way of supporting a more secular Arab self-determination. The doctor continued to slowly chew on his meat. 'There are many clubs, like Yarmouk, that are very Islamic. Islamic men, but very political too,' he added. He liked the devout teams, mainly because they made his job easier as *khat* use in more religious households, much like smoking, had always been frowned on. So far the new regime's net had started to catch the odd intransigent player leading to a number being banned from playing. 'We have had to throw players out. We have found a player chewing *khat* in front of the team's official. Even if they are famous, it's no excuse, the rule is the same for everyone.' This, I was about to find out, wasn't exactly the case. Hamid and I left to meet two of his best friends, both ex-Yemeni internationals who were now part of his new generation of officials trying to clean up football in the country. On the car journey north Hamid took the chance to rectify some of the misconceptions about Yemen: about how it actually pumped one million barrels of oil a day, the same as Iraq, but only declared 400,000, such was the corruption. That Yemen's Islam was actually far more relaxed than people assumed. That everyone had girlfriends and boyfriends. Drugs and booze were readily available and hip-hop was the soundtrack of choice for Yemen's twentysomethings. The bustle of Sana'a soon left us behind as we climbed higher into the sparsely populated mountains that protected the city. Decrepit oil tankers inched slowly in the opposite direction, one misplaced tyre away from a fiery apocalypse. Parked cars littered the side of the road in front of a magnificent, panoramic view of the city. As it was 2 p.m., prime *khat*-chewing time, I'd assumed it was the view that had attracted so many visitors there. But no. 'We have a lot of gays in Yemen,' he said, jutting his head towards the line of silent cars. 'No one cares, not really.' Just around the corner from Yemen's premier cottaging site, we arrived at our rendezvous. I'd assumed we'd meet at an office, or someone's house. Instead we were met by piles of rubble on the side of the road. Painfully thin stray dogs gingerly picked their way through the detritus, oblivious to our presence.

Khaleed and Fayad were already there, leaning against their 4x4s. It felt more like a mafia hit than a meeting. Both players were stars from a bygone era, playing in a team that hated itself.

Whilst East and West Germany were basking in the glory of the latter's triumph at Italia 1990 and looking forward to a peaceful and prosperous future together under one flag, a more low-key, dangerous and drugged up version was taking place in Yemen. Unification between the warring north and south, the south under the influence of Soviet communism, the north by religious jihadists, had uneasily taken place in 1990. The reunification of the national team was equally fraught. 'There were two teams, I was with the north, then after 1990 we came together and there were big problems,' shrugged Khaleed, a tall, studious-looking man who, despite a protruding bald pate, exuded youth. 'Politics has interfered with football too much here. A lot of political parties are involved. Some of the clubs have good relations with the regime and they support this club and some clubs follow the opposition and there are some problems. They are afraid but they support them through money. Ahli is the government team.' The only thing that anyone in the newly united Yemen national team could agree on was *khat*, which was chewed mercilessly in an attempt to qualify for several World Cups. 'I was one who didn't chew *khat*,' Fayad stressed, 'but everybody did when I played. Some of them chewed one or two hours before the games, others after. They thought it would give them more energy, that it would make them strong.' Unsurprisingly, Yemen's performances on the national stage were abysmal. Even Khaleed, a baritone-voiced, bald-headed ex-striker once considered Yemen's greatest player, admitted that he chewed *khat* before a game. 'Sometimes,' he shrugged, as Hamid glared at him. 'Maybe once a year, in the last years before I retired.' Khaleed pulled out a large plastic bag and handed me the reason why we had convened on top of a mountain near Sana'a's gay district. A dirty can of Heineken. He cracked it open, shouted 'Yallah, yallah, yallah' (come on, come on, come on) and downed it in one. 'Heineken is the best beer in the world,' he grinned. 'You can't get it in the shops, but you can from the discos, everyone knows where.' We sat drinking our beer as the bank of cars rocked to the motion of consensual gay sex below. It wasn't long before the subject of *khat* came up again. Khaleed asked me if I'd chewed, which

I hadn't. 'Drink, and then fuck, haaaahahaha. Yes?' It was only now that it dawned on me that I might have been dragged to an isolated spot for reasons other than an interview with high-ranking members of the Yemeni FA. Hamid jumped in to explain. '*Khat* is like Viagra, if a woman takes *khat*, it is potent.' Everyone agreed whilst frowning about the effect it has had on Yemeni society. 'We could achieve much more economically without *khat*,' explained Hamid. 'It takes so much money and time and we would have a big middle class with the power to buy commodities. It can take half your income. It's a curse.' The group solemnly nodded in approval before, a few moments later, Hamid dropped a bombshell with unexpectedly brilliant comic timing. 'OK, we will go to a restaurant, get some beer and chew some *khat*. OK?'

I'd felt oddly subdued on the journey back to the mountain. Hamid and his gang were singing along to their favourite CD – Eminem – as if they were preparing for a big night on the town. With Hamid's zero tolerance policy towards his players' use of *khat* and his explicit connection between Yemen's various failures and the drug, I was expecting a footballing Eliot Ness; a whiter-than-white enforcer, living by the same rules he implemented whilst shining the torch of justice under every last stone. He wasn't quite Al Capone in comparison, but it was akin to popping into FIFA headquarters in Switzerland and wondering whether Sepp Blatter fancied coming out for a spliff or two. We stopped at a nearby Chinese restaurant. The owner ran out and shiftily looked both ways before handing Khaleed a black bin liner full of Chinese beer. Abdullah, a fourth friend who had joined us, wearing a red-and-white headscarf and a long flowing kandoora, was dispatched to the market to buy the *khat*, whilst we went to Fayad's house. Like those of most affluent people in Yemen, Fayad's house was a white, expensive-looking homage to Mediterranean design stuck in the middle of a cesspool. Open sewers and shoulder-high piles of rubbish surrounded us. But regardless of how much your house cost to build, every home has to have its majlis. Fayad's was a large, open room, the edges skirted with cushions and the air full of sweet Yemeni incense, which before

the commodification of *khat* was the country's most valued
substance, making Yemen one of the richest places on earth.
Before the chewing could commence, we ate as much as we
could as *khat*'s main side effect is to suppress the appetite.
Abdullah arrived from his *khat* run hot and bothered. He'd
had to first go home to ask his wife's permission to come
and chew. She was a doctor and, unlike the national team's
medic, knew how harmful the drug was. With permission
granted, he assumed his cross-legged position at the edge of
the room. The ritual began. First, tissues and a small bucket
are laid out in front of each guest whilst the host empties
the *khat* into five equally sized bags. Each large green stem
looked like rocket, and the trick was to pick the right leaves.
The best and most potent were the small and slightly reddish
ones. Each leaf was pulled, cleaned between the fingers and
then jammed into the cheek, where it was chewed to a mush
before more was added, and then more, and more, until a
large ball of mush could be seen protruding from your cheek
like a particularly nasty abscess. At first, it tasted like shit, like
unwashed, bitter spinach, but once your mouth adjusted to
the sourness it had a smoky, nearly pleasant aftertaste. Then
you felt it working its magic: the raised heart rate, the loss
of inhibitions, the waves of pleasure that shook through you.
It seemed to be one part cannabis, one part Ecstasy, one part
speed. Suddenly everyone in the room was my best friend;
I was sitting with the wittiest people in the world. I felt
invincible. After spitting some of the thick green juice into my
bucket, we got down to the main reason why people chew
khat: to talk. The four men in the room were all desperate
to improve the image of Yemeni football. They couldn't have
found it in a worse state. Yet Yemen was due to host the Gulf
Cup in 2011, inviting the rest of the Middle East to view
the steps it had made. It would be embarrassing if the rest
of the region saw the current *khat*-addled mess. Although
for Hamid, the problems were bigger than *khat*. We had only
just got confirmation that Ahli and Yarmouk were to play
at 3.45 tomorrow afternoon, less than 24 hours before the
game. None of the teams had its own stadium. There was no

such thing as a match ticket in Yemen: fans just rolled up if they heard about a match on the grapevine and watched it for free. Violence, guns, knives and *khat* were commonplace. The government owned all the teams. And to make matters worse, unless you were at the game, no one would ever see it or have a record of it. Yemen's (one) state-owned television station got angry when the FA asked them to pay for the rights and had refused to show any more matches since. More and more *khat* was stuffed into our cheeks and as the night drew on we made an action plan. Hamid would rebrand the league, like the Premiership, and privatise the clubs. He would bypass the local television network and sell the rights directly to a pan-Arab satellite network. That would show them! Season tickets would be sold and for those that missed the game, no fear, a highlights show, an Arabic *Match of the Day*, would be the centrepiece of Yemen's Friday night television schedule. It would be a ratings hit! Fayad and Abdullah shouted ideas as the room felt the frenzied white heat of footballing revolution. 'That's what I've been saying!' they shouted over each other. 'Why don't we bring over big-name foreign players, like in Qatar?' another asked hopefully. Someone else suggested Sami Al Jaber, the legendary Saudi striker who had appeared in four World Cup finals. Why not? Why the hell wouldn't he want to play in Yemen?! 'How much would we have to pay him?' Hamid shouted excitedly. In the spirit of change, I suggested something a little leftfield. 'Allow women into the stadium!' The other four looked at each other quizzically. 'No,' Hamid eventually responded. 'This would not work.' But still, great work had been accomplished. At last, Yemen's footballing problems weren't as intractable as we first thought. In ten years Yemen would have the best league in the Middle East! No, in Asia! Everyone laughed, and slapped thighs, and clinked glasses. With these guys together we could save Yemeni football! The shout went up: 'Yallah, yallah, yallah.' All was great in the world.

Then the *khat* ran out.

Almost as soon as the last, sweet leaf had been chewed, the euphoria ebbed away and the depressing inertia that suffocated almost every single good idea in Yemeni society descended over the room. Sami Al Jaber wouldn't come here. What a stupid idea. Which pan-Arab network would want to pay to show Yemeni football anyway? If the government were so riddled with corruption, how the hell would we buy the football clubs off them? Where would the money come from? Everyone sat in silence, the same questions washing around their temples. What comes up, must come down. I felt utterly hopeless and desperate for more leaves to stave off the inevitable. But there was none left. The gang cleared up their stalks and shuffled outside into the cool Yemeni night. We said our goodbyes and retreated to our respective beds, spent. I knew that Hamid, Khaleed, Abdullah and Fayad would be having the same conversation in 12 months' time.

It was Friday and the big match was less than an hour away. As 3 p.m. approached there wasn't a bushel of *khat* in sight at the small football stadium on the outskirts of the old city. I'd had a fitful night's sleep, one of the drug's other side-effects, but I didn't have to walk far out of the old city to find the squat, condemnable wreck that passed for the testing ground for Yemen's new policy on cleaning up football. Soldiers with machine guns patrolled the front gates, taking guns and *khat* off anyone trying to smuggle them inside. But the main weapon against fan-on-fan violence was the Jambiya, and the police had a cunning plan. Rather than impound the knives, they set up a free cloakroom so the spectators could retrieve their knives after the games. The cloakroom was an engine-less Toyota Corona that sat silently as men streamed to the back window. Inside, two policemen poked their hands through a small crack in the window to receive each spectator's knife. In return they received a small plastic ticket. The system seemed to make sense, until I realised that each ticket appeared to be the same. Piled all around the policemen, the curved knives looked indistinguishable from one another. After being shaken down I took my position pitch side as the terraces filled green and red – the green of Yarmouk, the red of Ahli. Minarets protruded from the nearby slums like gleaming white skyscrapers as the basalt mountains watched over in the distance. Suddenly, the call to prayer wafted over the pitch from every direction. Most Islamic countries have employed a system whereby the call to prayer is called at exactly the same time. Some use a single recorded voice for uniformity. Others, like the UAE, make sure that it's not just the times and the voices that are in unison. Friday sermons are vetted by the government too and sent back to each Iman with the official imprimatur. Yemen, as with almost every aspect of its society, is gloriously oblivious to the technological evolutions in Islamic prayer. Each mosque still has its own muezzin, prayer caller, and each keeps its own time. Some calls to prayer start as early as 3.30 a.m. The result is a deafening, jumbled cacophony that has probably not changed for a hundred years. As the two teams warmed up a tall, balding man with glasses, wearing a long white kandoora and sporting a huge jambiya, stalked around the Yarmouk players. Abdul Aziz was still allowed to carry his knife because he was the vice president of the club. The Sudanese manager Mohammad Mahdawi circled the seated players in the other direction. Aziz spotted me watching his team talk and straightened his back before walking over. He seemed suspicious of my presence but agreed to talk to me. 'We established this club in 1968 with a group of people who had the same idea,' he explained, before spreading his arms and pointing to both sets of fans. 'We are all Muslims, but Yarmouk is more strict. We pray before matches and we are more strict with our values. We don't allow players to chew *khat* or smoke. Their behaviour is more important than the way they play. So we choose players on that basis.' It seemed unbelievable that a team could exist that was chosen not on ability, but on a player's degree of religious devoutness. But Yarmouk hadn't been doing too badly. They sat mid-table and had a reputation for playing fluid, attacking football without ever troubling the upper echelons of the league, a bit like an Islamic Tottenham. Abdul still seemed suspicious and was overly eager to point out that his team wasn't filled with extremists or corrupted by fundamentalist ideology. 'Since the beginning it was like this, not as fanatics but to respect the values [of Islam],' he replied when I asked whether a non-Muslim could play for the team. 'We have a Nigerian, but they are Muslim too. [But] we would have a non-Muslim.' I'd always found it odd that games were quite happily played on a Friday by devout Muslims, but that might have more to do with growing up in England at a time when opening a shop on a Sunday was thought on a par with adultery by some in the church. 'It is no problem at all,' he laughed, patting me on the back and walking back towards the players. 'Look,' he said, pointing back to the crowd. 'It will be full today.' He was right. Despite the short notice, the addictive draw of an afternoon's *khat* chewing and the demands of the mosque, 7,000 fans had packed into the stadium. It all seemed rather cordial as the players kissed each other's cheeks and rubbed each other's noses. Hamid finally arrived and we took our seats with the Yarmouk fans, who sang and shouted at the Ahli players, targeting those that had ponytails. 'You'll see a good game today and a good crowd,' Hamid assured me as the officials sorted out the paperwork. The linesmen sat atop the only three balls in the stadium as if they were rare and valuable eggs. Another official polished the brand new, $500 electronic substitutes board, Hamid's most recent attempt at modernisation. The referee blew and the crowd erupted. The Yarmouk fans flew the green flags of Islam and mocked any Ahli player who went down too easily. 'You're not hurt!' the 3,000-strong all-male contingent shouted. 'You have spoilt yourself.' Then, against the run of play, Ahli broke away with their star player Ali Al No No. 'No No' translates as 'baby' and Ali was the great hope of Yemeni football. He had moved to more lucrative and better organised leagues, first in the star-studded Qatari league, then in the less glamorous Syrian first division. He'd failed in both but in Yemen he was the closest thing they had to Ronaldinho, as he exhibited with a curling shot from all of 25 yards into the top corner just before half-time. The red half of the crowd exploded, the green half fell silent. With half-time approaching the third official struggled with the electronic board. Two more officials came to his aid, none able to get the requisite number of added minutes to be played displayed on its electronic face. Soon, a whole crowd gathered around, pressing buttons randomly and shaking the lifeless board before giving up and resorting to the numbered cards that had done them just fine for the past few decades. Hamid shook his head before bowing into his cupped hands and leaving the ground. In the second half, Yarmouk fought back and equalised, the goal sparking a riot in the Ahli stand behind the goal. Police with sticks waded in hitting anyone who dared show a lack of immediate respect. With order restored, the game wound down to its inevitable conclusion, just as dark clouds rolled over the stadium and the first spots of a cold, early spring rain started to fall.

Back in the changing room, Yarmouk captain Usman Salihu was happy with the result. Usman was Nigerian but had played in the region for the best part of a decade in Lebanon, Saudi Arabia and Syria for the army club Al Jaish – which literally means 'The Army' – before coming to Yemen and seeing the country's *khat* addiction first-hand. 'The players are not treated like professionals,' he said as we sat down in a large changing room, our voices echoing around the four peeling walls. 'The *khat* contributes a lot to the lack of performance in the team. I don't take it but from the people I know who take it, it absorbs their strength. They can't train. This is their main problem here.' His manager, who had earlier been stomping around his squad like a recently promoted army general, was equally clear on Yemen's problem. Madawi was a former assistant coach to the Sudanese national team but had been in Yemen managing Yarmouk for two years. 'Every year they say it will change but it doesn't,' he said, slumping slightly as he delivered the news. 'Even the [FA] committee get together to chew.' I shook my head and offered a faked look of shock in response. For the outsiders, it was obvious who was chewing and if the FA really wanted to make examples of players they could. 'I don't want to name any names, but I see those who chew. We know who they are. This is not something that is hidden. It is not like cocaine. It is allowed so they chew. And it is available everywhere.' Both Usman and Madawi hoped that Yarmouk's example would be the best way to exact change. One of the big advantages of only signing players that adhere to a purer form of Islam is that they would be fitter than the rest of the league. 'Every player prays before and after training and everything that religion doesn't allow, Yarmouk doesn't allow,' Usman explained proudly. 'Of course we are fitter because we stick to our religious obligations. We are seventh now but we hope to have a good position this season and maybe win the championship next year.'

This is arguably Yemen's best hope, that non-*khat* chewers lead by example, excel and are rewarded in whatever field it is they find themselves in, be it farming, journalism or football. I bade farewell to Usman and Madawi and their depressing take on Yemen's inability to break its *khat* thrall. Outside was anarchy. The crowd was still streaming from the stands to the exit, but an almost reverential clamour had come over them. Ninety minutes of *khat* denial was more than most men could stand. Almost every single pubescent male was filling his cheeks with the drug, secret stores that had somehow eluded detection from the armed guards outside. The pavement was dotted in the green effluence of Yemen's addiction. The crowd swirled around the engine-less Toyota Corona that doubled up as a knife depository like an unstable storm. Fans from both sides thrust their tickets through the window as the harassed policemen matched numbers to homeless ornate steel. The chaotic scenes sat in contrast to the lone man standing back from the pavement, watching from afar. Murat had been at the game, even though he was a Ahli Ta'izz fan from the south. Yet he didn't seem the slightest bit interested in joining in the melee. Was he not desperate for any *khat* too? I asked him. 'I gave up months ago, it broke my teeth,' he replied, before breaking into a bellicose laugh. His huge open mouth was devoid of anything resembling enamel. Murat had stumbled across a foolproof plan to kick his habit. After all, if you have no teeth, *khat* is pretty much off the menu.

My time in Yemen had come to an end. I checked out of the Taj Talha, said goodbye to Abdul, who was already on his first bag of the day, and hailed a cab on the Wadi Road towards the airport. Mujid picked me up in his ancient Toyota Corona, wearing the Yemeni uniform of white kandoora, blazer, headscarf and knife. 'Five hundred rials,' he said solemnly. Seeing it was a third of what I was being offered elsewhere, I agreed. The car lurched into life and spun off just before the other marauding taxi drivers could cut in and take his fare. Although, as I later discovered, they may have simply been trying to impart a warning. Mujid's car was, like every other in Yemen, on the brink of extinction. They regularly cut out down motorways and every Yemeni man seemed to have such a union with his automobile that he could sense the precise moment it would run out of petrol, ensuring that, as Mujid did, he glided into the petrol station on nothing but the most cursory of fumes. Mujid's luck had run out, though, as the car wouldn't start. 'Push,' he implored, poking me out of the car. I took my position behind, a passer-by on the right, and grunted. The car came back to life just as I trampled through a stinking, overflowing gutter, and jumped into the passenger side, Mujid speeding up as if he hadn't really wanted me to get back into his cab at all. He laughed, before narrowly avoiding a truck and asking me to give him all my money, using warped but impeccable logic.

'You will not need your money now because you are leaving Yemen.'

'But I can always change it at the airport,' I replied, sensing for the first time that perhaps Mujid wasn't the full ticket.

Stuck in a traffic jam, Mujid attempted to veer onto the pavement but slammed his brakes on, screeching to a halt in front of two Yemenis casually talking. This was clearly a provocation. Although the jambiya is a cultural accessory, it can be, and is, still used as a weapon to settle scores in Yemeni disputes under certain circumstances. I was pretty sure road rage wasn't one of them, but Mujid screamed at the two men before pulling out his jambiya, waving it inches in front of my face and stabbing it at the human roadblock. The two men responded, drawing their knives and thrusting them through the passenger window before clumsily jousting in front of me. I wedged myself back into the seat as far as I could and prayed to the God I had long ago forsaken to let me live through this. Being outnumbered, Mujid sped off, his knife narrowly missing my throat in the recoil, his cab narrowly missing a lorry as he veered away. Behind us the men continued chasing after the car. Somehow, no one had been stabbed and my face had remained unslashed. I had witnessed, a little too close for comfort, my first Yemeni knife fight.

An angry silence fell over us. 'Have you, erm, ever stabbed anyone before?' I eventually offered, still rooted as far back in my seat as possible. Mujid looked back blankly.

'Stabbed someone,' I repeated, making a stabbing motion with my arm at the same time.

'Yes,' he replied. 'I've stabbed many people. Now, give me a cigarette.'

Without hesitation I passed over a cheap Yemeni Kamaran Light and sat back in silence as Mujid swerved and shouted his way towards the airport, drawing his knife once more at another driver in a Land Cruiser that cut him up. The shell of a taxi careered into Sana'a International Airport. I handed over a 1,000-rial note and bolted, dragging my bag out of the back seat. The last thing I heard was Mujid screaming, demanding the rest of my Yemeni money. I didn't look back, and I didn't ask for the change.

SEVEN

Palestine

The protest was already in full swing when I arrived. Walking towards Bethlehem University, the low rumble of faraway raised voices could be felt, if not exactly heard, until the tall sandstone walls broke at the main gate to reveal the crowd inside. Dozens of young men danced in circles to distorted Arabic pop music, spinning their black-and-white keffiyeh scarves in the air. Those that didn't shook yellow flags. The flag depicted two fists, one clenching a bayonet, another a machine gun above a grenade. Behind the men, banks of women, some covered, some not, stood silently unmoved, as a demonstrator with a megaphone began shouting his call to arms, 'Allahu Akhbar!' God is great. The men mirrored his call.

'It was the student elections yesterday,' came a voice to my side, by way of explanation. It was one of the university's Christian brothers who administered the campus on behalf of the Vatican. This was a victory parade for Fatah, who had vanquished the likes of Islamic Jihad and Hamas to control the university's student body politic. It was a rare moment of success for Fatah – the nationalist party of Yasser Arafat and President Mahmoud Abbas; the party that had dominated Palestinian politics for the past 40 years yet had squandered the goodwill of their people through corruption and mismanagement. Hamas, the Islamic fundamentalist party still considered a terrorist movement in the West and by Israel, had picked up the pieces of discontent and was in the ascendancy after winning the 2006 parliamentary election. Hamas and Fatah had been rubbing each other up the wrong way ever since and had been fighting for hearts and minds in the West Bank and Gaza, sometimes metaphorically, mostly literally, one espousing a secular version of Palestinian statehood alongside Israel, the other promoting a vision of Islamic resistance and Palestinian statehood on top of it. It might have only been a minor student election, but Fatah needed all the victories it could get.

'I voted for Fatah,' said Jasmine, a 20 year old studying computer science, as she watched the rapturous scene unfold. 'Muslims and Christians vote for them, only Muslims voted for Islamic Jihad and Hamas. In other universities they have won, but not here. It's supported by the Vatican and Hamas would make us cover.' The screams from the victory parade couldn't be heard down in a basement office on the other side of campus. Samar Mousa was oblivious to the goings on in the main square as she shuffled important paperwork and fielded excuses from her students as to why they didn't have any kit with them for that day's physical education class. Short, with dark hair, piercingly friendly kohl-ringed eyes and wearing a fitted denim jacket, Samar welcomed me into her tiny office out of which she ran the university's women's athletics department. But that was merely a day job that helped her to build a subtler, but no less important, form of defiance: organising the Palestinian women's national football team.

Getting here had been a monumental logistical exercise. After fleeing Mujid – the mad taxi driver in Yemen – I had to somehow make my way back to Israel. My flight from Sana'a landed in the conservative UAE emirate of Sharjah, where I changed for Amman and took the well-trodden path from the city's Abdali bus station to the Allenby Bridge; over the border into the West Bank; through to Jerusalem; and then finally the short drive to Bethlehem, where the Palestinian women's team was based. Football had long been a man's game in the Middle East. Whilst women's football had exploded in popularity in Asia and the West, women in the Middle East still had to fight just to get a game. Not a single Arab team qualified for the Women's World Cup in 2007, which is no surprise given the reticence of governments and governing bodies towards the women's game. In Iran the authorities insist that women cover completely, only showing their hands and face. What's more, men are banned from watching them play. In Saudi, the authorities have banned national women from playing football completely. The national team is full of expats who play behind closed doors. In Egypt, one high-ranking FA official didn't even know there was an Egyptian women's team, even though they are arguably the best in the region and were ranked 85th in the world by FIFA. Kuwait's women footballers looked to have made a breakthrough when a member of the royal family, Sheikh Naima Al Sabah, announced that a national football team would be set up. Fans on message boards joked that it was probably the best chance Kuwait had of qualifying for a football World Cup again. The plan was quietly dropped when Waleed Al Tabtabae, a leading Islamist MP in the Kuwaiti parliament who ran a committee that monitored 'phenomena alien to society', forced the team to be banned by arguing that women's football was 'un-Islamic'. But even these barriers pale in comparison to those faced by the Palestinians, who have to fight, not just the restrictions of occupation, but also their own communities to play the game they love.

The seed of the Palestinian national team was planted over two decades ago, in Amman, Jordan, out of an injustice. 'I was studying there and they told me that I couldn't play football,' explained Samar cheerily as she ushered me into her windowless broom cupboard. Framed photos of her proudly standing next to the women's team littered the shelves along with dog-eared black-and-white prints of her family. 'They said I had to do aerobic dance, it made me mad so I made sure that when I was in charge, girls could play football.' It was difficult to imagine Samar getting mad; such was her soft, matronly demeanour. Yet her experience of being slighted as a young, football-loving student wasn't exorcised until four years ago. It was whilst teaching physical education at the university that Samar's dream came to fruition. And that was only when she met 23-year-old Honey Thaljieh – the team's captain and star striker. Samar ushered two girls into the room. 'We started with Honey,' she said, smiling at the brown-haired captain as she found her seat. 'Then we had three players, then five from the university, and then we spread the idea to other towns, in Ramallah, Jericho and Gaza. Now we have 20 players in all.' Honey and Jackline Jazwari, the team's left-winger, had come to the beautiful game from different places: Honey had played (and beaten) the neighbourhood boys in barefoot practice matches on the streets of Bethlehem almost as soon as she could walk. She was blessed with a powerful right foot and natural leadership skills, and Samar decided to build the whole team around her. Jackie, on the other hand, had never kicked a football before she met Samar. 'For me it was a strange thing to play football,' she recalled. 'But when I saw Miss Samar I was in the first year in university and I was playing in the basketball team and she said why don't you join our team? She said you'd love it and pushed me into it. I love her like my mother so I went to training, saw the girls and the spirit in the team and wanted to play.'

Despite having a strong nucleus of dedicated players, the practicalities of living in the West Bank made it almost impossible for them to actually play any football. To start with the only grass pitch was ten miles away in Jericho, which is largely inaccessible thanks to the ring of Israeli checkpoints that surround Bethlehem. Instead they practised on a nearby concrete court with pre-pubescent boys. No women's club teams exist, which meant no league, no cup and no competitive games. It was also impossible for the girls from Gaza to train with their counterparts in the West Bank without leaving the country. 'We went to Egypt to meet the Gaza girls before a tournament last year. It was the first time I had even met them,' Samar explained. 'We didn't know their names. It's strange playing together as a national team as we met the girls for the first time two days before our match. It was also the first time we ever played on a full-sized pitch once in Egypt. The girls didn't know their positions but they played by enthusiasm. We lost, but we didn't lose by that much.'

The biggest obstacle to progress, however, was Palestinian society itself, which hadn't exactly welcomed the women's team with open arms. 'At first it seemed weird, women playing soccer in our society because it has such a male mentality,' admitted Honey through her warm perma-smile, as we all sipped tea in the cramped office. 'Some families had problems sending their daughters to play football, some still face problems.' The resistance comes from a mixture of conservative social mores and a creeping religiosity that has spread from Gaza to the West Bank. Although five players were Muslim, most were drawn from the West Bank's small Christian community centred on Bethlehem. Some towns were so conservative they were totally off-limits for recruitment. 'We don't go to Nablus, Jenin and Tulkarem,' Honey lamented. 'We've had some difficulties. One player – her uncles said she shouldn't play. Then they said she had to wear the veil and kept putting barriers up. But they eventually accepted the idea. Step by step they saw what we were doing.' Then there's the issue of marriage. The team has already lost two first-team players to husbands who demanded their wives give up football for duties in the home, a fact that meant that Honey was the oldest of the team. She had vowed not to get married unless her future husband accepted her love of football. 'I'm single, but if I get engaged and get married I will still play. If he loves me he will love what I am doing.' Quite how football was any barrier for Honey getting married was beyond me. Aside from the fact that she was arguably the most beautiful woman I had ever met in the flesh, she was strong-willed, intelligent and obsessed with football. In other words, most men's idea of the perfect woman. Maybe Palestinian machismo was the answer. After all, if your fragile male pride can't handle a woman with her own ideas, it's hardly likely to survive being nutmegged by your betrothed during a kick-around. Marriage wasn't the only barrier either. The team's kit had become somewhat of an issue. Sepp Blatter may want to 'sex up' the women's game with a new kit that mirrors beach volleyball, but in the West Bank long shorts and over-sized shirts were still considered too risqué, especially for some Muslim families who regarded them as indecent. 'In the north of West Bank and Gaza they are a little stricter,' Samar said diplomatically, but with a wry smile. 'The problem is that they do not respect us if we don't dress honestly. We wear shorts near the knee. This is the biggest problem. But our coach is Muslim, a strict Muslim, yet he still coaches us.'

As if on cue Raed Ayyad, the team's 37-year-old coach, introduced himself. Quietly spoken and with a large barrel chest upon which his whistle lay, he smiled and stroked his thick beard when I asked whether his religious beliefs had been conflicted at all by coaching a team of inappropriately dressed footballers. He was new to the job. The vacancy had only arisen after the last coach quit when the Israelis detained him as he tried to leave the West Bank for a match overseas. It wasn't the inconvenience that made him leave, but rather the unfairness that his presence might hamper the team's attendance at tournaments. The new coach wasn't there for the financial benefits either, as the position was unpaid. Worse, he had to combat a whispering campaign as to his intentions in taking the job. 'It was difficult for me because all the people were gossiping that I was training girls,' he admitted, the fourth person in the room making it feel like a sauna. 'They would say "Why is he training girls? Football is rough, it's not good for them," things like that. I tell them, from a religious point of view, Muslim or Christian, no one has said that it is forbidden, that women can't play soccer. Islam says that sport is good for the body and if [the players] wear long clothes then it would not be forbidden amongst the Muslim community.'

Raed's moderate voice of reason had become more and more isolated in the previous months. Hamas' parliamentary election win had sent a huge signal to the rest of the world as to the changing nature of Palestinian society – it was becoming more religious, more conservative and more radical. Honey, for one, had noticed the difference, both as a footballer and as a Christian. 'Things are becoming more conservative under Hamas but not all women are the same,' she asserted. 'Some women believe that they can do something and won't just wait for their husbands to come along and make children. They believe that they can change something and I'm one of them, the rest of the girls too. It's one of the most difficult things we face. Sometimes we feel like we are fighting alone. We need some encouragement but you can't find it here. So it's about courage. If we have courage we can achieve anything we want.' Honey's articulate call to arms heralded the end of our interview. Samar had to get on with her athletics training and Coach Raed was preoccupied with training the university's men's team. As the only games Palestine played were international fixtures away from home it was impossible to see them in action, plus training was a few days away. But Honey and Jackline agreed to go for a kick-about in the basketball court outside. The basketball players stopped what they were doing and stared as Jackline teed up the ball and expertly transferred it from foot to foot, occasionally striking the ball higher only to control it back down to earth with her chest. Even within the university the team was considered something of an oddity. The ball passed to Honey who struck it with her ferocious right foot, the ball flying straight into my face. When the two had stopped laughing hysterically I arranged to come back to see training and interview more of the players. Holding my throbbing nose I climbed back up to the university's now empty main square. The detritus of the victory rally blew across the concrete floor. A yellow flag of Fatah lay crumpled and unloved on the floor. I picked it up, put it in my bag and left through the front gate.

It was a short walk down a steep hill to Manger Square. If there's one thing that defines the West Bank it is an inequality of altitude. The West Bank's uniquely coloured, yellow-white hills are the most coveted in the world, with the incremental battle for supremacy between Palestinian and Israel settlements taking place at their zenith. Each hilltop has its own urban snowcap, clinging precariously to its summit lest anyone replaced it when they weren't looking. Bethlehem's ancient foundations meant it could be confident of continuity, but others had not been so lucky. Silver-walled Israeli settlements rise up on nearby hills, all steel and superiority. At its base, the previous occupants scratched a living in huts made from discarded plastic and corrugated iron, waiting for the day they would once again claim the higher ground. Bethlehem will always be fixed in the mind as a place of worship for Christians and, sure enough, Palestine's shrinking Christian minority almost all live here. It was one of the reasons why the women's team could exist in the first place, operating as it does in a slightly, only slightly, more tolerant atmosphere. It was difficult to imagine such an endeavour being tolerated in the universities of Hebron, Nablus or Jenin. In one small back alley Mike tended to his customer-free trinket shop, St. Johns. 'Things here are bad,' he told me, lighting up a cigarette on the shop's step, revealing the large cross he wore around his neck buried in thick silver chest hair. 'Most Palestinian towns are industrial but we rely on tourism. The war in Lebanon really hurt us.' In fact, any bad news – suicide bombings, border restrictions, flare-ups in Gaza – was felt more keenly here than anywhere else. Once Bethlehem thrived on thousands of foreign tourists flocking here to see the Church of the Nativity, the site where Christians claim Jesus was born. No one comes any more. Bethlehem's nadir came in 2002 when a bloody siege between the Israeli military and suspected Palestinian militants took place, flashing images across the world of bloodshed on the doorstep of one of Christianity's holiest sites. 'It hasn't been the same since,' shrugged Mike, handing me a small wooden cross as a present. Sure enough the square was empty, the small door to the demure church clear apart from two Palestinian Authority policemen patrolling nearby. The only other life was a gaggle of American preachers dragging a large wooden cross with a wheel on it. Arthur and Joshua, a father-and-son preaching team from California, had been dragging the cross around the world since the 1970s trying to break the world record for the longest walk – feeling Jesus' pain before the crucifixion whilst spreading the word of God. Almost everyone had been photographed with him; even Arafat and Gaddafi featured in the black-and-white prints Arthur proudly showed me. I was half-expecting a grinning photo of him shaking hands with Saddam. Everything they talked about seemed to pertain to a bigger, higher question. 'I've never felt alone on my journey because the Lord has always been with me,' replied Arthur when I asked whether he missed a settled life. 'Jesus knows where I have been.' I could only think of glib responses – 'Shouldn't you take the wheel off to really feel Jesus' pain?' or 'Do you ever get stopped at customs with that?' But they were used to ridicule and wouldn't allow my facetiousness to get in the way of a possible conversion. 'Here,' Joshua offered. 'Try the cross on for size.' Too polite to say no and weighed down with the weight of the six-foot-long timber cross, it was impossible to escape without its smashing to the floor. I was a captive audience as Arthur gathered his disciples around in a circle: 'Let's pray.' His sermon was interjected by meaty shouts of 'Yeah!' from his followers every time he mentioned Jesus. 'Let Jesus into your heart,' Arthur intoned, holding my hand. 'You will never feel alone, amen.' Under my shades, my eyes were closed and I, like an unwitting victim of a hypnotist's stage show, had just replied in the affirmative. Amen. Arthur took his cross, thanked me for my time and skipped into the Church of the Nativity, continuing on his journey. I shook my head, laughed and continued on mine.

Both Palestinians and Israelis have a joke about Jericho. Three Palestinians are stopped at a checkpoint. The Israeli soldier asks where they are from. 'Jenin,' says the first. 'Get down and spread 'em!,' shouts the soldier. The second says 'Ramallah.' The soldier shouts at him to get down too. The third says 'Jericho.' The soldier hands him his gun. 'Hold this whilst I arrest the other two, won't you?' There has always been the suspicion amongst Palestinians that if Israeli collaborators were to live anywhere, it would be in Jericho. It isn't refuted by the town's aesthetics. The road from Jerusalem is littered with crumbling towns and dirt-poor villages populated by barefooted children and herds of goats. Once you pass the Israeli checkpoint, a different West Bank emerges, one that Jericho seems to be the only representative of. The streets were wide and clean. Grass and palm trees lined the roads. A swanky hotel and casino could be found on the outskirts. Whilst the rest of the West Bank reeked of poverty, Jericho had the air of a thriving oasis town. After visiting the Palestinian women's team I had been told that one of Bethlehem's local men's teams was due to play a cup match in Jericho the next afternoon, a rare occurrence in the West Bank. Since the so-called al-Aqsa intifada flared in 2000, movement restrictions between Palestinian towns had slowly strangled the life out of the Palestinian football league. With fans, teams and referees struggling to make it to matches, it was impossible to fulfil the league's fixtures. The FA eventually gave up, concentrating on smaller cup competitions to keep the clubs afloat until the day arrived when the league could return. The quarter-finals were due to be played between Tulkarem, a devout town in the north, and Wad Al-Nes, a small village on the outskirts of Bethlehem – two of the West Bank's best teams. Whilst the women's game had struggled to have its voice heard, the men's game in Palestine made international headlines after it tried, and tragically failed, to qualify for the 2006 World Cup. The national team had a higher purpose than most as it is in the unusual position of being a national team without a nation. So when FIFA recognised Palestine in 1994, it was a cause for massive celebration in the West Bank and Gaza. FIFA were, after all, one of the only international bodies to recognise Palestine's existence. Reaching the World Cup finals, the Palestinians reasoned, would ensure that the world couldn't ignore their claims for statehood any longer. With the UN refusing to grant it full membership, it was the next best hope. It all started so well too. FIFA had relaxed its rules on citizenship, allowing the Palestinians to call on its huge diaspora to fill its team-sheet. Adverts were put into magazines in Germany, Chile and the United States to attract players. A multinational squad was assembled, followed by an 8–0 thumping of Chinese Taipei and a respectable 1–1 draw with Iraq, two teams that had to play their home games in exile, on foreign grounds. Then the wheels fell off. Movement restrictions between Gaza and the West Bank, not to mention the restrictions within them, meant the team could rarely train together. Training camps were set up in Egypt, but the players from Gaza would rarely get through. The coaching staff, realising that nine-men training sessions probably weren't the best sort of preparation for an assault on reaching the World Cup finals, started picking more players from the West Bank, breeding resentment amongst the two groups of players and effectively creating two different national teams. The nail in the coffin was when some of the team were denied permission to leave Palestine to play Uzbekistan. Five Gaza-based players had been held at the border in the aftermath of a suicide bombing in Beersheba. The Palestinians could barely scrape together 11 players. It was a miracle they only lost 3–0. The campaign was over, the Palestinian dream of statehood through the back door shattered.

The national team had never really recovered after that, nor had local football. Back in the West Bank, the restrictions remained and a league was still a distant memory and a forlorn hope. The quarter-final was due to be played at the rather hopefully named Jericho International Stadium. Covered in smashed windows and looking little more than a derelict car park with a rectangle of grass and sand at its centre, it was hard to imagine the stadium having ever seen better days. Faded posters of Yasser Arafat still adorned the low walls that led to the stadium. Fans crushed through the single turnstile to pay their seven shekels for a ticket. Once inside they took their position in the one functioning stand at the side of the pitch, the Wad Al-Nes and Tulkarem fans separated by a thick line of Palestinian Authority policemen carrying clubs. A few left their seats to take their positions towards Mecca and pray in the bright, late-afternoon sunshine. 'This competition is a little like, how do you have, the Milk Cup,' Khaldom, a Tulkarem fan, told me whilst sitting in the stands chewing on a bag of sunflower seeds and showing an almost autistic grasp of mid-1980s English football. The stadium looked half-empty but Khaldom wasn't that surprised. 'It's a long journey and there are three checkpoints to get through. Luckily it wasn't too difficult for me and only took an hour.' The referee, on the other hand, wasn't so lucky. Half an hour after the planned kick-off and he still hadn't arrived. A few minutes later the rotund man in black came puffing onto the pitch to a wall of jeers. 'He got held up at a checkpoint,' Khaldom offered. 'But they are more free here in Jericho. In Tulkarem the police cannot work after 10 p.m., then the Israelis take over. But here they are everywhere all the time.'

Tulkarem were clear favourites. The team consisted of a number of Palestinian internationals and were coached by the current national team manager Mohammed Sabah. With the stadium not having any changing rooms, both teams received their last-minute instruction behind the steel fence that separated them from the fans. Finally the referee blew his whistle. The years of footballing frustration poured out. Tackles flew in, players rolled around on the floor as if they had been garrotted and yellow cards were brandished like confetti. Seeing that it could be months before the loser got another game, both teams were desperate not to lose. Off the pitch the situation was worse. One journalist sent to cover the match from Tulkarem was escorted from the stadium after he jumped on the pitch in a rage at one of the referee's many dodgy decisions, clawing at the air between him and the man in the middle as he was dragged away by the police. The armed police had to wade in to beat back a crowd of Tulkarem fans after the perimeter fence protecting the players from the terraces was stormed. Their flailing nightsticks carved through the mass until they stopped, confused. At its centre a wheelchair-bound supporter was repeatedly wheeling himself into the perimeter fence and hurling abuse at a Wad Al-Nes player taking a throw. 'Of course, some of these players are Hamas, others are Fatah,' Ahmad, a Palestinian journalist from *Al Hayat*, whispered to me as the match unfolded. 'But there isn't one team that is for Fatah, the other for Hamas. We are all Palestinians.' That might have been the case for the West Bank but I had originally wanted to visit Gaza to see how Hamas and Fatah rivalries were being played out in the football league there. One of the few benefits for Gazans in the chaos that had followed Israel's pull out from the tiny strip in 2005 was the absence of movement restrictions, which meant that the football league could go on unmolested. The Israelis occasionally still bombed the odd match – the main football stadium in Gaza had been hit by a mortar a few months earlier as a team trained on it – but other than that, the games and the league went on as planned. But Gaza had become totally inaccessible to Westerners thanks to the continued power struggle between the forces of Mahmoud

Abbas' Fatah and Hamas. A lawlessness had gripped Gaza as the two forces fought to exert what they saw as their mandate to fulfil the will of the people; the former presidential, the latter parliamentary. Matters were made worse since the BBC journalist Alan Johnston had been seized a month earlier and was still being held captive. I'd hoped that the Palestinian FA could have given me safe passage to the last game of the season, a title decider in the Rafah refugee camp. 'Not even the FA could protect you there,' Ahmad exhaled.

The game itself reached a frenzied conclusion, 1–1, extra time and then penalties. The two teams chose radically different ways to prepare. Tulkarem huddled, discussed the order of the kicks and took some last-minute instruction from the manager. The Wad Al-Nes players and staff, even a few of the fans, put their preparations into the hands of God. The motley crew knelt in a line and prayed in the near darkness, hoping for divine intervention. Football fans may talk about how unfair a penalty shoot-out is, but for the neutral penalties are the most exciting part of any match, like squeezing a whole tournament into ten kicks. But if it's your team, it's hell on earth. For one Wad Al-Nes player the tension was too much, and he sparked up a fag, smoking it surreptitiously in the cup of his hand so his coach didn't see. The goals, the saves and the misses ebbed and flowed. Finally, Wad Al-Nes scored the winning penalty to go into the semi-finals. The players bundled into one another on the floodlit pitch as the Tulkarem players sprinted away and jumped into a waiting bus, before speeding off minutes after the end. 'We played better,' explained midfielder Kader Youssef, grinning wildly as his team-mates celebrated around him. 'It is important to own the cup and it's great for our village and great for our people. Inshallah we will play Al Islam [next]. It's a derby.' Wad Al-Nes' prayers had been answered. Perhaps the England team should try it next time they reach the knockout stages of an international tournament.

With the match over and the onset of darkness now complete, I had been presented with another logistical problem: how to get back to Jerusalem. The buses had long ago stopped and I only had a handful of shekels left, not enough for a taxi. Salvation arrived in the form of a blacked-out BMW. 'I'm not going to Al Quds [Jerusalem], but I'll take you to near Bethlehem,' the driver intoned, sensing my desperation at being homeless for the night in the West Bank. Usually I wouldn't have considered climbing into a blacked-out car, with people I didn't know in a part of the world where kidnappings were commonplace. But I was skint, had no choice and had to trust the intentions of my driver. We drove through Jericho, the streets alive with activity after evening prayers, back towards the checkpoint we entered through. A huge tailback snaked back through the desert. It wasn't an obstacle. The BMW jolted left onto the bumpy sand and powered round to the Israeli checkpoint. The driver leant out of the window and shouted at the guard, 'Sahafi Britani!' – British journalist. Suddenly my purpose on the trip home made sense. I was a Trojan horse so that he could get home quicker. My usefulness spent, he dropped me off next to the wall and sped away before I could ask where I was. Isolated, with just ten shekels in my pocket (£1.50) and lost, I reasoned that if I followed the wall I would make a checkpoint eventually. But the wall towered above me, covered in the graffiti of resistance, giving no clue as to where it eventually split to reveal Israel on the other side. Suddenly, a small Toyota bus full of young men pulled up behind me. 'Where you going?' the driver shouted above the noise of crackly Arabic pop music. 'The checkpoint,' I replied.

'OK, 100 shekels.'

'I have ten.'

'OK – ten.'

I climbed in. It was my only hope. The van leant dangerously around corners as it clung to the tarmac. The men in the back only spoke English just enough to say 'fuck you' and laugh uproariously. I sat in silence, sweating until the familiar shape of Bethlehem's grey checkpoint loomed into view. The driver turfed me out and relieved me of the last of my cash. I didn't care. I had never been so glad to see a gaggle of Israeli soldiers in my life.

It would be a month before I made good on the promise I gave Honey and Jackline to return. Everything had changed. In the short time I had been away Hamas had unilaterally ended its ceasefire with Israel and its feud with Fatah was veering out of control in Gaza. The Palestinian movement was in the throes of a civil war. Gaza was tearing itself apart as forces loyal to Fatah and Hamas fought for control. With Hamas enjoying massive popular support, Fatah were taking a beating. Both areas had killed or expelled members of the opposite political party and their respective armed militias as Fatah officials fled to the West Bank. Extra judicial killings and revenge attacks were reported across both territories, even in Bethlehem. In return, the Israelis had cracked down on movement through the wall. You could gauge just how 'hot' a situation was – as the Israelis refer to it – by the number and thoroughness of Israeli checkpoints. During my last visit our blue-and-white bus had left East Jerusalem and climbed the steep hill to the walls of Bethlehem unmolested. Now the bus stopped on the Israeli side and weaved away to whence it came as everyone else was ushered through security and towards the wall. A sign that can only have been erected as an exercise in irony bore down on the Israeli side, in Arabic, Hebrew and English – Peace Be With You. I emerged on the Palestinian side, in Bethlehem, a mere few hundred metres from the university. It was Thursday, training day. Coach Raed stood alone in the middle of Bethlehem University's concrete handball court, a brush in his left hand, methodically sweeping broken glass bottles of soft drink into the dustpan in his right whilst muttering to himself. 'The boys,' he intoned despairingly of the teenagers who had made an overnight stop and smashed their drinks on the floor by way of a leaving gift. 'Sometimes they get a little crazy.' The girls arrived just as the sun began to dip behind the trees, casting long shadows over the hot gravelly surface. It wasn't an ideal place to give your national team a workout, but when you don't have a stadium, full-sized pitch or even a state to call your own, the small patch of grey was better than nothing. Raed complained that the surface exacerbated his players' injuries, but there was nowhere else to go. It was either here or the sand. All he could do was to arrive early for every

training session and clear the court to make sure the players
didn't cut themselves.

Dressed in her Palestine 'home' kit – coloured the red,
black, green and white of the flag – Honey was the first to
arrive, stretching and setting an example to the other girls,
some of whom were as young as 12. They filed through
the gates, one by one, some fixing their *hijabs* around their
heads before smoothing down long-sleeved T-shirts over thick
cotton tracksuit bottoms. It was prohibitively hot, even for
late afternoon, but 22-year-old defender Nevin didn't see her
veil as a hindrance. 'I played in the neighbourhood with the
boys and they accepted me. Nothing is forbidden, the veil is a
choice within my family,' she said, pointing out her uncovered
14-year-old sister Nadine, the second-choice goalkeeper, who
was diving around on the hard surface as Coach Raed powered
balls at her. Nadine flashed back at me, eager to explain. 'It's
the opposite to what people think. Wearing the veil gives me
power.' Raed began to work the girls, but only lightly. He had
told me earlier that he didn't want to scare any of them off by
being a disciplinarian. They didn't have enough players. 'You
can't be so rough with the girls, like the men's team, telling
them "don't stop here, don't walk here",' he said. 'We give them
recreational training, not like hard training for the boys.'

Only seven girls could make the training session. It was late
spring and exams were in full swing, but there were enough
present for a four-a-side game, if I played as well. 'Come on,'
Honey implored, dragging my arm. 'You can come on my side.'
This was something of a dilemma. I hadn't brought any kit
with me and my jeans had a large hole in the crotch. I was one
lunging tackle away from exposing myself to a devout Muslim
man and half a dozen teenage girls. But the main problem was
my complete lack of any discernible footballing talent. The
Palestinian team may be technically the worst national team in
the world, but I still wouldn't have made the cut, even if I had
possessed an extra 'X' chromosome. Within minutes it became
clear just how outclassed I was. Nevin nutmegged me and
Jackline sprinted past, leaving me for dead. Fida, Palestine's 21-
year-old midfield general, feinted. I responded by theatrically

falling over. She skipped around my prone, humiliated figure and powered the ball into the top left-hand corner of the small goal. Raed had a smirk on his face as Nevin held out a hand and helped me to my feet. Honey looked on disapprovingly from the half-way line, perhaps wishing I'd stayed on the bench. I was utterly humiliated and had blisters to boot. Predictably, my team lost, and with the sun fading from view the girls trudged back to the bank of waiting parents and their cars. The silhouettes could have been anywhere else in the world, of proud parents picking up their kids from football training in Colorado, Tel Aviv or Madrid. That was until the huge UN-marked 4x4 came into view. It belonged to Sami Mshasha, whose daughter Sarona was the youngest member of the team. Bald and in his late 40s, Sami worked for the UN agency that dealt with Palestinian refugees, the UNHCR. He too had seen Hamas' effect on the sport, but from a different angle. 'The prime minister [Ismail Haniya of Hamas] has done more than any other Minister [for football],' he said, lighting a fag as we pulled away from the other girls. 'He used to play for Rafah in his youth. He was a nasty defender too. He used to call them after every game, even now.' Perhaps less strangely given his custodianship of a hard-line religious party, the prime minister's help hadn't stretched to women's football. Sami had taken a keen interest in his daughter's dreams of footballing stardom, mainly by helping Samar to secure funding for the team. Few, he said, within the Palestinian Football Association or the government seemed that bothered. 'It's basically not their priority,' he shrugged as the Israelis waved us through the checkpoint. Travelling in a UN car certainly had its benefits. 'When I meet them [the FA] you can almost hear them snickering. FIFA allocate 20 per cent of their money for the team but they give Sanar no money. You can't have an open ended pro bono coach or rely on NGOs.' He also sensed the pressures that are on some of the other girls to give up the game. 'Palestine was always religious, but never conservative,' he said as he drove back along Hebron road towards Jerusalem's old city. 'Now the society is becoming more conservative, which is dangerous, but that tends to happen under occupation. You tend to become fatalistic and things can become violent. The interest is so high in football amongst the girls. And the commitment is there amongst the players. But most of them are over 20 so marriage will be knocking on their door whether they like it or not. The family pressure will start now, even amongst the Christian players.' The future, as he saw it, was in articulate, intelligent and determined players like Honey, to take on the next generation of players. 'Honey's the future leader of the team. She has to be smart and know the situation, know the politics. Unfortunately, the politics here in sport are as nasty as in national politics.'

I was back on the other side of the wall, back in Jerusalem, the only place in the world that felt like two separate cities superimposed on top of each other. Damascus Gate was buzzing with traders and old, black-clad women sitting on the narrow cobbled streets selling bread, mint, shoes – whatever it was they had got hold of that day. The old city is a claustrophobic place: dark and slippery, full of the smells that define that culture's quarter – be it raw halal meat from the Muslim butchers, or the incense that periodically catches you in the Armenian quarter. The Citadel Hostel just smelt of sewers, but it was the cheapest place in town. It had stood for the best part of a millennia and on its ground floor you could spend £2 a night and have a bed in the cavern dorm – a dark, dank cave with a toilet that always filled the room with the smell of sweet shit. The choices were to sit around breathing in the foul odour or to see what a Thursday night in Jerusalem had to offer. I wasn't expecting a lot when I took the road from Jaffa Gate towards Jaffa Street. Jerusalem is seen as the parochial little brother, in hedonistic terms, to Tel Aviv's towering excess thanks to the huge number of Orthodox Jews living there. This, as I was to find out in the Belfast Bar, mattered little. It was a little rock bar at the bottom of Jaffa Street. I'd never been to a Northern Irish themed bar before, although its name was more by accident than design. The owner, seeing how the Irish bars near Zion Square had cleaned up, decided to open his own homage to Guinness and the Emerald Isle. Unfortunately, his limited knowledge of Ireland and Irish politics meant that he strayed a little too far north. It would be the equivalent of opening an Israeli bar in London and calling it 'Hebron'. Or maybe they were being ironic. Either way, Belfast was packed with longhaired kids nodding into their bottles of Tuborg as 'Enter Sandman' by Metallica played in the background. I found a seat upstairs, next to a table of Orthodox Jews sporting the kippa, ringlets and tassels and cradling large glasses of beer. Their New York accents rose sharply. They were arguing. The youngest, with blond hair, wearing glasses and sporting the kind of beard that suggested it was his first attempt at growing facial hair, piped up, 'I'm just saying, if I was a Palestinian I would fight back too. We all would.'

'No way man, there's no way that justifies anything. No way,' replied another with dark hair and a manicured beard. They were having a philosophical discussion on the nature of resistance. 'Hey buddy,' the dark-haired guy said, turning to me. 'What do you think?' I had travelled enough to realise that getting into an argument about the nature of Palestinian resistance was to be avoided at all costs. It was almost impossible not to upset someone unless you began agreeing with the often heinous views that your host subscribed to. In Arab countries it was the same, with the same old accusations coming out: Jews controlled the media in the West and all the financial institutions. That's why they don't do anything about Palestine. Countering that one usually riled a few people. And in Israel even the most liberal of Israelis met the mere suggestion that the IDF (Israeli Defence Force) was a little heavy-handed with accusations of being a neo-fascist. You ended up upsetting everyone. The seven sets of eyes looked at me for an answer. Best to go for repetition. 'Well, I agree with you, we'd all fight if occupied, right?'

The blond-haired man, Yosef, laughed, shook my hand and invited me to join them. They were all young Americans who had recently emigrated to Israel – made *Aliya* – and were building new lives for themselves in Jerusalem. They had also brought some of their habits with them from the States. They were all drunk and started discussing what to do next. 'Man, let's go get some pussy,' shouted Abe, the dark-haired guy.

'Yeah, pussy, pussy!' agreed Shlomo, another, who, in another life, could have played the gangly loser in any number of Judd Apatow films. The group careered out of the Belfast and up towards Zion Square, shouting at one another and only stopping to take in a particularly attractive girl as she walked past. The talk was exclusively of girls. 'Are English girls hot? Israeli girls, man, they're tough'; and 'Where can we get some pussy tonight?'

We decided on a local pool bar. The group swaggered in like they were filming *Reservoir Dogs*. Yosef had clearly had enough. 'Man, I have a beautiful wife at home. I'm going home to get me some sex.' Everyone hi-fived him before he slipped me a piece of paper and left. Abe could barely take his shot thanks to a mixture of booze and the noise from another group of fedora-wearing Orthodox Jews playing pool on the next table. Words were said, voices were raised and a stand-off ensued. I quietly left the two groups shouting at each other across the pool hall as they made threats in Hebrew and thrust pool cues at each other, squabbling over turf like a Jewish version of *West Side Story*.

I awoke in my dark, stinking cave gasping for water. Sketches of the previous night flashed in front of my eyes – the pool hall, the pack of drunk and horny Orthodox Jews. Could that have really happened? Searching through my pockets I found irrevocable proof. A thin paper business card.

> Sarah and Yosef
> Please join us for Shabbas or Yom Tov!
> Have an iPod? We can fill it up with Jewish stuff

I had agreed to meet Honey and her family at their home. The scene from the night before couldn't have been more contrasted on the road back to Bethlehem. I had used the blue-and-white Palestinian buses that spread through the West Bank from East Jerusalem dozens of times, but I had yet to hear anyone talk. A suspicious silence enveloped the bus as we trundled towards the wall, carrying students, workers and mothers between the two different continents. But these were the lucky ones, the people who held Jerusalem ID and had permission to work outside of the West Bank. With the World Bank estimating that unemployment in the West Bank was running at 47 per cent with 44 per cent living below the poverty line, any job, even in the home of the Zionist enemy, was a job worth having. It is one of the great tragedies of the ongoing impasse between Israelis and Palestinians. The Israeli economy needs cheap Palestinian labour to thrive; Palestinians need remittance cheques from Israel to survive. Honey wasn't one of the lucky ones. Her home was just a stone's throw from Manger Square, where she met me. We walked the short distance to her modest maisonette where she lived with her brother, sister and parents. Outside the walls were covered in Arabic graffiti. Life had been tough for the Thaljiehs in recent years. Honey's father had been unemployed since the intifada erupted and both Honey and her brother Eissa were the only breadwinners. Being a Christian had also got harder, according to Honey's mother Nahada. 'The [Palestinian] authorities treat us differently,' she told me as we sat in her comfortable, immaculately kept front room. 'Two of our neighbours were caught speeding by the police. They brought them to the prison for one night and shaved their heads and asked them "Why are you Christians? It's easy the life for you, being Christian." And they beat them.' Eissa agreed that there is an unspoken tension between the groups that is forcing many Christians to flee. 'Day by day the Christians are leaving, emigrating. In 50 years you will not see any Christians in Bethlehem.'

Since graduating in Business Administration from the town's university Honey had worked for the sports charity PACE, whilst Eissa had the unenviable task of trying to attract tourists to the West Bank as a travel agent. But Honey's football had given the family hope of a better future. 'We used to play football together in the street,' Eissa recollected in the family's front room. On his arm he sported a large tattoo of a soldier of Christ carrying a cross, apt for a man whose name translates as 'Jesus' in Arabic. 'It wasn't strange for me, but other people thought it was as they were thinking that Arab girls shouldn't play. They got used to it because she was a lot better than everybody else.' Her mother had also got used to her footballing exploits from a young age. 'She started playing at nine but we thought she'd grow out of it,' she said. 'But she didn't. [What Honey] is doing is good for the women of Palestine. It's necessary to have football for the woman, especially outside America and Europe. It's good to have this team here.'

Honey's own aspirations are like those of any young footballer. She wants to travel to Barcelona to meet her idol, Ronaldinho. Before she can start dreaming of Spain, though, she has a training camp in Germany and a tournament in Jordan to prepare for. But deep down, despite the huge differences between the problems faced by the Palestinian men's and women's teams, their goals were remarkably similar. For Honey the big prize was one day reaching the World Cup and showing the world, and Palestine's fractured society, that football could triumph where politics had failed. 'The World Cup, that's what I'm aiming for. I was the first woman playing football in Palestine. There was no girl that knew how to play football before, even that women could play football.' She put down her mint tea and for the first time since I met her Honey dropped her infectious smile. 'It will be the next generation that will make it but hopefully I will be the coach then. I won't let the team die. Inshallah.' Outside it was getting dark, my cue to leave. Honey walked me back through the flickering streetlights and tightly wound alleyways back to the main road and my lift back to Jerusalem. As we said goodbye I noticed the same wall covered in graffiti that I'd passed when it was still daylight. 'What does it say?' I asked. Honey stopped to read the message, as if it was the first time she had noticed it. 'A Hamas member was killed by Fatah here,' she explained, her face blank. 'It says: "We will never forget. We will have our revenge."'

EIGHT

Egypt

After all his planning and high expectations, Asad looked like a man broken by the unforeseen. Face buried in his hands, he sat along with 40,000 fellow Al Ahly fans doing exactly the same. The vast stretch of red shirts and flags were motionless in their half of the Cairo International Stadium. The silence was stunned and awkward before a brooding malevolence rose, making me feel uncomfortable for the first time. In the distance, the white half of the stadium was a violent sea of celebration. Furrowed faces darted for explanation between friends and strangers alike. Al Ahly were 2–0 down thanks to a stunning goal worked by Mahmoud 'Shikabala' Abd El Razeq. This was a bad thing for two reasons. Being 2–0 down to anyone was bad enough, after all, Al Ahly weren't a team that did losing. In 2005 they broke the world record for the longest unbeaten run in club football, 55 matches, and only lost a game when they headed for the World Club Championships in Japan. But this was worse, much worse. They were losing to Zamalek, their hated Cairo rivals, their bourgeois city foes. More people watched this match than any another in Africa, and for the six-figure crowd that turned up to see it in the flesh, the derby meant more than just football. It was about politics, history, identity, colonialism, escapism and pride. And for Asad, leader of Ahly's hooligan brigade, the Ultras, the battle was equally important on the terraces as it was on the pitch. For weeks he and his band of die hard Ahly fans had been planning for the game by devising the best way to taunt the opposition's fans. They opted for a huge flag, designed to cover most of the north stand, mocking the 6–1 defeat meted out by Ahly in 2002. Proudly unfurled before kick-off, Asad looked behind at it now, an impotent heap of plastic and paint. It was time to go back to basics. The explosion was inevitable. 'Listen everybody,' he screamed defiantly, breaking the silence and the gloom. 'I'm going to beat Shikabala, the cunt. I'm going to beat him in the face!'

In Cairo you belong to one of two tribes, one red, one white: Ahly or Zamalek. There are other football teams in Egypt, of course. Ahly and Ismaily have a big rivalry; Alexandria has its Al Ittihad to support. But nothing gets the blood pumping like Ahly versus Zamalek. Almost every Egyptian has their allegiance pursed on their lips. On a taxi journey from Sharjah to Dubai four months previously my Egyptian driver had spilt his colours before he even told me his name. 'I am Ahly, of course,' he said proudly, before regaling me with stories of how 100,000 people would queue from the morning to get in, with another 100,000 stuck outside. Inevitably riots would break out. 'Do not go,' he imparted ominously as I handed over my fare. 'You will be killed.' His words came back to me as the plane landed at Cairo International Airport in the middle of the night. Arriving at Cairo airport is like turning up on the set of a 1970s British light farce about the last days of the empire. Jack-booted soldiers march around in ridiculously ornate uniforms. Men sit at desks where papers and passports are passed along a large line before disappearing into an unmarked bureaucratic hell. Everything, the walls, the desks, the light, was coloured brown and grey and beige. The humid weight of early summer kept the city's overpowering odour of sewage, and the border guards' incessant cigarette smoke, at ground level. Once this was the personification of modernity; a bright vision for visitors arriving in a vibrant and upwardly mobile city. Now it was as if a pane of drably coloured glass had been placed in front of the eyes. I collected my bag and walked into Cairo's night. It was Friday, the day that Ahly and Zamalek should have played each other. But the authorities had got canny about avoiding violence and had moved it to an early kick-off on Monday, hoping that thousands would be put off by the awkward timing.

'Ahly or Zamalek?' I asked the taxi driver after our conversation in pidgin Arabic, and then pidgin English, had ground to a halt.

'Ahly,' he replied with a shrug, as if there could be only one answer.

The roots of the rivalry can be traced back to when the British army walked the streets of Cairo. Football was almost universally regarded as Britain's only popular cultural import and Al Ahly was started in 1907 as the first Egyptian-run club. The name translates as 'The National' and Ahly, wearing the old red colours of the pre-colonial flag, was seen as a team for the nation, a bulwark against occupation and a chance for the average man on the street to come together for a common nationalistic cause. Zamalek, wearing white, was considered the team of the foreigner (read the British), the unpopular, the outsider. Originally called Mokhtalat, the hated King Farouk agreed to have the team named in his honour, before Farouk was changed to Zamalek post-abdication. The team traditionally attracted not just the occupiers but also the people who had got rich by what Egyptian nationalists called 'collaboration'. It was also home to the awkward squad: the authors, poets and intellectuals who were uneasy with Egypt's new-found nationalistic confidence. As much as the Cairo derby was about nationalism, it was also about class: the truly loyal man on the street versus the effete, shabbily wealthy liberal. But it has always been bloody. Like with the majority of the world's great derbies, violence has featured prominently in past bouts. Such is the ferocious hatred between the fans that since the 1990s, no Ahly versus Zamalek match has been played on their home grounds. Instead, all games have been played at Cairo's huge Olympic stadium. The referees are not beyond suspicion either and foreign officials were bused in to take charge of proceedings. Egypt's notoriously baton-happy riot police took the threat of disorder very seriously and swamped the matches any time the two played. In fact, Egypt's riot police had become even more proficient with their batons in recent months. Hosni Mubarak, Egypt's stalwart president, had recently won what opposition parties called a sham election and had fought off two rival threats to his power; one from the liberal movement Kefaya (which means 'enough' in Arabic), the other from the Muslim Brotherhood, a well-organised radical Islamic movement with links to Hamas. Police prevented voters from reaching the polls, intimidation was rife and opposition candidates were either locked up or denied the chance to stand. Mubarak walked it with 89 per cent of the vote. From what a friend who was working on the *Daily Star* in Cairo had told me, the city felt desperate and hopeless; intractably poor and squeezed between an authoritarian government and Islamic fundamentalism. The hostel where I was staying, the Sara, didn't seem too bothered by goings on in the outside world though. Five young men and a bald pensioner sat in the reception area quickly smoking short joints, giggling hysterically. The pensioner passed me the joint without saying anything. The keys dropped into my hand as I sucked in the first breath. Welcome to Cairo.

It's hard trusting strangers in Cairo. Waking up with a thumping hash hangover, I had to go and find a phone to arrange to meet Ayman Younis. Ayman knew a thing or two about the enmity between the two sides of Cairo. As Zamalek's star striker in the late 1980s, and a regular in Egypt's national team, Ahly fans targeted him in ever more elaborate, vicious and sometimes hilarious ways. These days he was the main anchor for Egyptian and Premiership football on state television whilst supplying 3-D advertising mats for sports pitches, as well as being on the Egyptian FA's board. If there was anyone who could get me into Ahly and Zamalek's training sessions – which were heavily guarded in fortified complexes – it was Ayman. But first I had to find a phone. It's not that there was a paucity of phones in Cairo but rather that every single man in Cairo seems to be intent on selling you something. '*Habibi*, where you from, England?' asked a voice to my side as I walked down an identical side alley. Hassan, a tall middle-aged man with a wide gut and a long white shirt had sidled up next to me and started talking in perfect English. 'I lived there for eight years in Leeds. Come, come, let me give you a business card.' A phone, I was assured, was nearby, next to his oil shop no less. Before I knew it I was sitting down flicking through pictures of the shopkeeper as a young man with an assortment of young British women sporting horn-rimmed glasses and beehive haircuts before he handed over his prized possession. A black-and-white photo. Muhammad Ali stared back, standing in the very spot I was in, looking at a bottle of oil. 'He liked it very much here,' intoned Hassan, grabbing the photo back before I could work out whether Ali's head had been superimposed. The Egyptian hard sell is a little like watching a schizophrenic trying to get a date. It begins with lashings of unexpected kindness, conversation and coffee before the goods – bottles of oil and perfume – are quietly introduced. 'I'm really not interested,' I offered in the most plausibly genuine manner I could muster. The shopkeeper's face dropped, as if I had disrespected his father. 'I am not trying to sell you anything!' I was his friend, he explained, and just liked helping tourists out. The bottles kept coming out, each getting smaller and smaller like diminishing Russian dolls. 'This,' he said hopefully, nursing the smallest, 'is only 50 [Egyptian] pounds.' Even this couldn't procure a sale, and the shopkeeper disconcertingly walked me back to the door, waving me away as if he were crushed I hadn't bought anything.

At least he hadn't lied about the phone. I called Ayman from the cigarette shop next door. He had some bad news. 'There is no training today,' he said. There could have been any number of reasons: the clubs had swapped venue or date to flummox Egypt's vicious sports press. Or, worried about fan violence, training might have been cancelled. The answer was far more surprising. 'It's the FA Cup final, Chelsea versus

Manchester United. All the players and the coaches want to watch it.' Ayman invited me over to watch the match at his place. I agreed, not having the heart to tell him that any final involving Chelsea's brand of anti-football was likely to be as riveting as watching pandas mate. His villa was on the outskirts of Cairo, towards 6 October City. This was where the moneyed middle classes chose to live these days, away from the dirt, noise and poverty of Cairo in a newly built and rapidly expanding settlement. It derived its name from the date that President Anwar Sadat – the man who made peace with Israel – was assassinated. It was as if, rather than struggling to integrate into Cairo, the wealthy had instead decided to rip it up and start again somewhere nearby. Short and with tightly curled black hair, Ayman welcomed me into his huge house as if I were a long-lost family member. His three-storey home told me that, post-football, Ayman had not struggled. Back in the 1980s he was a fast, skilful attacking midfielder who had an uncanny ability of turning it on for the big derby. 'I think I played maybe 11 derbies between 1983 and 1994,' he explained. 'Then I moved to Saudi. But I scored four times. I was lucky, I always played well in these matches.' It wasn't enough to take his word for it. Handily Ayman had set up his large entertainment room, which doubled up as his trophy cabinet, so that I could experience some of his magic on television. He sat me down, passed me a Pepsi and slid the first videotape in. The screen blinked to life, initially a distorted mess of popping feedback, Arabic and neon-green. It was a compilation of his best goals: a scissor kick against Ahly in 1988; goals in the African Nations Cup; the final of the African Champions League. He looked on engrossed, oblivious to my presence. 'Mubarak was there!' he shouted, pointing at the screen, lifting himself out of his seat at the same time. 'There, he was there!' The crackling Arabic on screen gave way to a Brazilian-esque surge from the over-excited commentator: 'Ayyyyyman Yoooooooooooounis!' And there he was, with his tight retro-shorts, large Afro and barrel chest, wheeling away in celebration after volleying it into the top left-hand corner. The camera focused in on the mass of white celebrating the goal. Men were standing on the terraces holding their babies up in almost sacrificial celebration. 'Ahly fans say this goal was offside,' he said, turning around, breaking his grin and taking on an air of seriousness. 'But it wasn't. That was the goal of the season. But 1990 was my best season, I scored a horrible number of goals.' His best form coincided with Egypt's only World Cup appearance, at Italia 1990, and the stage was set for Ayman's goal-scoring prowess. But he never made it onto the plane. 'I was in Scotland for the last [warm-up] game [before the World Cup] and the fucking number 8,' he spat, still angry at the memory of Egypt's 3–1 victory in Aberdeen 18 years later. 'The number 8 [according to the Scottish FA, the number 8 that day was Aberdeen and Rangers midfielder Jim Bett] had a problem with me, he kicked me in the knee and *khalas*, finished, I had to go to Germany for an operation.' Jim Bett may never realise it but he might indirectly have had a hand in England's greatest World Cup performance since 1966. Egypt had a strong, defensive-minded team that drew its opening two group games with the Netherlands and Ireland. The crunch match came against England, which Egypt lost thanks to a solitary Mark Wright goal. The group was so tight that if Egypt had won 1–0 England would have finished bottom of the group. But Egypt had struggled to score goals without Ayman and, as one of Egypt's most creative forces, he would almost certainly have played in the final game. A 1–1 draw would have created a first in World Cup history: every team finishing on the same points, with the same goals scored and the same goals against. England, Egypt, the Netherlands and Ireland's World Cup future would have been decided on the drawing of lots.

The next season Younis went back to being a constant thorn in Ahly's side on the pitch, but he was made to pay off it. 'If I go to the stadium I have to go without my car as they break everything,' he said of Ahly's fans who, to this day, still hound him in the street for his efforts on the pitch two decades previously. 'When I was playing I had a lot of problems with Ahly fans. In 1990 I found my BMW car on its side and they signed it "Ahly fans". And that was when we lost, 2–0, but they remembered that I scored in the first game earlier in the season.' That, however, wasn't the worst of it. 'Then there was the time they attacked me in my home. I had to phone the police. Five thousand Ahly fans came to my street and shouted against me, my wife and kids, throwing things at us.'

The FA Cup final turned out to be as turgid as feared and, with the game instantly forgotten, Ayman offered to drive me back to Cairo. For Ayman his love of Zamalek, along with its fans, transcended nearly every other impulse in his life, even religion. 'Ask a Zamalek fan, can you change religion?' he said as his sleek black BMW pulled away down the empty highway. 'He wouldn't answer. But you ask them can you change Zamalek, they'd say "NO!"' And if you see a policeman, they won't ask you whether you are Muslim or a Christian, they'll ask you whether you are Ahly or Zamalek. It's true.' But there was a historical demarcation when it came to religion. 'Fifty years ago Ahly became the team of the devout [but] Zamalek was the team of the middle classes.' The car's average speed dropped exponentially as we neared Cairo. I told him about my travels through the Middle East. It was probably a mistake to mention Israel. Ayman sucked air sharply through his teeth. 'If you have been to Israel, trust me, someone is following you.'

'What, even now?' I asked, looking around for any suspicious black cars keeping a steady distance behind us.

'I hate Israel,' Ayman continued. 'Not Israelis, but Israeli politicians and the wars. We've had three of them and lost something like 15,000 people. Everyone has lost someone.'

Ayman's BMW pulled to the kerb when we reached Zamalek Island. He offered me his card and pulled out a fat wedge of Egyptian notes, counting them out in front of me.

'Do you need any money?' he asked. 'I can give you money.'

'I'm OK, Ayman, I have money.'

'Are you sure?'

He looked a little offended. 'OK, but if you need anything, ANYTHING, call me. If you need something, tell the person you're a friend of Ayman Younis. Exactly that.' Ayman was a useful person to know given his status as the Egyptian Alan Hansen. On Monday he would be giving his thoughts in front of the biggest television audience of the year. As much as he was a White Knight to his marrow, he begrudgingly recognised the hold Ahly had on Cairo. Their support was drawn from Cairo's vast working poor, meaning that Ahly's fan base represented one of the few growth areas in Egyptian society. They had already wrapped up their fourth consecutive title to boot, long before the game. 'Ahly already own the championship,' he conceded through his car window. 'So whatever happens tomorrow, Cairo will already be red.' He pulled away into the stream of traffic and left me on my own, on the pavement checking over my shoulder for spies.

Zamalek's training ground looked like it was about to collapse. With Ayman as my golden ticket I'd arrived at their huge grey complex on Zamalek Island, by far the most run-down structure on what was an upmarket and aspirational part of town. Outside a couple of hundred of Zamalek fans had turned up to catch a glimpse of the players as they arrived. One man grabbed my arm as I was walking through the gate. 'We are Zamalek.' He looked confused as he tugged on my red T-shirt. He slowly repeated his statement assuming I was retarded. 'Za-ma-lek.' For the second time, I had forgotten the cardinal rule of attending any football function in the Middle East: never wear the opposition's colours. Thankfully the crowd was good natured compared to the rioting hordes of Beitar Jerusalem fans who had accosted me the previous year. But they did have good reason to be more optimistic than Ayman about the derby. Rumours had surfaced in that day's papers that Ahly, who were fighting for honours on four fronts, were to rest the majority of their first team. Even more encouragingly, Manuel Jose – their crackpot Portuguese manager who had won them their four successive championships and back-to-back African Champions League titles, and regularly boasted he was a better manager than his compatriot Jose Mourinho – was out of the country. He was on holiday, apparently, although most fans believed he had been asked to step down for a few weeks after infuriating Egypt's religious conservatives by stripping off on the touchline during a league game in protest at a poor refereeing decision. Still, Manuel claimed that his players were 'bored of success' which had in equal parts infuriated Zamalek and given them a glimpse of their first derby victory in over three years. But they didn't want to look overconfident and their recently appointed and notoriously secretive manager, Frenchman Henri Michel, had banned his players from talking to the press. Michel was one of those managers that stalked the leagues and national teams of Africa, taking one generation to the heights of World Cup qualification before dumping them and moving on to the next African job. His last job was taking the Ivory Coast to Germany in 2006, where they were knocked out in the first round despite having a team that included Didier Drogba, Kolo Toure, Emmanuel Eboue and Yaya Toure. They were, however, in the same group as Argentina and the Netherlands. The only player who would talk to me was Mahmoud 'Shikabala' Abd El Razeq, Zamalek's best player who was in his second spell at the club after playing briefly in Greece. 'I came back because I played with Zamalek since I was very young and Zamalek is my home,' he admitted outside the dank, damp changing room. 'The derby is like a championship in itself: if you win it you win the biggest trophy since football started in Egypt. The players will do their best to win tomorrow, Inshallah.' At least he was more communicative than the manager. I'd patiently hung around by the side of the pitch waiting for Michel to walk back to the changing room so that I could catch him and interview him. It was his first Ahly versus Zamalek derby and I wanted to hear his views on the rivalry. He waddled past and held out a hand, before quickly removing it when he heard I was a journalist.

'No, no, no, no, no!' he shouted as he walked away.

'But I've come a long way, Henri, from England, to speak to you,' I shouted back.

He dismissed it with a nonchalant wave of his hand.

'That's not my problem, that's your problem,' he replied over his shoulder before disappearing down the tunnel. He obviously had more important things on his mind.

On the other side of Zamalek Island, things were equally tense at Ahly's purpose-built 25,000-seater training ground. Security wouldn't let me in until I lied and said I was from the BBC. But that was just the first layer. Inside three separate flanks of security guards were on hand to keep the press away from Ahly's players whilst they trained. The closest I got was when the team boarded the bus to leave. Even Ahly's genial Vice Captain Osama Hosny, famed for his strict adherence to Islam, impeccable manners and beautiful singing voice, looked guiltily at the floor as he appeared, mumbled an apology and climbed onto the coach. He had recently become one of the most famous voices in Egypt, not for what he had achieved on the pitch, but through his second career as a pop star. Sort of. Osama had rolled his love of Islam and his magnificent voice into one package and released a tape of him singing passages from the Koran. The tapes were selling like hotcakes. 'He always speaks to me [but] the press get so crazy that the players have stopped talking to us before the match,' sighed Usama, a journalist for an Ahly news website who had hung around for the past three hours just to get a few scraps of gossip. With any hope of a quote gone, we walked to a nearby café to talk about tomorrow's game. 'Ahly and Zamalek hate each other,' he told me over a mud-thick Turkish coffee. 'Is there much trouble at the games?' I asked. Usama grinned. 'Ahly has an Ultras group, they're crazy and they hate Zamalek. I can't tell you how much they hate Zamalek! At the Ahly versus Sfaxien [African Champions League final in 2006] match they had a lot of bombs and flares and entered with them into the stadium and when Ahly scored . . . well, the Ultras were the only fans who had travelled to the game and when the goal went in they let off the bombs.' It was the first time I'd heard of the Ahly Ultras but their reputation seemed to be legion. 'The Ultras are everywhere,' continued Usama, partly in disgust, partly in admiration at their commitment. 'Cairo, Alexandria, 200 km away, everywhere. There are maybe 200 officially but a lot of fans want to go with them when they travel so it's a lot more. You have to see them.'

Asad readily agreed to meet me. After a few phone calls I'd managed to get through to the Ultras' self-declared leader. But it all seemed a little civilised. 'Of course, you can come with us, it will be a pleasure. Do you need a lift?' Asad asked politely. 'Er, yes, thanks,' I replied. 'Cool. We'll pick you up at Falaky Square, you know where that is? 5.30 p.m.' Perhaps it's years of conditioning in British football that makes you expect a football hooligan to look a certain way: fat, skinhead, tattoos. But the hierarchy of the Ahly Ultras looked like they'd just finished a shift at Cairo Library. Asad, tall, painfully thin and wearing thick-rimmed glasses, jumped out of the car and shook my hand before we squeezed into the car with Mohammed and Ishmail for the short drive to the stadium. 'We are very unique, we are the only club who have several Ahlys named after it in Jeddah, in Yemen, Libya, in the Emirates, Qatar. But Ahly is THE Ahly, it was the first ever in the whole region to be the first 100 per cent Egyptian so it is very nationalistic,' he explained. 'Zamalek have changed their name so many times we sing: "You used to be half-British, you guys are the rejects." In Arabic it's the plural of "Small dirty houses".' The Ultras are the exact opposite of what you would expect. The hardcore are all university educated, with good jobs, moderately liberal views on women, religion and drugs. Asad started organising the Ultras after spending time studying in England and immersing himself in the football cultures of the Premiership and *Serie A*. It was time, he reasoned, that Ahly had its own fan movement that was separate from the sycophantic organisations that tried as hard as possible to 'suck up to the board'. They have a lot of things to rail against, but Zamalek is at the apex. 'In the past Zamalek used to be the bourgeois club, and Ahly the people's club, although that's changed a little these days,' explained Asad. Zamalek, however, still couldn't shake the foreigner tag which had existed for over 100 years. 'Now we mock them and say they are the door tenders club because it has such popularity amongst Sudanese security guards. Seriously. They still think they are high-class.'

As we neared the ground, I asked Asad why Ahly were so

popular today. 'The two biggest political parties in Egypt are Ahly and Zamalek. It's bigger than politics. It's more about escapism. The average Ahly fan is a guy who lives in a one-bedroom flat with his wife, mother-in-law and five kids. And he is getting paid minimum wage and his life sucks. The only good thing about his life is that for two hours on a Friday he goes in the stadium to watch Ahly. That's why it is such an obligation to win every game. It makes people's lives happy. We are probably the only club in the world where we [the fans] expect to win every single game. Ahly is the only thing that makes people happy.' And with the frustrations of modern life comes the inevitable violence. 'You're asking the right people!' Asad exclaimed. 'Between Ahly and Zamalek the stadium is segregated now so we don't meet and with so many police it's difficult. So we take another route and the violence happens in all sports. There is attacking each other's buses or going to the basketball derby between Ahly and Zamalek.' Mohammed, who with his large beard, baggy fatigues and baseball cap, looked like an East Coast stoner, agreed. 'Egypt is like a police state, they are the most powerful institution in Egypt without doubt,' he said as we got out of the car. 'So you can't even reach a Zamalek fan, but you can be as open as you like and say what you like in the stadium.'

It became clear as we pulled into the stadium what he meant. Thousands of black uniformed riot officers stood menacingly as a deterrent from the main road up to the stadium entrance. Plain-clothed security officers in dark glasses darted between them, asking suspicious-looking fans for their ID papers and tickets. Twenty thousand fans were already inside Cairo's vast national stadium chanting songs against their hated rivals: 'you are the white bitches', and the catchy 'come on, come on, come on, fuck the mother of Zamalek'. The Ultras took their usual place at the back of the lower stand and discussed the best way of unwrapping their vast flag, the highlight of their achievements thus far. The stadium's huge electronic screen fluttered into life. There was Ayman, his face now the size of a bus, talking the audience and the crowd through great moments from Ahly Zamalek derbies of old, many concerning his input as a player. The Ahly fans jeered and whistled when they saw him appear. 'He was good, but he was always fat,' retorted Mohammed as the rest of the Ultras, now 50-strong and rapidly growing, broke into hysterics. The reverie was broken by the piercing sound of the call to prayer. The more devout rush to the nearest piece of flat ground next to the popcorn sellers. In the absence of a prayer mat, they use the next best thing: Ahly flags. Minutes before the game and the Ultras launch their flag. It's vast, far bigger than anything else at the ground, and provokes rapturous applause from the Ahly fans. Asad looked on proudly at his creation, his little piece of Milano that he'd brought to Ahly's terraces. It's the last time I saw him smiling. From the minute the whistle is blown, it's clear that Ahly are in trouble and are playing like a team that have made nine changes. Shikabala is everywhere, first to every ball, quickest down both wings, spurred on by the abuse hurled down on him. By the time he had helped Zamalek take a two-goal lead, he was on his knees, bowing in front of Ahly's fans, infuriating the Ultras and sparking Asad's outburst. 'Why do Ahly hate him so much?' I manage to ask amid the uproar. 'He is pure Zamalek,' spat Asad. 'I had a run-in with him once, when he was playing for the under-20s. There's always horrible fights there. I was by the tunnel and I heard Shikabala say bad things about Ahly so I spat in his face. He tried to slap me so for three months we chanted: "I'm going to beat Shikabala, the cunt, I'm going to beat him in the face." I heard he wants to get me but I'll just beat him up with my car and he'll never play again.' It kind of sums up Egyptian football. Hatred, spitting and violence at under-20s youth matches. Like a particularly virulent type of moss, Egyptian hooliganism had popped up wherever it could find a weakness. It made sense of why a ring of black carrying shields and helmets had circumnavigated the stadium.

The second goal had started to divide a fan base unaccustomed to losing. 'It's only one loss,' a man in a suit offered. 'One loss!' exclaimed Asad, screaming before admonishing him for his low standards. A Luxor Egyptian, his head piled high with a sloppily arranged head scarf, shrugged and pointed at the sky. 'I hate Ahly, but what can I do?' The game ended 2–0. Ahly was vanquished for only the second time in three years. Yet the fans refused to recognise the defeat. As Zamalek paraded in a lap of honour, Ahly's fans refused to leave, screaming out their chants louder than before, over and over again: '1,2,3,4,5,6, Ahly!' Bottles and cans rained down onto the pitch and onto the line of black, keeping the Ultras from the pitch. A bottle fizzed past my nose and cracked on the shield of a policeman cowering under the barrage. An unknown signal ushered the crowd outside and the jeering, seething mass, thousands strong, rolled out of the stadium. Momentarily, I was on my own. Fights broke out between police and fans. Fists flew and blood was spilt, but still the fans marched on, chanting: 'Ahly, Ahly.' Asad, Mohammed and the Ultras were nowhere to be seen as the mob carried us out of the stadium towards the main road, too big even for the phalanx of nearby riot policemen to contain. I spotted a gap in the crowd where the Ultras were waiting, panting. 'It's going crazy around there, we smashed up Zamalek's team bus and managed to get away,' Asad boasted, although not entirely convincingly. From the muddy patch to the side of the concourse the human river of red rumbled defiantly, and noisily, on. Ayman Younis was right. Whatever the result, Cairo was always going to be painted red.

We stood in the sand car park until the last of the crowd passed by and the Ultras packed their banner back into the car. They had lost, but claimed an immoral victory, deciding to celebrate by getting some beer and getting stoned. 'Until the 1980s it was virtually legal,' laughed Mo when I mentioned that I was surprised so many people smoked hash in Egypt. 'Everyone smoked it [hash]; Muslims, Christians, but even now the police don't care as long as you don't make trouble. My last dealer? Man, he was a sheikh from a local mosque.' We drove back through Cairo's thick, polluted air to Asad's flat. Rather than arriving at a modest apartment, the car pulled up in front of a walled compound, complete with guards. It turned out that Egypt's notorious hooligan brigade had come from high stock: Asad's father was high up in CAF, Africa's football confederation. He didn't have a clue that his son led Africa's most notorious hooligan gang. We sat in Asad's bedroom, blowing out blue smoke and drinking some hastily arranged beer. On the television a famous Egyptian movie from the 1960s was playing. 'You look at any Arab television channel at 7 p.m.,' explained Asad. 'Eighty per cent of the films or programmes are from Egypt. We've been making films for 100 years. All the musicians are Egyptian too.'

'What about Nancy Ajram?' I offered. Ajram was arguably Arab pop music's biggest star. She was also Lebanese. 'Ahh, but her mother was Egyptian and she was born here.'

It's not unusual to hear this kind of thing anywhere in the Middle East. The Saudis have an authority bequeathed by Mecca and Medina; the other Gulf states have fabulous oil wealth and the arrogance of their new economic miracles; the Iranians have the legacy of the Persian empire, of poetry and literature and modern irrigation; the catchphrase for the tourist board of Syria is The Cradle of Civilisation; the Iraqis have 'zero' to be proud of (the number rather than a paucity of achievements) and proto-atomic physics. And the Egyptians can point to a very real, very modern legacy too. All Egyptians revel in their past brilliance. A common refrain, as Ayman had told me, was: 'I'm not African, I'm not Arab, I'm Pharaonic.' To the Egyptians, most modern civilisation comes from them and the now-booming Gulf would be nothing if it weren't for their engineers who had built the infrastructure in the first place. These days Egyptians, like most other Arabs living or working in Dubai or Doha or Manama, were treated like third-class citizens, making a mockery of any lingering remnants of a united Arab body politic. But at 7 p.m. every night, the proof of Egypt's greatness was there for everyone to see.

By 3 a.m. it was time to leave the Ultras and head home. Outside I stood on the pavement and tried to hail a cab. The bookshop behind me was covered in posters of Osama Hosny. His almost-handsome face and ginger hair was advertising his latest tape singing the passages from the Koran that had made him famous. I got into a taxi and left Cairo. The driver and I sat in silence as neither could fully communicate with the other.

'Ahly or Zamalek?' I finally proffered.

'Ahly,' the driver replied.

Of course he was.

NINE

West Asian Championships

It was the hottest day in Amman in 90 years and Jorvan Vieira had taken refuge in the looming shadow thrown by the King Abdullah stadium. Around him his squad of young footballers joked and chattered in accelerated Arabic, stretching in the green-and-white colours that had always covered the Lions of Mesopotamia. They didn't know Jorvan well; he wasn't too familiar with them either. It was only the second time he had met his new charges, a few weeks after the thin, stubbly-faced, small-framed man with bookish glasses and a wide cheeky smile had landed himself the most difficult job in world football: coach of the Iraqi national football team. 'This is the hardest job in the world, definitely,' Jorvan agreed as we stood pitch side – waiting for the Jordanian national team to finish training. They were running late after insisting that they prayed in their dressing room, as they did before every training session and match. The Iraqis didn't want to pray. Or rather, they weren't allowed to pray. It had been decided long ago that religion, such a divisive force in their homeland, should be kept out of the team's pre-match preparations. 'These boys,' began Jorvan absentmindedly as the Jordanians stretched in front of us, 'I have to deal with many, many problems: social, political, internal. Most of these players don't know where they are. Every minute the situation changes.'

Jorvan wasn't new to the vagaries of Middle Eastern football politics. A Brazilian Muslim, he had spent most of his career coaching in Saudi Arabia, Oman, Egypt and Morocco. He was fourth choice for the job, and he was only given a two-month contract, but for the FA that was preferable to having an Iraqi coach again. I had spoken to the last one, Akram Salman, before he was sacked after he had watched his team being knocked out of the Gulf Cup six months previously. Jorvan was brought in to guide the team at the Asian Cup being held in Indonesia, Thailand, Malaysia and Vietnam. It was the region's top tournament, Asia's equivalent of the European Championships or the Copa America, and second only to the World Cup in importance. The Iraqi FA didn't have high hopes for the tournament and Jorvan was soon given a reminder as to the huge obstacles that faced him and his team. 'We lost our physio, two days before we got here,' he explained as his charges trotted onto the field. 'A bomb exploded in Baghdad and he was passing by. He was on his way to the travel agent to buy his ticket to come here.'

The Iraqi national team had eluded me until now. For six months I had been chasing an audience with them through three countries: first Iraq, then the UAE, before finally catching up with them in Jordan. It would have made sense to bypass the other two and head straight for Amman. Since the war as many as one million Iraqis, fleeing the anarchy in their homeland, were now living in Jordan, an island of peace in a sea of instability. To its east, Iraq slowly imploded. To the west, the West Bank crumbled under the weight of internecine warfare between Hamas and Fatah, agitating Jordan's already sizeable Palestinian-descended majority. Israel, Syria, Lebanon and Saudi Arabia – all with their own internal problems – surrounded it. Yet somehow Jordan had gone about its business, made deals, played countries off against each other and generally done anything it could to survive. Much of the credit sat with the wily King Hussein, father of the current monarch, King Abdullah, who could keep all the diplomatic balls in the air at the same time; making peace with Israel, keeping the Americans onside and staying friends with Saddam Hussein.

No wonder Jordan has long been thought of as the quiet man of the Middle East. Huge portraits of both men peered down as the Iraqis trained below.

To make the Iraqi diaspora feel even more at home their national football team had decamped there as well, meeting up for training and playing its competitive matches in Amman, waiting for the unlikely event that peace would take hold so they could return to Baghdad, Erbil or Basra and once again enjoy home advantage. This time, though, they weren't here merely for the sunshine and the easier living. They were preparing for what must constitute one of the most potentially explosive football tournaments to ever be organised. I'd heard about the West Asian Championships, a bi-yearly tournament that brought together the Middle East's best teams for a knockout tournament, the previous year. It had been due to take place in Beirut but the war with Israel made that impossible. Instead it was postponed and moved to Jordan. The problem was that the teams competing all had colourful histories off the pitch: Iran, Iraq, Syria, Lebanon, Jordan and Palestine. Almost every single permutation was charged with political significance. Iran and Iraq had fought a bloody, attritional war in the 1980s, a war that claimed as many as a million lives. And with Iraq degenerating into an inter-sect civil war, the country's Sunni minority feared the influence of Iran – who they suspected had more influence over Iraq's Shia majority than the government – more than the Americans. Syria had long had a hand in Lebanese politics, occupying the country from 1975 until 2005, and only pulling out after the country's security forces had been fingered for the assassination of ex Lebanese Prime Minister Rafik Hariri. One of the UN's investigations into his death put the blame squarely on the shoulders of the Syrian secret service, whose influence many in Lebanon believe still looms large. The Syrians, of course, deny any wrongdoing. The Jordanians and the Palestinians also have a turbulent history. The creation of Israel saw hundreds of thousands flee to what was then known as Transjordan on the East Bank of the River Jordan. The many wars and conflicts that had arisen since 1948 had seen a steady trickle of Palestinians enter Jordan, changing its ethnic mix. Now, depending on who you listened to, Palestinians make up anywhere between 45 and 75 per cent of Jordan's population. Fearing being overrun, political power consolidated in the hands of ethnic Hashemite Jordanians whilst Palestinians struggled against discrimination – as in many other Arab states – to get work, housing or any education. Instead, the Palestinians excelled in making their own future and were known for their successful business interests, further antagonising the 'true' Jordanians. One hundred and fifty thousand Palestinian refugees still lived at the nearby Wihdat refugee camp in East Amman. They even have their own football team, Wihdat FC, who played their home games at the King Abdullah stadium. They had won the title two years in a row, much to the chagrin of Al Faisaly, the team of the king, of the Hashemite Jordanians. The only time the low-level, unspoken discontent between the two groups was visible was when the two teams met.

If the potential for a feisty tournament was already there, several developments had made the tournament potentially even more explosive. Two players from one of Lebanon's top clubs, Nejmeh, a Shia-supported but Sunni-owned club, were killed in a car bombing targeting one of Lebanon's Christian opposition MPs. Again, the finger of suspicion pointed at Syrian involvement. In Gaza, open warfare had broken out between Fatah and Hamas, the lonely, overpopulated strip having been cut off from the rest of the world in response. But Jorvan was preparing for his next game, a must-win match against Palestine for a place in the semi-finals, with by far the most difficult set of circumstances to overcome. Almost every single player in the national team had now left Iraq. The league was only operating in the northern town of Erbil, where the Kurdish Regional Government could ensure relative safety. Every player had been touched by tragedy, threatened by insurgents or feared kidnap by criminal gangs. 'How can they come through? Where can they train?' replied Jorvan when I asked how the next generation of players could emerge under such anarchy. 'Iraq will miss one or two generations because of the war. How can they develop sport in Iraq? Did you hear about the boys from taekwondo? It could happen with any player here.' Hours before Iraq kicked off the tournament against Iran, news reached the squad of the fate of the 'boys from taekwondo', illustrating just how dangerous it was to be a sportsman or woman in Iraq today. In 2006, 15 athletes aged between 18 and 26 were kidnapped in Western Iraq on their way to a training camp in Jordan. A year later, their remains were found in a ditch near Ramadi. All had been shot in the head. The team wore black armbands during the diplomatic 0–0 draw.

The dangers were such that most players chose not to return home and those who did soon regretted it. Goalkeeper Noor Sabri had seen his brother-in-law killed a few weeks previously. Midfielder Haitham Kadim watched as gunmen stormed onto the pitch during a match in Baghdad to execute one of his team-mates. 'I'd lost two members of my family,' explained Hawar Mullah Mohammad, the team's Kurdish striker who had been so revered back in the Iraqi Kurdish capital of Erbil when I was there to watch the Gulf Cup six months previously. The executions, bombings and insecurity had got so bad he left his home in Baghdad and signed for Al Ain, an oasis club in the middle of a desert in the UAE, to ensure his safety. 'It's difficult when you have no safety. Cars explode all the time. I had to pick up my two guns before going to practice, because I'd been threatened,' he said nonchalantly as he was warming up. 'You can buy guns anywhere in Baghdad. You need them. I don't go back any more.'

With the Jordanians finally departed, Jorvan started running the team through its paces. It wasn't lost on him just what a potential powder keg the tournament was. 'All it takes is one match,' he said grinning before rejoining the squad on the pitch. 'And then, BOOM!'

The Iraqi team's coach moved quietly through the Wihdat refugee camp, over the still-intact tracks of the old, largely defunct Hejaz railway – the great, crazy Ottoman project designed to link Istanbul to Mecca – and into the centre of Amman towards their hotel. The players and coaching staff, exhausted by training in the heat, dozed as the bus rocked and bucked through the traffic and badly tarmacked roads. The only man alert was first-team coach Ahmed-Rahim Hamed. Captain Rahim, as the players referred to him, was a legend of Iraqi football. He had played in the great Iraqi team of the 1980s, considered to be Iraq's finest crop of players after they reached the World Cup finals in 1986. Back then he was a 23-year-old striker and one of the youngest in the squad, playing alongside the current head of the Iraqi FA, Hussein Saeed Mohammed. The team narrowly lost all three games by a single goal against Paraguay, Belgium and hosts Mexico. To the outsider this was a respectable result for a team from a part of the world so maligned by FIFA that Asia received just two World Cup spots. But the players knew that anything less than silverware would upset the man who had been put in charge of Iraqi football: Uday Hussein. Saddam's bloodthirsty eldest son had a myriad of interests – torture, extortion and football. After proving that he wasn't quite yet ready to take the mantle as Saddam's chosen successor by beating to death his father's chef in front of horrified guests at a party hosted by Egyptian President Hosni Mubarak, Uday was imprisoned before being sent to Switzerland to lie low. When he returned, however, he was handed the keys to Iraq's sporting empire, which he used to feather his own nest as head of Iraq's Olympic committee. He also used some of his unique motivational skills on Iraq's footballers. Hussein didn't want to talk about Uday's legacy when I had met him in Abu Dhabi during the Gulf Cup, but Rahim was still upset, mainly because Uday had put paid to his homage to his favourite player. 'You knew that if you didn't play well, Uday would do something bad,' said Rahim, running his hands through his dark hair. 'I loved Kevin Keegan, he was my best player, and I had a perm like him. After one game [that Iraq lost] Uday shaved everybody's hair. That's when I lost my perm.' Uday may have been killed in a hail of American bullets but Rahim and the rest of Iraq's football community were still being punished for their involvement with the national team. Rahim had to move to Erbil after he received one death threat too many. 'I got a letter that said we will kill your children and . . . make something . . . with my daughter. They fired at my house twice. So I moved to Erbil. I'm Shia. I don't care, I'm

Muslim and Iraqi. But now I sit in a small flat in a dirty area. It's expensive. My rent is more than my brother's rent in Holland.'

The bus dropped me at the team hotel and I got a taxi back to my down-at-heel but eminently cheap hostel in downtown Amman. In the reception, an excited gaggle of men had gathered, flicking through the channels on the small television screen that sat in the corner. 'What are they looking for?' I asked the bookish-looking man behind the reception desk. 'Real Madrid and Barcelona play tonight,' he replied. 'But we can't get it here. He's a Real Madrid fan.' The receptionist pointed at a tall Syrian man looking agitated at the prospect of missing his team's crucial match. It was the dénouement of *La Liga*'s most exciting season in years. The two arch rivals both had a chance of securing the title, Real Madrid with a resurgent David Beckham looking for his first piece of silverware since moving to Spain, Barcelona seeking reward for possessing arguably one of the finest forward lines in football history of Messi, Ronaldinho and Eto'o. Desperate not to miss the opening salvos, the Syrian Madrid fan grabbed my hand and dragged me out into the street. He spoke no English, and I little Arabic, but it was clear he had a plan. Across the street a dirty concrete stairwell led to the top floor. It was brightly lit and buzzing with anticipation. The packed room was full of 150 or so men smoking water pipes in front of a large screen showing the match. It turned out that Spanish football, rather than the Premiership favoured by much of the rest of the Middle East, was Amman's game of choice. The atmosphere was subdued as Mallorca quickly went ahead against Real, but the melancholy was shattered when Barcelona scored. The 50 or so Barcelona fans blew their cover as they jumped in the air. It didn't last long. Madrid's equaliser was always coming, but the two goals that followed turned the shisha café into a roar of celebration. Accusatory fingers were pointed by men wearing dark blue and maroon stripes as the title slipped away from them. When Madrid's victory was confirmed, the Syrian joined the white half of the room jumping around in ecstasy, before tripping on his chair and flying backwards, crunching to the floor. He got up gingerly and continued to dance, albeit with a slight limp in his leap. As the revelry – every bit as genuine as the dancing in Madrid's Cibeles Square that night – abated, a young Palestinian man explained why Madrid had come out on top. 'You see, it all changed when Fabio Capello took off Beckham,' he said, analysing the game at a far deeper level than I had bothered to. 'Beckham is slow and was fading but bringing in Reyes changed everything.'

Amman's Madrid fans went home happy. I went back to my hotel room and discovered that I had been an inadvertent drug smuggler. The night before arriving in Amman I had been at a wedding, where a friend had a gift for me: a well-rolled joint. This I pocketed in my suit, thinking it would make a nice post-revelry comedown. But on the way home I had got into a stinking row with my fiancée who stormed off home, leaving me abandoned at Victoria Station. With nowhere to go I travelled to Heathrow, changed and slept in my clothes at the terminal. It wasn't until I had passed through customs, flown to Jordan, arrived in Amman and, now, finally unpacked my suit a week later that I realised that the offending jazz cigarette was still there: an offence that could have cost me four years at least in a grotty Jordanian jail. Panicked, it wasn't immediately clear what to do. Initially I had contemplated flushing the evidence. But the risk of its bobbing up later in the night was too great. So I decided on the only course of action available to me. Dispose of the evidence by power-smoking it. This was easier said than done. First I tried the roof, but fearing getting caught by the smell, I ran into the street and up towards Jabal Amman, the hilly, upmarket quarter of the capital, where I found a derelict building and disposed of the evidence. A few seconds later and the full force of the drug hit me. And with it paranoia. I ran back to the well-lit roads of downtown Amman, only stopping to buy a plate of *knafah*, the Palestinian sweet made of goats cheese, fried wheat and pistachio nuts, before finding refuge back at the hotel. On the television Patrick Swayze's *Road House* was showing. Normally anyone in possession of even the most basic motor functions would dismiss this slice of American trash cinema. Tonight, though, the few other people still up watching it with me couldn't understand why I found it the funniest film ever made.

I shouldn't have been that surprised to find so many Iraqi fans sitting in the afternoon sun on a working day waiting for their team to take on Palestine. Amman's International Stadium looked like it had been futuristic once in the early Nineties, with its plastic-looking cladding hiding an ugly concrete and iron frame. But it was suspiciously busy for a mid-afternoon kick-off with Iraqi fans milling around in their hundreds outside. The answer was simple. 'Jordan is good,' said Nasir, an Iraqi Christian, with the kind of intonation that you knew would be followed by a 'but'. 'But the government doesn't let us work. I brought my savings because if the government catch us working they send us back. It's a hard life, but at least it's safe.' Another spectator with time on his hands had brought his entire family along for a rare taste of Iraqi pride. 'I've been here a year. I had to come here when my brother was kidnapped,' said Essam, a Sunni sewing-machine salesman who was there with his wife and two kids. 'When we see our team we feel like it's home.' Given the huge Palestinian diaspora, I had expected thousands of fans supporting the old country. But the only Palestine fans I could find was a gaggle of angry-looking youths who couldn't afford to get a ticket. 'We can't watch because they doubled the prices because the Iraqis are here and they are very rich. It's not fair, it's like 6 JDs [$9], we have no oil, the Palestinians don't even have money to buy cigarettes,' spat Salman, a Palestinian student living in Amman, who wanted to show solidarity. 'This team is important because it brings us together, Hamas and Fatah. This team is unity, this team will give us attention.'

It was an important time for unity. The civil war between Fatah and Hamas, between the West Bank and Gaza, had created an almost total, intractable separation between the two groups and two territories. Salman, who spoke in a strong North American accent from his days studying in Canada, knew who was to blame.

'Who's at fault?' I asked as his friends gathered around and unfurled a huge Palestinian flag that the national team's players would never see.

'Israel and America.'

'Not Hamas?'

'Not Hamas, my friend, when you have poverty and unemployment anything can happen. They [Israel and America] have deprived the Palestinian people of everything.'

The football team, though, seemed to be functioning Ok despite the chaos back home. The team's Gaza contingent, 13 players in all, managed to make it out before the border was shut.

'Why can they share a football team but not a government?' I asked.

'Why?' repeated Salman before answering his own question. 'Because the football team is from the people. Fatah and Hamas are made from the Israelis and the Americans and we know who they are. Trust me. The solution is for the refugees to go home. I'm a refugee. I was born a refugee, my father was born a refugee, my grandfather was born a refugee and I would not give up a single piece of my land. The UN can sort out Jerusalem, but I just want to go back home. I would die for it.'

'How old are you?' I asked, surprised that Salman would still consider himself a refugee.

'Twenty-three.'

He wouldn't tell me which side he plumped for although he gave his allegiances away somewhat when I asked him about Fatah President Mahmoud Abbas. 'I wish he was dead,' he replied deadpan. 'He is a faulty sperm. He shook hands with the invaders. The South Africans didn't shake hands with the whites, the Vietnamese didn't shake hands with the Americans. He is a disgrace to us. So was Arafat.'

Palestine's luck didn't get any better on the pitch. The game itself was a scrappy affair. Even though the Iraqi side of the stadium was full, compared to the 12 Palestinian fans who could afford the steep entry price, the Lions of Mesopotamia were devoid of creativity and had no idea how to get through a Palestinian side that put 11 men behind the ball in searing temperatures. At half-time the fans had had enough and started shouting for their favourite player: Hawar Mullah Mohammad. Hawar had been on the bench resting an injury, Jorvan had told me. But an Iraqi journalist covering the match for an Australian newspaper had revealed that he had thrown a strop when he wasn't made captain and been dropped as punishment. With things going badly Jorvan didn't have a choice. Hawar came on and swiftly dispatched an 86th-minute – twice taken – penalty to break Palestine's resistance 1–0. Later, Hawar was mobbed by more than a hundred fans who had waited for him to appear by the team coach, a swirling pack of Iraqi flags, digital cameras and mobile phones preventing him from leaving. Hawar didn't mind. The adulation was probably vindication for being upset about the captaincy. It took the police to eventually drag him out. He reluctantly stepped onto the team bus.

The country names clustered in groups in the lobby of the Arena Hotel. Each group of footballers was demarked by what was embossed onto the back of their tracksuits – the Syrians sticking together in one corner, the Palestinians in another, the Iranians in yet another. The gangs didn't mingle, only giving a cursory nod as they swaggered past one another in twos or threes. Sitting down sipping on a thimble of Arabic coffee, with a shining bald pate and a moustache that made him look a little like Mussolini, was Emile Rustom. Emile was the head coach of the Lebanese national team, a Maronite Christian. This usually wouldn't warrant a mention but in Lebanese football, the demarcation between religious and political groups was arguably more pronounced than even in Iraq. 'Anywhere we go to play everybody says "are you still playing football in Lebanon?",' he laughed. 'We are living day by day in Lebanon, we don't know what will happen tomorrow. Every day is a dramatic event.' The problem, Emile told me, was that each team had a strong link to each of the country's competing communities. And when Sunni, Shia, Druze and Christian teams met one another, it tended to end in bloodshed on the terraces. So much so that the authorities banned fans from attending games, such was the fear that inter-religious fighting could spark wider instability at a time when Lebanon was still weak internally, both politically and economically, and vulnerable. 'There are teams for Hezbollah like Al Ahed. But it's a good thing if Hezbollah gives money for a club to help football. Mr Hariri [Saad, Rafik's son] is giving money to Ansar and Nejmeh. We don't have the basics. We don't have sponsors, no money. If this political party is giving money then that is good.'

But Emile insisted that, within the national team, there were no differences. To prove his point he called over three players: Paul Rustom, his young son who was a striker for the Maronite Christian team Sagesse; Ali Yaacoub from the Shia-dominated Al Ahed and Bilal Najarin from the Sunni-owned team Nejmeh. 'When we play against each other me and Bilal make trash talk against each other in the game, but we are best of friends afterwards,' explained Paul, the three chatting easily together. 'Our teams are a symbol for the community. Sagesse is a Christian team [but] we [Christians] are eight out of thirty. There are six or seven Sunnis, one or two Druze and the rest are Shia. We all go out with each other.' The problem was that this fraternity hadn't transferred onto the terraces. 'It is because of Nejmeh versus Ansar,' said Bilal. 'Forty-five thousand would attend the game and half of them would be Shia, half of them Sunni. They would fight.'

'The political problems are reflected between the fans,' continued Paul. 'If the Sunni and Shia leaders have a disagreement, there's trouble. This season the fans were forbidden but next season they will hopefully be back.' Ali, whose team was funded by Hezbollah, agreed but played down the role of the political organisation.

'The club is for Hezbollah, yes, but they do not interfere too much. They give money but they let the club spend it on players.'

'Does Nasrallah go to the games?' I asked.

'No!' shrieked Ali, the others laughing at the thought of Hassan Nasrallah on the terraces. 'The Israelis will get him!'

Things hadn't started so well for the Lebanese at the West Asian Championship. The death of two Nejmeh players after training two weeks before in a car bombing – team-mates of Bilal's – had dampened the mood. Worse, with Syrian involvement being blamed for the spate of targeted assignations against politicians, who all happened to be from the anti-Syria bloc, the fixture list had thrown up their Eastern neighbour in the first game. They promptly lost 1–0, which didn't go down well back in Beirut. 'The fans were blaming us,' said Paul. 'They said: "Why did you lose? You could have lost to anyone by 100 goals, but not against Syria."' But there was, according to Emile, little animosity between the players. 'This is a political problem,' he stressed, finishing up his coffee and gathering his players for their early-afternoon rest. Tomorrow they had to win the game against hosts Jordan. A victory was the only chance they had of making the semis. 'It's true that the Syrian army in Lebanon made many mistakes against the Lebanese people. They were abusing their power to have money, to kill people, to jail people. It happens during the occupation of any country, thirty years of occupation [but] we met the players before and it was a clean game. Many people back home wanted us to win against Syria. Sports people don't think in the same way.' With that, the quartet got up, hugged me one by one, and left. 'Call me the moment you get to Beirut,' Emile insisted, giving me his phone number and promising to show me around. 'The season will start in September, hopefully, and the fans will be back too.' His son was less sure. 'September? With Lebanon you never know,' Paul added mischievously. 'There will probably be another war in Lebanon in September.'

Another coach with off-the-field worries was Mohammed Sabah. His Palestine side had narrowly been beaten by Iraq the day before but his players had other things on their minds. 'The main problem is the situation in Gaza as we have 13 players from there,' he told me. Mohammed was in the lobby and reading the paper, trying to devour as much information as possible on what was going on in Gaza. It seemed that finding out about the political turmoil was equally important a job for the manager of the Palestinian national team as keeping tabs on training. 'What has happened in the past week means they are very worried, stressed.' The tensions between Hamas and Fatah that had simmered since the former's parliamentary victory in 2006 had finally exploded and reached some sort of end game. Hamas was, after weeks of bloody fighting that had killed several hundred Palestinians, in total control of the Gaza Strip. The Israelis responded by closing all the borders and isolating Gaza. Effectively, there were now two Palestinian governments. 'It's very difficult at the moment as some of the players and coaches wanted to go back as their minds and their hearts are with their families in Gaza but they can't because the border at Rafah is closed,' Mohammed explained. The schism had long existed for the Palestinian national football team. Unable to travel between Gaza and the West Bank, there were essentially two national teams, one set of players training in Gaza, the other in the West Bank. They only met together a few days before a match in a third country, usually Egypt. Yet Mohammed was positive that within the camp there was no Fatah-Hamas rivalry. 'I think that a Palestinian team makes a unit for the Palestinian people,' he said when I asked whether any disagreements had broken out. 'The players are close, they are sharing rooms, training. Every player here is an ambassador. When you represent your country you must be good in every way. No players say I am Hamas, I am Fatah. Yes, some are members, but they are friends. If the people were like the Palestinian team there would be no problems.' He brought out his captain, Saab Jende, who played for Shajaiya in Gaza City, to prove his point. He refused to say whether he was a member of Fatah or Hamas. All he cared about was the safety of the people he had left behind. 'Every second I am thinking about my family,' he said. 'Every time I'm here I'm calling them in Gaza asking about the border, when they are going to open it and whether my family has food or not. In the past two days it has been difficult for them to get food and I have five very young kids. And my salary from the government hasn't been paid for ten months.'

Oddly, as the West Bank and Gaza indulged in civil war, a star-studded Real Madrid side fresh from winning *La Liga* was making its way to Israel for a peace match against a mixed Israeli Palestinian side, hosted by Israeli President Shimon Peres and his Peres Centre for Peace in Tel Aviv the next day. It was odd because Mohammed didn't seem to know any of the Palestinian players taking part in the match. Stranger still, the official press release with biographies of the Palestinian players taking part stated that they were Palestinian national team players playing in the Palestinian First Division – which had had to be abandoned several years previously due to Israeli movement restrictions. I emailed the Peres Centre and Roni Kresner gave an explanation:

> None of the players were from Gaza. Due to the present situation in the Gaza Strip, we were unable to include players from Gaza. That is, had they participated, they would have been severely punished for taking part in such a match. [Due to the dominance of Hamas in the Gaza Strip.]
>
> As for the players being part of the national team, there is a Palestinian national squad, and the coach selects players from the squad for each game. You are correct in stating that there was a match in Amman the same day. Players from the national squad played in that match. Similarly, players from the national squad took part in our match at Ramat Gan stadium. The coach, who is linked to the Palestinian Football Association, is looking for a way to punish these players for participating in a mixed Israeli-Palestinian team (a sad state of affairs!).

For Mohammed, though, the issue was cut and dried. 'No, I'm not sharing [a pitch with] the occupation,' he said when I asked why none of his squad was in Tel Aviv. 'The Israelis must know that when we have our rights we can play. But when we are killed and they make checkpoints so we can't play like in other countries. In my club [Tulkarem], many times they stop us going to the match, turn us away and arrest some players. It's very difficult to play and want peace when they won't give us our rights. I want peace, two states, but until now we cannot move freely, we cannot go from city to city. It's difficult to a share a team over here, when over there they arrest my brother.' Mohammed's sentiment summed up what I had heard from virtually everyone I had spoken to who was connected to Palestinian football. For them, football was about attaining international recognition and achieving internal unity. Football wouldn't be used to attain peace with Israel. In fact, Iraq, Lebanon and Palestine all had very different problems to deal with, but had one thing in common. All represented a forlorn, distant hope for unity in their homelands. In Lebanon and Iraq's case, the national football team was a rare chance to build some form of nationalistic pride by bringing together disparate, competing sectarian groups under one flag, something that a weak central government had singularly failed to do. For Palestine, the national team had always given the illusion of that elusive prize: statehood. But now, more than ever, it had to also try and engender its own form of common cause, bridging the ever widening gap between the supporters of Fatah and Hamas which had threatened to drive a permanent wedge between the West Bank and Gaza and undermine the great prize of a united Palestinian state recognised by the UN.

That night another group of Palestinian footballers also had to deal with the grim reality of division back home. I'd received an email from Honey, the captain of the Palestinian women's national team. After we had said our goodbyes in Bethlehem a few months previously, Honey and the rest of the squad had been invited to Germany to take part in a three-week-long training camp in anticipation of the women's West Asian Championship taking place in September. Now, however, they were stuck in Amman.

The players' floor at the Sandy Palace Hotel was buzzing with activity, girls darting in and out of the different rooms as Coach Raed stood in the middle like some kind of pushover physical education teacher at St. Trinians. He nodded his head in recognition and disappeared into his room, unable or unwilling to control his hyperactive players. Samar Mousa, the matriarchal team manager, and Honey sat in a large, modest suite on their own, chewing on the detritus of an Arabic fast-food meal. They both looked worn-out after 20 days of intensive training and media attention. After such a high, Amman must have proved somewhat of an anti-climax. None of the players knew if they would be allowed back into the country. In Bethlehem, Samar told me, armed Fatah militias were roaming the streets rounding up Hamas members in retaliation for the latter's Islamic coup in Gaza. Not only that, two players and one coach from Gaza had been affected in different ways. One player had been refused permission to leave in the first place thanks to an over-protective father who disapproved of her playing football. A second didn't know how to get home as Israel had closed the border. The coach had to leave early after hearing that an Israeli rocket had destroyed her home. Now, all the girls crossed their fingers and hoped they even had homes to go back to. Honey soon perked up when we talked about Germany. 'What was the best part of it?' I asked, before leaving them to try and negotiate safe passage home. 'To taste freedom,' she replied quickly. 'To not have to carry my passport wherever you go.' I left her sitting on the floor, staring at a faraway spot on the opposite wall.

The Iraqi team bus pulled through Amman's city limits, rocking to ear-splitting Arabic music. Training had been light this time, and with good reason. The team was recovering from their best performance of the tournament so far, a 3–0 victory over Syria. The game was held on a Friday yet, unlike every other single Middle Eastern football crowd that gathered on Islam's holy day, nobody prayed. The fans had taken on board the same mantra as their football team: keep religion to yourself. I had sat through the drills, patiently waiting to talk to more of the players. But on the bus, I was expected to dance. It felt like an ambush. As soon as the bus had started, music from the famous Iraqi singer Hussam Al Rassam screeched and crackled through speakers that couldn't handle the volume. Drums rattled like gunfire as the players danced and shouted in delight, occasionally getting thrown into the lap of a team-mate as the coach driver veered around a corner. Younis Mahmoud, the team's star striker and captain, and Nashat Akram, looked at me strangely. 'Come on,' Nashat implored, taking my hand and leading me to the centre of the bus. 'You can dance.' It didn't seem like a bad idea to be part of the whole team-bonding ritual. Little did I know that it was a thinly veiled trap. The whole team circled around as best they could and clapped me in. 'I don't know what to do,' I shouted over the noise. Defender Jassim Gholam took the lead, hauling his shirt off over his bald head, bowing slightly, circling his fingers and jutting his neck from side to side. Every few beats he would slap an arm across his chest. I tried to mimic his actions. The whole coach descended into mocking laughter as the players started to mimic my rigid movements. Those that weren't dancing were filming the humiliation on their mobile phones. Jassim took things a step forward, pulling at my T-shirt and slapping his chest whilst urging me to join him in his semi-naked revelry. Standing in the middle of the wild-eyed circle, I had no choice. I slowly peeled off my top, revealing painfully white skin, and stumbled along to the beat as we slapped each other's backs. The two minutes seemed to go on for hours. The only thing you could hear over the sound of the music was the sound of laughter. Nashat slapped me on the back and ushered me back to the seat. Behind me a group of players were watching the video back – me, pasty white, red neck from sunburn, dancing like a middle-aged woman who had just discovered drum-and-bass for the first time. Jorvan surveyed the scene and gave a wry smile. 'We have to give the Iraqi people a good mirror. Inside the national team there are no differences between Shia and Sunni. I was asked, how can you coach Iraq? I said "I don't have ammo, no grenades, no M45, no axe." I'd like victory to bring peace to Iraq. They don't have to pay me if I can help bring peace.'

Mohammed Nasser and Nashat talked business as we trundled through Amman's darkening early evening. Both had negotiated their way out of Iraq: Mohammed to Apollon Limassol in Cyprus, Nashat to Al Shabab in Saudi Arabia. The key, they said, was getting an agent. 'Most Iraqis don't have one but it's crucial because he can drop you in any country,' said Nashat. He had grounds to be more optimistic than most though. Nashat had been promised a top-four club in Europe. What he got was a visit from Sunderland, which was stretching the definition of top-four somewhat, but it at least meant that he was on the Premiership's radar. Nashat had even heard rumours that a Sunderland scout was at the first Iraq–Iran match. 'Iraqis can play anywhere in the world, but it would be a dream to play for Roy Keane,' he said, ignoring the fact that he would also have had to live in Sunderland. 'I sent them my DVD and, Inshallah, I'll hear something.'

Mohammed had also been made some grand promises. He was promised Europe, and he got it, sort of. 'No one can see me play in Cyprus,' he complained. 'So I sacked my agent. I have one at the moment, an Iranian, and he's promised me a top-four club in Greece, England or Spain.' There were other cultural reasons why Mohammed had wanted to leave Cyprus. 'In Iraq you have your wife and maybe five, six, seven, eight girlfriends. You just don't do it in front of her. She might know, but she'll look away. She needs to feel special.'

'What happens if a wife takes a boyfriend?' Mohammed bristled as if it was the first time he had ever considered such a possibility.

'Then [the husband] cancels her,' he replied. 'It's different in Cyprus, in Europe. There you have one woman, one boss, the captain. I have a girl in Limassol and she always says: "Why can't I live in your flat?" But if I did she'd be in charge. She doesn't know about the other girl in Nicosia.' Still, life was preferable to back home for Mohammed, a Shia who lived in Basra. As a footballer who earned a handsome wage in Europe, albeit in one of the continent's lower leagues, he was a target for criminal gangs looking to kidnap players and make anything up to six million dollars per footballer. 'When I go home,' he said, 'I just stay indoors. It's safer that way.'

After forcing me to dance, captain Younis Mahmoud now sat at the front of the coach on his own. Younis was arguably Iraq's greatest hope to make it on the European stage. He was top scorer in the star-filled Qatari league and scorer of 30 goals in 49 internationals. French first-division clubs had come in for him yet it was unlikely he was going to arrive in Europe soon. 'Of course I want to play in England or France,' he said, 'but my family is my priority and if I sign for a club in Europe, I can't take my family. In Qatar, it's no problem: they say "Bring everyone!"' The EU's strict work permit rules meant that if

Younis signed for an English or French club, his family would stay behind. Worse, with no reason to stay in Qatar, it might mean they had to move back to Iraq. It wouldn't be the last time an Iraqi player had been stung in this way.

For the players left behind in Iraq not lucky enough to get a move or well connected enough to get a decent agent, there was a different set of priorities. Second-choice goalkeeper Ahmed Ali was one of only four players in the Iraqi squad for the Asian games who plied their trade in the Iraqi league. He stood between the sticks for Al Zawraa in Baghdad and his day went something like this: 'I wake up at 9 a.m., I go to practice at 3 p.m., go home at 6 p.m., lock the door and don't go out.' I suggest that he must have some security at games, and the players around him howl with laughter. 'I earn $100, a bodyguard gets $1000. I'm not David Beckham! My friend was shot dead during a game once, and they also dropped bombs, five of them, mortars I think, onto the field. It's very dangerous.' The bombs, the revenge and the war were a long way away now, though. The victory against Syria meant that the tournament was going to end as it had begun, against arch rivals Iran. This time there had to be a loser. The Lions of Mesopotamia were ready.

The noise from Iraq's fans could be heard nearly two kilometres away. From the outskirts of the sprawling, wooded Sports City complex, where the Amman International Stadium sat at its centre, the distant noise of drums and chanting grew louder and louder as I approached the front of the stadium. It was still two hours before Iraq were due to take on Iran but as many as 8,000 were already in the ground. Outside hundreds of men crushed at the single ticket booth desperate to snap up the last of the tickets. Their wives, daughters and young sons, holding miniature Iraqi flags, stood respectfully back, away from the unedifying scene. It was as if the Iraqi flag had been grafted onto almost every single available surface. The red, white and black, embossed with the three stars that represented Saddam's Ba'ath party and laced with Arabic script – Allahu Akhbar – was etched everywhere; on large pieces of cloth; on handheld banners; on hats; dresses;

children's faces. Back home large-scale pride in the national flag was a distant memory, from a time five years previously when hope and idealism of a new post-Saddam Iraq ran rampant. But here, in Amman, for the Lions of Mesopotamia, Iraqis picked up their flags once again in the biggest outpouring of nationalist sentiment since the bombs stopped falling on Baghdad. The terrace inside the stadium was frightening, a deafening noise that hadn't been articulated into any single song or chant. The years of frustration and isolation, of living in their own private hells of repression, humiliation and poverty, poured out, one third of it coming with a female timbre. Twenty Iranian fans, the only ones who had made the trip from Tehran, looked on from beyond the wire fence that separated them in awe. A young boy, wrapped in the Iranian flag, stood at the front with tears in his eyes. For some, it got too much. A group of men hoisted a different flag high up on a pole they had somehow smuggled into the ground. It was red, white and green and blazed with a golden sun at its centre. It was the flag of Kurdistan. 'We fly this because we are Kurds and Iraqis, but we fly it for Hawar [Mullah Mohammad],' the young man responded when I asked why. I didn't get a chance to ask his name. The smiling Kurd's face turned as, out of nowhere, a sick-looking middle-aged bald man – his face deeply etched and mean like a caricature of an officer in the Republican Guard – defied his frailty to leap down two rows of seats and lunge at him, knocking me out of the way. With one hand he had the Kurd by the throat, with the other he had ripped down what he saw was an affront to Iraqi unity. The Jordanian riot police quickly waded in and forced the man outside, still bucking and screaming at the indignity. The Kurdish flag wasn't seen again that night.

The teams emerged to a one-sided roar. Hundreds of fans were still outside when the national anthems were sung. Iran's was booed mercilessly, so much so that the music was drowned out by the screams, causing the Iraqi bench to turn around appalled at the spectacle. On the pitch the Iranian players looked at each other as they struggled through the din, shocked by the outpouring of vitriol. They put their indignation to good use. Within two minutes they had sliced open Iraq's defence, one that hadn't conceded a goal all tournament, and taken the lead at the opposite end of the pitch. There were so few Iranian fans, and with the large LCD screen broken – from which a sign hung that pointed out it had been 'Donated by the People's Republic of China' – no one was sure what had happened. By the time the screen fluttered into life, Iran were two up after a mistake by the goalkeeper Noor Sabri. The crowd began to turn on their heroes, raining plastic bottles down on Mohammed Nasser, who wasn't having his best game, when he came near to the fence to pick up the ball. Even the previously untouchable Younis was booed when he got booked. The second half pacified Iraq's travelling fans somewhat and even gave them false hope of a victory with an 86th-minute penalty. But Iran had done enough and when the final whistle blew they ran to Iraq's fans to bow in mock appreciation, sparking a fight between them and some of the Iraqi players who ran to intervene. Nashat consoled his devastated team-mates while Younis – topless and bearing a tattoo of Iraq on his left arm – harried the players to thank the fans, who had stayed in the stadium even as the Iranians collected their trophy, soaking up every last minute of national pride. Mohammed Nasser was distraught, standing on his own by the dugout, his white tracksuit limply hanging off his shoulders. Tears mingled with salty white beads of sweat that streamed down his face. 'Are you Ok?' I asked. Mohammed opened his mouth, but was unable to respond. Finally he choked out what he wanted to say: 'The Asian Cup. We . . . we still have the Asian Cup.'

And he was right, they did. Iraq's tepid 1–1 draw with Thailand in Bangkok in the opening game didn't give a hint of the glory and the tragedy that would follow. First the glory. Iraq pulled off the shock of the tournament, beating favourites Australia 3–1. Vietnam fell in the quarters. They were to meet South Korea in the semi-finals. The game finished 0–0 and went to penalties. No sooner had keeper Noor Sabri saved the deciding penalty than tens of thousands of fans poured out into the stifling Iraqi summer to dance and sing. For a brief, all too fleeting moment, Iraq was united, celebratory bullets being fired high into the late afternoon sky, the tracer fire from Kurd, Shia and Sunni indistinguishable from one another. Which is exactly what the insurgents feared. Tragedy was the only conclusion. As the revellers rejoiced, a suicide bomber quietly approached an ice cream stand in the well-heeled Mansour district of Baghdad, destroying himself and 30 football fans with him. That night twenty more fans were killed across town in suicide attacks, as were five more, accidentally, when gravity reasserted its will and the bullets of victory fell back to earth. The squad, ecstatic in the aftermath of triumph, were shattered by the news that their victory had indirectly led to the deaths of dozens of their compatriots. The team held a meeting to discuss pulling out of the tournament, but the players, spurred on by a bereaved mother who had begged the team to continue in memory of her murdered son, chose to play on.

On 29 July, the Lions of Mesopotamia proudly marched out into the Bukit Jalil National Stadium in Jakarta to face Saudi Arabia. Younis was the hero, heading the game's only goal and sparking joyous scenes. Suddenly the intractable differences that had blighted Iraq didn't seem that intractable any more. Back home, the fear of attack wasn't enough to dampen the mood. The team and their remarkable achievement was suddenly the biggest story in the world, Younis gracing the front page of the *New York Times*, television crews from Japan to Brazil wanting their story. Crowds celebrated on the streets from Erbil to Basra. Increased security measures meant just seven people were killed by insurgents, but it would have been many more had police not averted an attempted suicide bombing in Baghdad. The risk of such activity meant that celebrations on the team's return home were subdued. The Prime Minister's reception had to be held in the heavily fortified Green Zone in the centre of Iraq, away from most civilians. One person who wasn't there was the hero, Younis. 'I wish I could go back to Baghdad to celebrate, but who will secure my life?' asked the captain. Typically, every silver lining has a cloud. Jorvan quit after the match as he had promised, despite pleas from fans, players and even the prime minister. 'If my contract was for six months and not for two, they would have had to take me to the hospital for crazy people,' he explained. For some of the players it would be the making of them. Some were signed to regional teams in the Gulf on lucrative contracts. European teams courted others, like Younis, after he had been nominated for FIFA's prestigious World Player of the Year award. One player, Nashat Akram, went one step further. Sven Goran Eriksson's big-spending Manchester City side had offered him a lucrative contract to become Iraq's first Premiership player. The significance of the move couldn't have been overstated. At a time when Britain's standing in the Middle East was at its lowest ebb, huge numbers of Iraqis would watch their hero gracing the grounds of some of the world's most popular football clubs week in, week out. Or they would have if the British government hadn't refused Nashat a work permit on the grounds that Iraq weren't good enough. Despite just picking up the Asian Cup and surviving against all the odds, Iraq were below 70th place on FIFA's ranking, the minimum required by the British government to award a visa.

But as Younis, Nashat, Jorvan and the rest of Iraq's national football team walked off the pitch at Amman's International Stadium, no one could have predicted what they would achieve in four weeks' time. Outside the ground, the procession of fans who had gathered in Amman in their thousands for every match had pushed into the streets, singing once more. This time, the incoherent noise had morphed into a single song, sung over and over. 'Do you know what they are saying?' shouted Salif, a 16 year old who had fled Baghdad with his family. 'They are singing against Iran. "The Sunni and Shia and brothers. We will never sell Iraq."' I stood on a concrete bank, high above the crowd and the police below, and watched as Amman's street filled with red, white and black, the drums beating victoriously in defeat long into the night. Five hundred miles to the east a dress rehearsal was under way as the guns of sectarian conflict finally pointed to the sky.

TEN

Lebanon

I awoke when the wheels of the plane hit the tarmac. It was 3 a.m. and, out of my window, I could feel the presence of dark, foreboding hills, lit up by a patchwork of crisscrossing lights. It felt like I had been here before. Almost a year ago I had sat in my flat in Dubai, watching CNN as Israeli planes unloaded their missiles into the very same tarmac I was currently taxiing on at Rafik Hariri Airport. Anyone with a keen eye on the Middle East probably didn't watch the unfolding carnage with any measure of disbelief. Lebanon, after all, had for many decades been a geographical joke. Like 20th-century Poland, Lebanon was coveted, fought over and taken by the neighbours that surrounded it. Lebanon was a place other people went to fight their wars. But for me, I had heard only of the boom times, of the economic revival of the 1990s, of tourists from the West flocking to witness its shabby café charm. The Paris of the Middle East, they called it, and it was surely to return to its former glory. Then the Israelis came again and reset the clock to 1982, the last time forces from the Jewish state headed north. A year on Beirut was still trying to get back on its feet. The flight was empty. Not many people wanted to come to Lebanon any more. Even the weary-looking border guard happily stamped my passport despite the fact I had an overland exit visa from

Taba, Egypt, into Israel. They didn't even ask for a visa fee. Once they could have been discerning enough to turn me away.

After watching the final of the West Asian Championship, and the aftermath of Iraq's stunning, against-all-odds victory in the Asian Cup a few weeks later, my thoughts turned to Emile Rustom, the head coach of the Lebanese national football team. We'd met in the hotel in Amman where all the teams were staying and he explained just how divided Lebanese football was. In many ways it was an exact mirror of the political crises that had afflicted it over the years. Each football team had been co-opted by a sectarian group and politicians had fallen over themselves to fund teams in the hope of increased popularity that might one day translate into votes. The country's biggest club and current champions, Al Ansar, had traditionally been a Sunni club, funded by ex Prime Minister Rafik Hariri. After his assassination his son, Saad, continued to give money to them, as well as Nejmeh, a team that was Sunni-owned but supported mainly by the Shia. Saad had also dipped his toe in with the Christians, funding the Orthodox team Racing Beirut. Hezbollah had got into the game too, funding their team Al Ahed. The Druze community had Al Safa whilst the Maronites backed Sagesse. Every Saturday was derby day in Lebanon, where Sunni met Shia, Shia met Druze, Christian met Muslim. Violence was inevitable. With the dust still settling after Israel's 2006 bombardment of the country, Lebanon was on a knife-edge. The central government and its army had been humiliated by its impotence both in the face of the Israeli onslaught but also by the power and organisation of Hezbollah's guerrilla army. The West demanded that Prime Minister Siniora reined in what was effectively an army within an army. The problem was that Hezbollah's stock – both within the Shia and non-Shia communities – had never been higher after their successful act of resistance. They were also a legitimate political party, with elected members of the Lebanese parliament. Siniora's hands were tied. The only thing he could do was tinker around the edges. So he banned all football fans from attending football matches, lest their sectarian rioting produced the spark that blew his country wide open again, this time from the inside.

This year it was supposed to be different. I had flown in for the first weekend of the Lebanese season and this time, I had been told, the fans would be back. Or so I'd hoped. I was also flying in to the biggest political crisis to rock Lebanon since the war. However, given that the Lebanese are forced to experience exponentially greater crises every year, there was bound to be another one along in one shape or form. But this one was serious. Ever since Rafik Hariri's 2005 assassination blew away Lebanon's post-civil war innocence two political groups had formed and vied for political supremacy. On one side was the anti-Syrian 14 March group, made up mainly of Sunnis like Rafik Hariri's son Saad and his Future movement, the Druze and some Christian groups. On the other stood the pro-Syrian 8 March group, an alliance of convenience between the Maronites led by General Aoun and the Shia militia Hezbollah led by Sheikh Hassan Nasrallah. Lebanon's constitution had been drawn up on sectarian lines, with each community given a slice of the political pie. The Maronites, who had fought against Lebanon's Muslims and, by proxy, Syria in the civil war, had now jumped into bed with the Pro-Syria camp. Although the Maronites constitutionally hold the post of president, no one could agree on a suitable candidate – fearing it gave Hezbollah and the pro-Syrians the whip hand. The election was supposed to be held in September but it was postponed and a new date set. It had created the last thing that Lebanon needed: a power vacuum. The football season was due to start on Saturday, but the presidential vote was on the following Tuesday. The timing couldn't have been worse. I got into a taxi and headed for the Christian area of Ashrafiyeh, home to two of Lebanon's most bitter footballing rivals, Racing Beirut and Sagesse, who were to kick off the season against each other. Traditionally, Paul Rustom, Emile's son and Lebanon's international striker, had told me back in Amman it was Lebanon's answer to Scotland's 'Old Firm'. Only this time the Christian rivalry was between Orthodox and Maronite Catholics. Like the Glaswegian version, from an outsider's perspective, both teams seemed to have more in common then they cared to admit: both were from the same small hill in northern Beirut, both were on the same side during large swathes of the country's bloody civil war, both were Christian. The crucial difference was that the Maronites were an Eastern sect of Catholicism allied with Rome whilst the Orthodox Church broke links with the Pope in the 11th century. Both now celebrated different Christmas Days and, in Lebanon at least, rabidly supported different football teams. As I sped through Beirut's deserted suburbs, I didn't share Paul's confidence that the fans would be there to see it.

Beirut by daylight is a beautiful thing. The small narrow streets of Ashrafiyeh were filled with stylish old Mercedes Benz. The buildings – with their little art deco iron balcony railings and wooden shutters – were magisterial, turn of the 20th-century concrete palaces that had only been enhanced by their corruption over time and by conflict. They wore the scars of civil war well. It wasn't until I walked outside into the unseasonably hot autumnal morning that I realised that the façade of the hostel I was staying in was riddled with bullet holes. The telltale dimples seemed to be clustered around the window of the dorm I was staying in, as if my room was once the workplace of a hard-to-dislodge sniper, methodically picking off his prey whilst his increasingly desperate enemies indiscriminately sprayed bullets back in return. The main street of Gymnazie is quiet in the morning. This wasn't its time. The idle bars and clubs that are packed on either side tell you that life doesn't truly fill its streets until somewhere around midnight. But even for Hassan, who worked in a mobile phone shop on the street, and Nader, a club singer, it was still unusually quiet. 'Watch what you say, everybody is tense,' warned Nader, a Sagesse fan, when I asked for directions. 'Tuesday is an important day for the country, maybe after Tuesday, no one will be safe.' Eventually I found my rendezvous point on a dual carriageway near the hostel. Emile pulled up in a brand new, black 4x4 wearing a Lebanese national team training top, tracksuit bottoms and trainers. There hadn't been training that day but Emile was evidently a man who was always ready to kick a ball, no matter where he was. Emile was a Sagesse man, an ex-player who still coached and helped out at the club but the financial hardships – no fans, after all, means no revenue for the turnstiles – meant that for the first time in his adult life Emile would be starting a football season with no football club, which made his full training ground attire all the stranger. 'It is still not decided [about the fans] as we are waiting to hear from the Ministry of the Interior,' Emile declared as we drove up the hill that Ashrafiyeh lived on. He didn't seem to think it was that bad a thing. 'Because of the bad political situation the fans are fighting [especially] the Shia and the Sunni. So the FA was ordered not to create more problems. I think they will not change this decision. They will make the clubs wait.' Emile lived in the tallest building in northeast Beirut, a huge tower block that dominated all around it. Out on the balcony, the Mediterranean stretched out before us. 'We didn't leave here [during the 2006 war],' he said, looking ruefully out towards the horizon. 'We just watched as the planes came and bombed over there.' He pointed towards the port. 'That was the closest they got.' He continued to storyboard Lebanon's bloody recent history across the panorama: in front, where Israeli planes unloaded their missiles into Beirut's dock; over there, to the left, where Rafik Hariri was assassinated; over here, slightly closer now, the huge Mohammad Al-Amin mosque which Hariri helped build and where he was buried. 'He didn't see it finished but he was buried in it.'

Over the past 30 years Emile had seen it all, experiencing the country's bloody civil war first hand. 'I played in 14 Sagesse versus Racing derbies – the first in 1966,' he said as we drank cold water on his balcony. Emile had been a cultured centre-back who had turned out for the national team at a time when there was scarcely a nation. 'We lost many players at that time, five were killed. Once during practice a bomb went off injuring several of us. We were targeted because we were Christians.' Between 1975 and 1990 Lebanon was plunged into a vicious civil war pitting Christian and Muslim communities against each other as outside powers, in particular Syria, Israel, the USA and the Palestinian Liberation Organisation (PLO), tried to manipulate the situation for its own ends. An estimated 100,000 people were killed by the time a ceasefire was brokered leaving Syria in custodial occupation. The war saw the country divided into two, the north controlled by a Christian government, the south by a Muslim parallel administration. Lebanon's football league also split, with Sagesse and Racing competing in exponentially fiercer derbies. Even though they were both Christian teams that should have been united by a common enemy, the rivalry between Maronite and Orthodox remained fierce. 'There was no solidarity between us, even in the war. We hated each other more when there was a war between Muslims and Christians.' Even those involved in the game were puzzled by the hatred. 'I don't understand it,' Emile admitted, shaking his head. 'It's the 21st century and we still make a difference between Maronite and Orthodox. It's a shame to have two Easters. What, Christ died twice? We make the sign of the cross with a hand, they make it with three fingers. That's it.' Emile had agreed to make some calls and arrange for me to meet some of the players. With Emile and Sagesse parting ways, he arranged that we visit Racing Beirut. Racing didn't have a training ground. Instead they trained on a rented sand pitch at a local school at the edge of Beirut's Christian district. The drive there was illuminating. The closer we got to the sand pitch, the higher the density of bullet holes in the buildings. Just behind the pitch was Damascus Street, which separated us from the Shia area on the other side of the road. This was the frontline for the civil war and some derelict wrecks still stood here, missing chunks of concrete thanks to the blast of tank shells. One building closest to the road looked little more than a shell, with front rooms that once housed life clearly visible through the blown-off façade. The building looked derelict until you realised that up on the third floor, a line of children's clothes hung messily between two concrete pillars. At its base, someone had spray-painted a huge red cross. Given the building's proximity to the front line, it wasn't clear whether this had been a foolish act of Christian pride or something more sinister, a cross perhaps to mark out the building as a legitimate target.

Racing Beirut's pitch looked like it had taken a few hits

itself. With no nets and large holes gouged in its surface it was virtually unusable for football. If Saad Hariri was funding Racing, he wasn't giving them very much. Walking over to the penalty area I noticed something sticking out of the ground: a used hypodermic needle. What looked like a sewage truck rumbled onto the pitch in an attempt to make it playable, spraying water to dampen the coarse surface. Baha Salem Hanoun, the team's Iraqi coach, stood by waiting for his team to arrive. He was used to working with this sort of privation. 'We have gifted players but the situation is ruined here by politics,' he said as the truck bounced through the uneven pitch, leaving wet tyre prints in its wake. 'But they keep going. The players and coaches of both sides serve the country better than the politicians.' The team's captain, Tony Mikerai, was the first player to arrive. Unsurprisingly given the political problems that had surrounded the first weekend of the season, he tried to take the sting out of the weekend's biggest potential flash point. 'We must not look at this game as a rivalry, simply as three points,' he said before the rest of the squad arrived and began stretching on the potholed surface. 'We play football because we love it. You don't get a good salary but I thought, when the war finished, the whole country will be good, and football too. But there was too much fighting so if the fans are there it will make problems for the country.'

The comparison with Ansar couldn't have been starker. We drove south, past the Shatila and Sabra Palestinian refugee camps and around a broken-backed bridge that was still to be rebuilt one year after it had been destroyed. 'Nothing rebuilt by the government has finished yet,' lamented Emile. Anything that had been finished had been organised by Hezbollah, using money either from prominent local businessmen or outside sources. Sure enough, we passed under a brand new pedestrian bridge bearing the legend: 'Donated by Tehran Municipality.' Emile pulled his 4x4 into a car park surrounded by rubble. Expensive cars sat juxtaposed sharply to the blackened concrete and rocks that surrounded them: BMWs, convertible Mercedes, blacked out 4x4s. In front of us sat a pristine football pitch, with grass, floodlights and a stand full of well-dressed spectators in expensive suits and smoking Western cigarettes. From the podium we watched as the players below were run through training, including Emile's son Paul. When I had last met him at the West Asian Championships the previous June he was playing for Emile's team Sagesse. Now he turned out for the Champions, for Rafik, and now Saad, Hariri's favourite team. 'Football is a reflection on society, definitely [and] I can't deny that we are a Sunni club,' explained Mahmoud Natour, a member of Ansar's board who was there to check on his team's progress before the first game of the season. 'But we have mixed players, especially here in Ansar. Our board members are Shia, Sunni, one is even Jewish. We care more about football. It doesn't mean [because we are a Sunni club] we are doing anything for politics. We are trying to build a professional club.' Without the Hariri family's money, most of the football teams would go to the wall. Even Ansar would struggle without the fans being allowed in. But they had recently proved that they couldn't be trusted when football matches were being played, even when they were cheering on the same team. 'We did have a problem with the national team when the fans fought in a game [against Kuwait] because of the political tension,' Mahmoud admitted. 'The government aren't happy with that. It's whether football fans [use] the political tensions on the field to start a fire, that's why the government is doing this. You never know who will use it.'

The club that had fascinated me most, however, was Al Ahed, Hassan Nasrallah's team and a club that I had heard was heavily subsidised by Hezbollah. Hezbollah translates as Party of God in Arabic and was set up as a militia to protect Lebanon's Shia – allegedly with Iranian monies – after the Israelis invaded Lebanon in 1982. The Shia had good reason to seek protection. For them, the threat was four-fold – the Israelis; the Americans; the Christian north; and the Sunnis. For 1,500 years the two major branches of Islam had bristled next to each other. The split revolves around an issue of succession over who really embodied the true Islam when the Prophet Mohammed died. Without a son to take the mantle as a natural successor, two sides emerged: those who believed that the line should pass through Mohammed's cousin Ali and those who believed that the lead should be taken by the most suitable person chosen from the Prophet Mohammed's close personal cadre. The former were referred to as Shia (which comes from Shiat Ali which roughly translates as 'followers of Ali'); the latter Sunni (which roughly means 'the words and deeds of Mohammed'). The two took different paths and had been in conflict almost constantly ever since. Today, Hezbollah was the best-known and best-organised militant organisation espousing Shia Islam and the West still considered it a terrorist organisation. The Americans had a particular axe to grind after 300 soldiers and civilians were killed by a suicide bombing attributed to the organisation in 1983. But as the insecurity and anarchy grew in Lebanon during the 1980s, Hezbollah started to achieve a form of legitimacy by excelling in overground politics, by winning hearts and minds in their own communities by providing essential services the central government wouldn't or couldn't – water, healthcare, education and other social and sporting projects. Now many within Lebanon and most countries in the Middle East regard it as a legitimate resistance force. And despite still holding on to its arsenal, Hezbollah had an important presence in the Lebanese parliament too. Blue-and-yellow signs that sit on street corners in Beirut's southern suburbs – two yellow hands enveloping a small, blue collection box – sum up Hezbollah's raison d'être: 'The hand that fights, the hand that builds.'

Hezbollah's finger prints were also on Al Ahed's training complex. It was a stone's throw from Ansar's, across the main highway south out of Lebanon, just on the edge of the Shia stronghold of Dahiya. To the left of the entrance a large banner hung with Nasrallah superimposed onto a Hezbollah flag. Inside, Haj Mohammad Assi, the club's general secretary, sat in his large, white office. It was harshly lit, the strong strip lighting bouncing off the white tiles and abundance of silverware on show. Behind his large, brown wooden desk hung two flags; one the Lebanese standard, the other Hezbollah's distinctive yellow insignia. But Mohammad wouldn't be drawn at first about his club's connection.

'We are a team of all Beirut,' he replied when I asked him to describe Ahed's catchment. 'This is the Shia area. But the fans of Ahed are not just Shia; they are from all the political parties. But here we don't talk about politics. This is a club of football, and a good club.' Yet all around him more subtle evidence of Hezbollah's connection presented itself. Next to his desk a table was clustered with photographs in wooden frames. From where I was sitting it looked like a picture of a football dinner of some kind, with a visiting foreign dignitary. It was only on closer inspection I realised who it was.

'Is that a picture of Hassan Nasrallah?' The bearded, turbaned nemesis of Israel was a picture of rude health in the shot, kissing a young girl, Mohammad's daughter, in a touching show of affection.

'Yes, the leader of the resistance. This is after the war with Israel.'

'And this is a picture of Imam Khomeini?' Two large portraits hung on the far wall, one of the leaders of Iran's Islamic revolution, the other of his successor. Like reading a *Where's Wally* book, Nasrallah's face suddenly jumped out from every corner, on every wall.

'I take it he's a big fan of the club,' I asked. Mohammad ushered me outside his office and pointed proudly at the large team photo that hung at its entrance. It showed Al Ahed's victorious Lebanese FA Cup-winning squad of 2005. In the middle Haj pointed to a picture of himself, standing next to the grinning face of Nasrallah who had dropped in to congratulate the team.

'This isn't an office for the football club though, I would not be able to hang all these pictures, see,' Haj admitted, looking slightly guilty. He had been slippery about Hezbollah's involvement in the club ever since I had arrived. 'This is the club office.' He pointed to the lobby outside his office. It was pretty unconvincing, although not entirely surprising. Hezbollah had always been cagey about the scale of its social projects and worked hard to present itself as the party of resistance for the whole of Lebanon, not just the country's Shia community. Anything that seemed too sectarian from the party's members

– and Haj was a sports officer for Hezbollah after all – was decidedly off message. And there were few things in Lebanon more sectarian than football.

'Hezbollah don't give money to us, not like Hariri gives to Ansar and Nejmeh,' Haj continued, trying to distance himself and Hezbollah further. 'He gives money and those in the club are now for him. [Walid] Jumblatt [the long-standing leader of Lebanon's Druze faction] and his party is the same, giving money to Safa. When Nejmeh get money they send a communiqué to all the media that they [the Hariris] are backing this club. In this team we have many forces within the team. The players are free to believe in what they believe. Hezbollah is backing the team.' He paused, perhaps realising the futility of arguing away Hezbollah's involvement in front of a picture of him with his arms around Nasrallah.

'When we need help, Hezbollah is backing us.'

'In what way?' I asked

'I am the sports officer for the Hezbollah party. I am taking care of it.'

'But what kind of help?'

'If we need any help, administrative help, to push people to back the team with money. They know that the team gets help from the party, and they respect the party, so they come and help the club.'

Despite the obvious discomfort about the explicit link between Ahed and Hezbollah, Haj and the team were still excited about the prospect of Nasrallah dropping in to see them. The problem was that, with Hezbollah's Secretary General under constant threat of assassination, he couldn't give forewarning. 'Everyone can expect Mr Nasrallah, but we don't know when or where!' Haj laughed when I asked whether he'd be there for the first game of the season. 'It is very dangerous. He would love to be here. He is very normal. He supports the team and gives orders to support them.' Still, even if he weren't watching Ahed's opening-day fixture, he would still no doubt be getting his footballing fix, although it would be from an unlikely source. 'He likes English football too, the Premier League is on Al Mansar [Hezbollah's own television network, itself listed as a terrorist entity by the USA, and which boasts 10 million viewers worldwide] every weekend.' But like most things with the mysterious Nasrallah, no one was sure where his allegiances lay. 'I think maybe Liverpool,' one of the club's members interjected when I asked who he liked to watch in England. 'I like Steven Gerrard. My father likes Michael Owen but I don't like Wayne Rooney. He is Manchester.' Clearly the enmity between Liverpool and Manchester had even reached Beirut, and the smart money was on Nasrallah being a Liverpool fan. But this wasn't that unusual. Most of the big four have their own pariah supporter. Famously, it was alleged that Osama Bin Laden – like Fidel Castro – was a keen follower of the Arsenal. It was even alleged that he watched four games at Highbury in 1994 when he was briefly residing in London. But I wanted Nasrallah as one of my own. 'Do you think he could be a West Ham fan?' Haj smiled a knowing, sympathetic smile. 'I will ask him. But it is unlikely to be West Ham. He will need a lot of persuading.'

The club agreed to allow me to see the rest of Ahed's ground and outside the front gate I was confronted with an odd sight: a blond-haired man speaking in a thick German accent. 'At last! An English accent!' he boomed as he grabbed my hand with a Teutonic fervour I hadn't felt since Manfred Hoener almost ripped my arm from its socket back in Qatar. It turned out to be the team's manager, Robert Jaspert. Robert was an Australian-born German coach who had worked with the South Korean national team until, out of the blue, someone from Lebanon called. 'I got a call and was asked if I wanted to coach Ahed,' he explained happily as he slowly walked me around Ahed's vast training pitch. The complex was even more impressive than Ansar's, with two pitches, a stand and a fully equipped gym. There was even a heated swimming pool. Ahed had got his number after Lebanon had played South Korea and he had met some representatives from the club. Unbeknown to him when he accepted the offer, they were also representatives of Hezbollah. 'I'm not very political so I was on the plane on the way over here and I was sitting next to a Lebanese guy. He told me about Hezbollah and I thought:

"What am I doing here?'" Almost immediately Robert was immersed into Lebanon's complicated football politics when, back in March and after only a few days in the country, he was caught up in the car bombing that killed two of Nejmeh's players. 'Everyone talks politics, even on the football shows. It was March and my hotel room was wrecked. There was glass everywhere. We all went to the funeral, which is something I will never forget. Now, with the presidency, we do not have spectators. We are artists and need to perform to people.' It wasn't the only difference that Robert noticed. Any ostentatious religious symbols were banned. 'I have to keep this covered,' he told me showing the silver cross he wears around his neck. And Nasrallah was everywhere and nowhere. 'We have a few Sunnis [in the team] but everyone in the club loves him so much. We have a television show that gives awards for the best players. They all dedicated their awards to Nasrallah.' If success followed on the pitch, Robert was even told he might meet the man himself. 'I was told: "If you get to the cup final again we are sure Nasrallah will meet you and shake your hand." In Germany they have the wrong journalism about Hezbollah. They think it's like Al Qaeda. It's not, they do a lot of social work, for orphans.'

Robert disappeared to prepare his team for their first match and I was left to roam the grounds. It was inconceivable that the money for Lebanon's most advanced training facilities had come from anywhere other than Hezbollah. Through a metal door that was left ajar, I walked into a high-walled gym, itself bigger than Racing Beirut's small, sand football pitch. On the back wall two more portraits of the Imam and the Ayatollah looked down. Unsurprisingly given the plethora of Shia imagery Al Ahed's main support came from the nearby suburb of Dahiya. I had struggled to find it on the map, until I realised that it actually wasn't there. It was as if it had been wiped off. But every Lebanese knows where it is. It is Hezbollah country and allegedly the place where Western hostages like Terry Waite had been taken and imprisoned during the civil war. Emile wasn't sure it was a good idea I went when I phoned him and asked for directions. 'Be very careful around there, they think everyone foreign is an Israeli spy,' he said. I took a service bus with Andrew, a young Hungarian student. He was a militant Arsenal fan. 'Who do you support?' he asked me. 'West Ham,' I replied. 'Fuck off,' was his abrupt conclusion. He was headed for the same destination as me, a touching exhibition that had been organised by Hezbollah called House of Spider. It was an exhibition that celebrated the 'divine victory' of Hezbollah over Israel, so called because Hassan Nasrallah had said that Israel was 'weaker than a spider's web'. It was touching because it didn't really deal with any heroic acts of bravery. Instead it exhibited pieces of captured Israeli hardware whilst showing pictures of children mutilated by Israeli munitions. Dahiya was also famous for bearing the brunt of the civil war and of Israel's 2006 bombardment. In both cases Dahiya was impossible to subdue, and as our taxi inched through the lunchtime traffic, it was easy to see why. With its identical, sand-coloured tower blocks and warren-like alleyways, it was almost impossible to navigate on foot, let alone in a tank – Dahiya seemed to have been designed with guerrilla warfare in mind. Compared to the excess and the revelry in Ashrafiyeh, Dahiya felt like a different country: gone were the church steeples, gone were the countless impossibly beautiful women with long, tumbling dark hair, gone were the bars and the clean Parisian streets. In their place stood minarets, *hijabs*, shisha cafés and poverty. The unmistakable yellow flag of Hezbollah fluttered on every street corner. Down one road, every two metres, hung a huge photo of a Hezbollah fighter martyred in the last conflict with Israel. The district, though, isn't as densely populated as it used to be. Every three or four buildings, a sudden gap appears, the footprint of an Israeli rocket attack that destroyed the tower block that once lived there, a reminder that the vast majority of the 1,000 Lebanese killed perished in Dahiya. 'That was where Hassan Nasrallah lived.' The taxi driver pointed to his right. Two large tower blocks loomed over a patch of twisted steel and sandstone blocks. The exhibition itself was on a patch of rubble too. From the outside, the House of Spider had been arranged like a battlefield. Green-and-brown military netting rose up

on either side of the main path inside. To the right sat the
broken propellers of a downed helicopter, to the left a trench
full of boxes that once held ammunition. There was activity,
but not as we expected. A pack of bearded men had formed
a line and were quickly passing broken pieces of military
hardware towards the truck. When it had first opened it had
made international headlines for its lurid exhibitions and for
its gift shop, where you could buy a copy of a computer game
where you played a resistance fighter who hunted down and
killed 'Zionist pigs'. Now they were less pleased to see tourists.
One of the men spotted us surveying the scene and turned
around. 'We are closed, *khalas*, it's finished,' he barked angrily
before turning his back to us once again. We stood there for
a few moments, hoping he would change his mind. I offered
that I was a British journalist. The back remained unmoved.
Andrew said he was a tourist. Nothing. Then Andrew had a
cunning plan. 'Allahu Akhbar,' he shouted. 'Khomeini Rahbar!'
As if we had just said a secret password, the man turned
around and ushered us inside. 'What did you say?' I asked
Andrew incredulously. 'I learnt it in Iran. It means "God is
great, Khomeini is the leader."' His little homage to Imam
Khomeini, the late spiritual leader of Iran and a poster boy
(man?) for revolutionary Shia everywhere had done the trick.
Inside, men rushed past us with hastily packed boxes. 'You can't
go in there, only here,' the worker intoned, a little softer now
that we were deemed friends of a sort. The centrepiece of the
exhibition was a huge crater where a captured Israeli tank sat
inside. Around it dismembered mannequins, each with its own
Star of David painted on it, were strewn around, as if they
had been blown outwards by whatever force had stricken the
prone tank. Its own Star of David was burnt and forlorn, the
blue only visible on one side. As I inched closer to the crater
my right foot clanged on something metal. I knelt down and
picked up a spent rocket launcher with instructions on the
side written in Hebrew. Within seconds a guard snatched it off
me and carried it outside. The room next door was off limits
but I managed to creak the door open just enough to poke
one eye through. The large white room was empty except for

some large colour prints hanging on the walls. Each depicted a different scene of Israeli misery: a crowd of crying Israeli soldiers hunched over the body of a fallen comrade; a party of Israeli women crying in grief thanks to the destructive power of one of Hezbollah's katyusha rockets. I had seen enough. Andrew and I left them to finish off their packing. It was clear why they were leaving. If I could find my way here on the back of the press House of Spider had got, Mossad would have no problems. We walked through the district safely, past the new offices of Hezbollah's media office, until we found a local souvenir shop. The shop was a homage to Hezbollah – mugs, key rings, Nasrallah prayer mats. On the floor, in a big pile, I saw dozens of Lebanese flags. They weren't selling too well. 'We sell three times as many Hezbollah flags as Lebanon flags,' explained the young shopkeeper, not moving his eyes from the newspaper he was reading. That said everything about where Dahiya's heart was. I bought a Lebanese flag and a Nasrallah key ring before leaving.

Finally, on Saturday morning, the first day of the Lebanese football season, a decision was made. Rahif Alameh sat at his desk in the Lebanese FA's smart offices on Verdun Street with a face like thunder. The FA's general secretary had been forced to make a choice he didn't want to make, even if he understood why it had to be made. 'Football is a little dangerous,' he sighed as I sat in front of him to pick up my press pass and find out whether the fans would be let in or not. Football was indeed dangerous in Lebanon and to illustrate the point he stood up, removed a photo that hung on his wall and passed it to me. It was a picture of Beirut Sports City Stadium, the 60,000-capacity national stadium I would be heading for later to watch Nejmeh take on Shebab Al-Sahel, after the Israelis had destroyed it in 1982. There was no pitch, nor any grass. Any that had survived the bombing had been grazed to dust by the herds of cows that lived amongst the blackened concrete pillars. They belonged to the owners of the shabby tents that surrounded it. In the aftermath of the attack it had been used as a makeshift camp housing refugees from Palestine, Lebanon and

Syria. 'The prime minister [Fouad Siniora] directly interfered in this case. We said: "Every club should have to decide how many spectators they can accept on his responsibility, to help the government as the situation in Lebanon is not safe." But everyone is looking for the [presidential] election.'

The decision had far larger ramifications for Rahif. The game itself was under threat in Lebanon. Even in the darkest days of the civil war, matches would be organised and thousands would turn up for a distraction from the horror. Not any more; the lack of fans had strengthened the hands of those seeking to fund football clubs for political gain. With no money coming in from the turnstiles, the clubs were even more dependent on handouts from sugar daddies eager to secure votes. 'It's not healthy. If the assistance is based on politics it's dangerous. Excluding maybe one team I think all of the clubs receive political money,' he said, signing press accreditations for the game.

I told him of my visit to Al Ahed and how they had tried to deny that they received any help. He could barely hide his anger.

'Of course they get help from Hezbollah!' he said. 'Look at their ground: they have two pitches, a swimming pool and are building an indoor gymnasium for the winter. It's against the future of the game what we do now. If no one can come to the stadiums they will forget the football. Once there would be 40,000 to 60,000 at a game. They will choose another way, like drugs or fighting.' Or basketball. With the prospect of a second season of no football, many fans had started watching Sagesse's basketball team instead. It didn't help that they added a little bit more glamour than their footballing namesakes thanks to their regularly being considered one of the finest teams in Asia. The Lebanese national team had enjoyed some success too, qualifying for the 2006 World Championships, the World Cup of Basketball, and only narrowly avoiding the knockout stages after beating France and Venezuela. There was less trouble in the domestic league, and the authorities hadn't felt compelled to intervene. 'Basketball,' snorted Rahif handing me my pass. 'It's a big joke.'

It only took a few hours for the word to get out, but some fans already had a well-prepared plan. In a small, dusty building back in Ashrafiyeh, the Sagesse Fan Club was holding their annual pre-season meeting. Like any fan meeting, the ten-strong delegation discussed the basics of fan politics: from the crisis the club found itself in now that Emile had left the coaching side to the less arch but no less important dilemma of who would play the tabla in the team's band. The Sagesse fans, you see, weren't going to let anything as trifling as a government ban, heavily armed troops or arrest deter them. But that plan was further down the agenda and things had already started to get heated. An argument had broken out and swiftly been ended when a gun was pulled out and slammed onto the table. Samir, a board member who had produced the offending weapon, was forced to act. 'We thought we'd agreed 500 fans with [Lebanese Football] federation,' screamed Bashir, a huge bear who looked like he had slept rough the previous night and who was in possession of a voice so deep you suspected that in his tender moments only oceanographers would be able to pick up the growls. He was responsible for leading the terrace chants during games, which had pretty much made him surplus to requirements in recent months. Another season of inaction was unthinkable. 'It's not the federation, the government didn't allow it,' replied Patrick Aoun, the young, clean-cut president of the fan association. Joseph, Patrick's grey-haired deputy, tried to calm Bashir down by covering his mouth. The room descended into farce as clipped Arabic effortlessly segued into French and occasionally English. Six conversations rose at the same time, in three languages. It was chaos. The club's vice president, there to give 'The Management's' perspective, gave up and walked out before Samir pulled out his gun and used it on the table as a makeshift gavel. He didn't say a word. Calm was restored.

'In Ashrafiyeh, you're either a Sagesse fan or a Racing fan, there's nothing else and after the games there were too many problems, fights. It was really a derby in every way, like Barca and Real. Look at how much this club means to us.' Patrick qualified the point by sweeping his arm in front of the packed table of arguing fans who were filing out into Beirut's steaming late summer. But Patrick had a plan. 'This is a secret,' he said, lowering his voice, 'as we don't want any Racing fans to find out. At some grounds they have a motorway which is a little bit higher than the stadium so we are using guerrilla tactics. It would kill some people to know Sagesse are playing without them so we are going to watch it at the highway and if the army won't let them we will go to the roofs of tower blocks around the ground. We know the owners. Although we won't bring the band as we don't want to make noise and upset the residents.' I took a mobile phone number and was told to call his right-hand man Joseph when I got to the ground. Samir walked by, prominently clutching his gun. He didn't usually have a habit of turning up with a weapon to football functions, apparently. He had just finished his shift working as a bodyguard at a foreign embassy. 'Here, you want to fire it?' he asked, forcing the gun into my hand. It was heavy and powerful. I felt weak holding it, as if it controlled me, not the other way around.

'Where shall I shoot it?' I asked, looking at the kids standing by the entrance of the building unfazed, as if men swinging pistols was a normal thing around these parts. Samir looked over his shoulder, kicked open a shoddy-looking white door in front of us and pointed at the pathetic-looking cistern: 'Fire!' Nothing. I couldn't do it. It wouldn't have mattered if I had. Samir laughed, taking the gun out of my sweaty grip, holding up the missing clip in his right hand.

The silence that followed Ali Nasser Eddine's goal covered the empty Sports City Stadium in a dark melancholy. Ali wasn't sure what to do at first. The pure, blind ecstasy of scoring had led him to perform an act of gymnastic heroism, flipping backwards in perfect circles. But then the silence caught him too. His celebration was in vain. No one would ever see his back flips, his team's initial adulation or his goal. Ali trudged back up the pitch, shoulders hunched, head down, as if he'd just watched the opposition score. The shouts of the few soldiers allowed into the ground – the same stadium that had once been a shell housing broken refugees in the mid-1980s and now rebuilt into a new, all-seater stadium – were well-meaning but only provided relativity, a bench-mark with which to measure the stadium's vast echo. It was Nejmeh's fourth goal against a fellow, predominantly Shia-supported side, Shebab Al-Sahel, in the first game of the season. Shebab had already had a player sent off early in the first half for comically diving and handballing the ball on the goal line. Nejmeh missed the penalty but proceeded to destroy their opponents. It was 4–0 and there was still half an hour left. The first day of the Lebanese season had started with footballing fireworks. But it felt like a pyrrhic victory.

After meeting with Sagesse's guerrilla fans, I hailed a cab and went south again, this time to the Beirut Sports City and the first game of the season between Nejmeh and Shebab Al-Sahel. As soon as I approached the roman façade of the national stadium, the troops loomed into view. APCs scuttled at its base, carrying troops brandishing automatic weaponry. For the first time at any match in the Middle East I saw tanks, six of them, parked to one side. The teams came out just as I had taken my seat in the only place in the ground that exhibited any sign of life, the press bench. The Nejmeh players carried on a long, plastic poster eulogising their three fallen comrades who had lost their lives pre-season. 'I think it's better now [the fans are banned] because you know it won't be a massacre,' argued Pauline Sahyoum, a reporter for the *An-Nahar* daily newspaper, who was sitting next to me. 'Before, the fans beat the fans. Even the army couldn't stop them, especially when Nejmeh played Ansar, there were too many of them. So the Ministry [of the Interior] had to make a decision.' The sun was setting now, and the minarets began their call by the time Ali had scored his goal. The game ended in a rout, 5–0. I was used to a crush leaving a football ground but outside was dead, the troops still clustered around the entrance whilst the distant beeping of incessant traffic heralded the Lebanese rush hour. At this game football had become everything and nothing. On the one hand, the fingerprints of the game's importance were there: the need for troops, the banner honouring the innocent bystanders of

Lebanon's increasing anarchy. Yet on the other, it felt futile. Who was this game for if no one was there to see it? Football for these two teams had been so removed from the terraces, the weight which tethers any club to reality, that soon you feared these teams would be playing on empty pitches in parks. A new generation had begun to desert the game, not knowing or understanding what it was to collectively love a team that you could actually breathe in and almost touch. The players too had begun to feel the disillusionment that this might be a permanent state of affairs for Lebanese football. As I was walking back to the main highway, a figure wearing Nejmeh's kit walked past, looking for his car in the dark. It was Ali Nasser Eddine, the player who had celebrated his goal in vain. 'Normally I score and I am so happy because everyone knows we have the most fans in the East,' he said ruefully when I asked about his celebration. 'But without the fans I score and it feels like I have died.' Ali continued to look fruitlessly for his lift home. Behind him the army stoically remained, as if not fully believing that Nejmeh's faithful weren't planning a final sneaky attack on the stadium's entrance.

Sunday was an apt day to hold Beirut's most prominent Christian derby. Like the previous day's match, the army was out in force outside the ground. An hour before kick-off heavily armed soldiers patrolled the Bourj Hammoud stadium, lest any fan dared get near the ground. Inside, the vast ageing concrete structure was alive with activity. Through a half-open door, I watched as the referee and his assistants prayed to Mecca in their office. A solitary Racing player did the same on the pitch. Meanwhile Christian players from both sides sporting large Jesus tattoos got dressed in their respective changing rooms. Sameer Nagim, Sagesse's team manager, stood guard at his team's door, refusing entry to anyone but players. He apologetically explained that the stakes were too high to risk letting outsiders in. 'Every year one of us would get relegated, so we haven't played each other for so long,' he said, clearly relishing the opportunity to continue the tradition. 'The rivalry is still there, Maronite versus Orthodox, and fighting was normal. I used to be young and run from the police. This is football in Lebanon. We have to do it today, especially for the people of Ashrafiyeh.' The Racing management were less worried about their tactics being leaked to the opposition and let me sit with the players. The atmosphere was thick with Deep Heat, almost blinding, as Rabih Abouchaaya, the team's midfielder, explained Racing's religious mix. 'There are maybe ten Christian players, ten Shia and four Sunni,' he said, although even this basic explanation sparked a political debate between the players about the up-and-coming parliamentary elections. 'I'm with General Aoun [the Maronite presidential candidate supported by Hezbollah],' exclaimed Rabih. 'The majority here is with him because we are Christian and we have a bond with the Shia.' Joseph Attieh, the team's long-haired left-back who wore a huge cross on his arm, agreed. 'I'm with the General too,' he admitted, just as other players walked in to admonish him. 'We're not all with him! I'm for Hariri,' shouted the midfielder Moursri. All mention of politics abruptly ended as the coach began the team talk, mapping out the 4–3–3 formation he hoped would bring Racing its first derby victory in close to a decade. There was just one last thing to do before kick-off. The Racing team huddled in the changing room, with the captain instructing the players to 'each pray to their own god'. For a brief few moments, the eleven men were tightly locked in a circle, three different prayers to three different creeds rising from the group. They shouted: 'Oh Mary, Oh Mohammed, Oh Ali, 1,2,3 Racing!' and ran to the tunnel. Sagesse were waiting for them. 'We are all Ashrafiyeh,' an anonymous Sagesse voice implored. 'Let's take it easy, OK?' The two sets of players got the nod and walked out into the empty stadium and to the faint, almost inaudible hum of applause.

High up on the nearby overpass, Joseph and the Sagesse Fan Club were there in force. Despite the government ban and the threat of arrest, hundreds had avoided the army directly outside the stadium and made it to the overpass that skirted the northern end of the stadium. The rooftops were dotted with more fans, all cheering on their team from their precarious vantage points. On the overpass cars flew past and swerved to avoid the growing crowd on the road. 'It's dangerous, there are mad drunk drivers driving past,' shouted Jeffery, a Sagesse fan clinging onto the crash barrier. 'You can't blame the government. People are afraid of the fights, some people are crazy and mad [but] I've supported this team for 40 years. Can I stop now? How can I stop now?' Joseph, fiddling constantly with rosary beads, looked on proudly, smiling at the large contingent of support he'd brought. The vast majority were Sagesse, with a few Racing fans thrown in. 'Aren't you worried they'll fight?' I asked him. 'No, I don't fight here. I used to fight for real.' With that he lifted the sleeve on his right arm, revealing a tattoo of a skull, with a red beret and two swords. I didn't recognise it, but Gaith, an Iraqi photographer who had accompanied me on the trip, did. 'That's the insignia of the Lebanese Forces.' The Lebanese Forces were the feared armed militia of the fascist-inspired, avowedly-Christian Phalange political party. They were widely believed to be responsible for the brutal Shatila and Sabra massacres in 1982, one of the civil war's bloodiest atrocities where anywhere between 400 and 3,500 Palestinian men, women and children were executed. It gave a new, wholly unexpected meaning to the phrase 'guerrilla fan'. Perhaps the presence of a potentially genocidal maniac could explain the rather genial peace that had descended on the crowd although, as Jeffery explained, just as Racing missed the first chance of a heated opening few minutes, there was a far more mundane reason. 'The truth is that neither of us, Sagesse or Racing fans, have anywhere else to go.' Sammy, a Racing fan, agreed that the government ban has forced the two groups of supporters to accept each other just so that they can watch the teams they love. 'I'm happy we are playing in the first division again, but I'm happier just to be watching. I don't care if there are any Sagesse fans here any more.'

The game descended into a brutal battle of attrition. Players were stretchered off and yellow cards brandished. Ironically given the pre-match talk, there was far more animosity on the pitch than on the makeshift terraces. Finally the deadlock was broken by Racing's Sierra Leone striker Donald Massinter running through and coolly beating the keeper. Suddenly the Sagesse fans came to life, screaming at their own team for their inept display: 'You are playing like kids!'; 'I'm too angry to swear at you!'; 'Your mother's cunt!' Things got worse when Sagesse went 2–0 down, Massinter again the scorer. It could have been four. The final whistle went and the Racing players celebrated like they'd just avoided relegation. Joseph flung his arms in the air and stormed off without saying another word as the rest of the Sagesse fans negotiated the perilous path back down the overpass, back to Ashrafiyeh. There were no fights and no arguments. It had taken every ounce of effort just to be there, let alone rekindle decades-old antagonisms. But it also constituted a hope of sorts, that football wouldn't be forgotten, even if it took an underground resistance movement to keep the flame alive.

And what of the presidential vote? Tuesday was tense but passed peacefully even if the vote was postponed again, further deepening the country's political crisis and leaving Lebanon in a precarious, rudderless position. As I write this, the election has been postponed 18 times and street-to-street fighting was being reported between Hezbollah's forces and pro-government militias in Beirut. 'It looks like it's going to be a long, hard winter,' shrugged Jeffery as he finally let go of the crash barrier that had kept him safe for the previous two hours. He was right, in more ways than one.

ELEVEN

Syria

Colonel Hassan Swaidan wasn't best pleased and wanted to see me straight away. Outside the training complex of Al Jaish, six armed soldiers had surrounded me, shifting awkwardly from foot to foot. They knew what the rules said, and the rules were the rules. This was the army after all. 'Did you take a picture?' the taller of the six asked, as another went into the guard post to phone his superior. There was no use lying: I'd been caught red-handed. After being dropped off at the training ground I had walked past the heavily armed entrance to the club, the first time I'd ever seen a football club protected by such a show of brute force. But then Al Jaish wasn't any normal football club; they were one of Syria's most decorated teams. They were also the team of Syria's huge and all-powerful army. Al Jaish literally means 'The Army', and the club had long dominated Syrian football, like the army had dominated Syrian society, winning ten league titles and at the beginning of the 20th century winning the AFC Championship, making them the best team in Asia at the time. They weren't run like other clubs either. Al Jaish was run by the Ministry of Defence, with a strict chain of command. A general sat at the top whilst The Colonel took the role of technical director and oversaw the day-to-day running of the team. Every aspect of the team was run like a military operation, even player recruitment. It was a beautiful arrangement. As Syria still enforced national service, every 18 year old had to complete two years' military service. So as soon as a good player hit 18, Al Jaish would force rival clubs to hand over their star man. It was no wonder they had enjoyed such dominance on the field. It was more the dominance off the field I was worried about. The soldier repeated his question. 'Did you take a picture?' A few scenarios ran through my mind. I could run and jump into a taxi. But I'd probably be shot before I got off the kerb. I could lie. But then, I had already lied to get into the country. I'd arrived in Amman without a visa after an attempt to secure one was scuppered in London, when they asked for a letter from my work. As soon as they found out I was a journalist I was kicked into a bureaucratic jungle from which my visa never emerged. The shared taxi left Amman and headed north, to the Jaber crossing with Syria. I had begun to formulate a story, one which the border guard, sitting in his smoke-stained white formica booth in the arrivals area, didn't have time for. He visibly slumped as I jovially explained that I didn't have a visa, his balding head slapping into his palm, as if my arrival was more work than any one man could possibly expect to handle. The arrivals hall was empty. He composed himself, straightening his back along with the green starchy uniform that covered it. 'What is your profession?' he exhaled.

'I'm a call centre administrator for a bank,' I replied, using my alternative identity. 'I am travelling around the Middle East and I hear that Damascus is the most beautiful city in the world.'

The guard looked back blankly, unimpressed by the attempted sycophancy. He returned his gaze to the passport, flicking past visas from places that no one in their right mind should ever want to visit for pleasure: Iraq, Saudi Arabia, Kuwait, not to mention a small but deadly exit visa from Egypt to Israel, which had so far gone undetected. 'Why you no get visa in London?' he quickly asked, as if he'd found the silver bullet that was to reveal my duplicity.

This had me stumped. I should have had a good excuse, but I didn't. So I thought of the first thing that came into my mind. 'My sister,' I stammered. 'She was involved in a car accident.' It wasn't my proudest moment, but it was the clincher. He nodded, sucked out the last column of smoke from his dying cigarette and told me to wait. By the time he returned, someone in a no doubt equally smoky back-room had given me a sympathetic nod. I was in.

I had been desperate to get to Syria ever since one of Yarmouk's players in Yemen had told me about his previous club Al Jaish and how it had used its position to recruit conscripts to its cause and sweep all before them in the Syrian league. It seemed to encapsulate something about a heavily militarised country that possessed an army numbering close to half a million and was still technically at war with Israel. This fact is drilled into every Syrian's psyche, not by propaganda but by geography. The long road to Damascus is dominated by the eerie, snow-capped mountains of the Golan Heights, policed by the peak of Jebel Al Sheikh. Israel won the Golan Heights in the 1967 Six Day War and, for Syrians at least, it's a line in the sand for any potential peace deal. You understand why it is so important when you reach the outskirts of Damascus, where you can see the ancient city spill out of its crater like slow-moving lava, and the heights mockingly smile down at all those that pass.

It was when I reached the Al Jaish training ground that the real problems started. If they arrested me at the front gate and found out I was a journalist on the sly then my trip was over, at least. I could have offered a bribe. But I only had three dollars and a few Syrian pounds in my pocket, about £2 worth. I would have been laughed at all the way to solitary confinement. I came clean. 'Yes, I took a photo.' They had me bang to rights. The soldiers had watched as I approached the entrance to the training ground, stopped to see whether I'd been seen, and taken a photo of a sign that said: 'Military Zone, No Entry, No Cameras.' 'You can't do this!' the young soldier shouted, more out of exasperation and fear than anger. 'The Colonel, if he found out he would . . . ' His voice trailed off as he crossed his wrists in an unambiguous sign that transcended any language barrier. Jail. 'Give me the film,' the shortest soldier, carrying a chipped machine gun, demanded. I considered handing them a roll of unprocessed film, hoping they wouldn't know the difference. Instead, I pathetically blurted out the first thing that had come into my head. 'Please, I was just taking a picture of a kitten.'

'Give me the film,' the soldier reaffirmed, more menacingly than the first time. Just as I was about to hand over my camera, a breathless young recruit with a sketchy teenage moustache ran into the crowd with new orders. The tallest soldier seemed relieved. 'The Colonel will see you now.' The gateway cleared and the young recruit led me into the complex, past the stone frieze dedicated to the president, Basheer Assad, past the huge, Lenin-style bronze bust of his father, the late President Hafez Assad, through a trophy-room fit for a champion. He marched me up the stairs, along a dark corridor that stank of fresh detergent, the smell you imagine a windowless room deep in the bowels of a football stadium in Pinochet's Chile smelt like just after it had been cleansed of a recent and horrific torture. His shoes squeaked as they met the linoleum-covered floors. The walls were pasted with the Syrian flag every two steps. We walked past banks of troops as they sat at desks, craning their necks to see who the new arrival was. This was it. The end. Deportation at least. If not more. The look of fear in the soldier's eyes at the gate told me The Colonel was not a man to be messed with. Yet here I was shitting on his parade. The soldier stopped abruptly, pivoted 90 degrees, knocked on a door and walked in. The Colonel was sitting behind a large desk, in a grey lounge suit. The soldier immediately stiffened his back and offered a salute. The Colonel rose and turned towards me. He was short, with white hair and a round cheery face. Out of uniform, he didn't look so intimidating. 'What are you doing here?' he asked in perfect English. 'I'm an English journalist, writing a book about football in the Middle East,' I said. 'English . . . ' He replied, letting the nationality hang in the air for a few seconds. 'Where else have you been?'

'Oh, Lebanon, Egypt, I . . . Iraq,' I had almost said Israel.

'How did you go to Iraq!' he laughed, guessing correctly that I obviously wasn't a man of military bent. 'The Americans

and the English have made such a mess with their stupid war!'
He nodded at the soldier to leave, who saluted and spun out
of the room. 'Sit,' he ordered. The Colonel squeezed behind
his desk. 'You shouldn't have just come here without a letter,
without permission. And you cannot take pictures here. This
is the army, there is discipline here.' He said the last sentence
as if he wanted to smash his fist on the table to emphasise the
point, but couldn't quite bring himself to do it. 'But I was only
trying to take a picture of a kitten,' I persisted, trying hard
to convince myself. Behind him a large portrait of President
Assad loomed over us. His piercing blue eyes were deliberately
hung forward so that it bore down on the viewer, making him
look like Vigo, the omnipotent dark lord whose soul lived in
a painting in *Ghostbusters 2*. The Colonel smirked and reached
under his desk. He pulled out a small, wooden box and placed
it in front of him. About the same size as a revolver, I thought,
as he lifted the lid and stared at its contents before looking
up: 'Sweet?' I could have cried with relief. With the tension
broken I brought out my notebook, thinking I had crossed
some kind of Rubicon with the man. 'Stop!' he shouted, picking
up the phone. 'I have to verify who you are.' It seemed like a
good idea to turn on the dictaphone I still had in my pocket,
seeing that I wasn't allowed a written account of proceedings.
The Colonel made a call, and was quickly assured. Content
that I wasn't a spy, he called the soldier back into the room.
'I will ask whether you can talk to the players, but there is
a procedure, rules to follow' – he was a stickler for the rules.
He left the room, leaving my baby-sitter and I on our own.
The Colonel's room was adorned with dozens of pictures of
the president. A large squad photo of him with the famous
Al Jaish side that won the Asian cup hung behind me. He
was sitting pride of place in the middle, where the manager
should have been sitting. 'President Assad,' I said, pointing to
his portrait in a futile attempt to make conversation with the
soldier. He placed his right hand over his heart. 'I love him,'
he instinctively responded in Arabic. The Colonel returned
with a decision. 'The general will see you now.' The general?
I was to be shown into the office of a Syrian army general,

with a voice recorder still whirling in my pocket. There was no way I could turn it off without The Colonel and the soldier realising my error. Taking photos of a military zone was bad enough, but recording the voice of a bona fide syrian Army general was bound to be some kind of criminal offence. The general's office was at the end of the corridor. Dressed in a green military uniform, left breast sagging under the weight of military honours, he sat behind a large, expensive-looking desk as soldiers buzzed around, handing him pieces of paper for his perusal. Each was read and promptly dispatched into the shredder that sat next to him. Even sporting secrets were state secrets. Behind him hung more photos of the president, several of the general shaking hands with the great man himself. He stopped midway through signing a letter when he realised I was in the room. Words weren't necessary. His well-fed jowl, grey side parting and red, important-looking epaulets smacked of a man who had been suckling the rich teat of the military's creamy nipple for decades. He didn't like surprises any more than The Colonel. He merely went about his business as I sat there, with more soldiers buzzing in with more pieces of paper. They too met with the shredder. Eventually he stood up, walked around to the front of the desk, asked who I was and then announced: 'I'm not a big fan of football. I am more of a track-and-field man. I used to run the marathon.' And that was it, my cue to leave. A decision had somehow been made. I wouldn't be allowed to visit the training ground or see the players. The day after tomorrow, maybe. If I get the right letter. In Arabic. Then we would see. No promises. Maybe. He shook my hand and I was bundled out. The Colonel walked me back to the offices, arranged for my escort to the front gate and made his own excuses to leave. 'How many generals are there in the Syrian army?' I asked. 'Ahh,' he winked. 'That is a state secret.' The soldier saluted, turned on his heel and walked me quickly back down the corridor, back down the stairs and through Al Jaish's trophy room. I stopped briefly to see what they were for. One seemed to be an unmarked plaque adorned with the Olympic rings with a bayonet and a rifle pushed through them. The soldier ushered me forward, out into the spring sunshine and through the front gate. He saluted me before turning and disappearing back into the building. I didn't take out my voice recorder until I was safely in a taxi and well out of shooting range.

Damascus is a city that walks to a military beat. It is often said that the Syrian capital is the world's oldest continuously inhabited city, although pretty much every regional metropolis with a walled old city seems to lay the same claim. What can't be denied is Damascus' turbulent and bloody history; of wars, massacres and a merry go round of owners from the Romans to the Turks to the Persians. The forces of Arab nationalism, and the secrecy and authoritarianism that followed its failure, have moulded modern Damascus. Down every Damascene street you'll find soldiers on patrol. Whole districts of the city make their living from clothing the country's newly minted conscripts. An inordinate number of amputees go about their daily business, selling newspapers or cigarettes or pushing a cart full of fruit with their one good arm – testament to Syria's past, unsuccessful, conflicts with its quarrelsome neighbours, Israel and Lebanon, to its west. You can imagine, however, that Damascus' ancient streets had always been filled with soldiers, its tailors drawing a wage from its warriors, whether sewing camouflage trousers or tunics. With the army so ubiquitous it's no surprise that little dissent is tolerated in Syria, either of its political institutions or its armed forces. But then, five years ago, opposition came from an unlikely source: the Syrian football association. Al Jaish's player plundering had reached critical level. The league was still amateur, which meant there was no compensation. As it was the military doing the taking, there was no argument. By sucking up the league's talent they won honours and attracted huge crowds, whilst the other clubs had to keep a lid on their simmering discontent. The FA decided that enough was enough. Syrian football was going pro and if Al Jaish wanted to take any club's players, then they'd have to bloody well pay for them. 'Before, they took all the players,' admitted Taj Addin Fares, vice president of the Syrian Football Association, when I visited their headquarters down the road from Al Jaish's training ground. 'Any good players, they would just take them and if they played for Al Jaish they played for the national team too.' The military had successfully turned what should have been a partisan league club into a de facto national team, flying the flag for Syria at home and abroad. Not supporting them was akin to treason. 'More than 80 per cent of Damascus used to support the army club,' said Toufik Sarhan, the FA's general secretary who, with his salt-and-pepper hair and thick-rimmed black glasses, looked like a Syrian Michael Caine. 'But now many of the clubs are as good as Al Jaish, if not better, because we made the league professional. Rich men started to support their clubs. Football is much better now.'

Just how much Al Jaish's stronghold had been broken became clear the next day, on match day. Friday. My taxi arrived at Damascus' biggest stadium, the Abbasiyyin. Most Middle Eastern stadiums smell the same, of roasted nuts and weak piss. The Abbasiyyin Stadium was no different. Hundreds of troops had been drafted in to police the match even though a paltry 1,000 Al Jaish fans had turned up for the Damascene derby against title chasing Al Majd. Ten years ago all 45,000 seats would have been taken. The Colonel was out on the pitch early, dressed in a neat grey suit whilst keeping half an eye on his team warming up. Anonymous, well-dressed men wearing sunglasses approached to kiss him on both cheeks. The coach was nowhere to be seen. With The Colonel otherwise disposed I had the freedom to roam. In Al Majd's dressing-room the players were raucously preparing to go out on the pitch. 'It always was a big rivalry,' explained Ali Refaie, a Syrian international, as he put his shin pads on. 'I was in the army for two years but the people don't like the army, so they see us or Al Wehda instead.' In the Al Jaish dressing room, the atmosphere couldn't have been more different. The room was empty, except for the forlorn figure of Ahmad Rifat, Al Jaish's experienced Egyptian coach who had been conspicuously absent from his team's warm-up. He'd been in charge of the Egyptian and Syrian national teams and had been sacked from both but was enticed back into Syrian football with the prospect of building a team that was capable of breaking Al Karama's monopoly.

Now he sat in the changing room as The Colonel strode around outside sucking up the plaudits. Yet according to Rifat, it was he who had implemented the changes that the army had previously refused to admit needed to be made. 'When I got here last year Al Jaish's results were not good,' he said. 'I made a young team – only two players are above thirty, the rest under twenty-three. I'm here for two years and Inshallah I hope that next year we will have a good team.' He insisted that he still picked the team and that The Colonel was the team manager off the pitch but he still found it something of a culture shock managing an army team after spending his managerial life looking after civilian outfits. 'It is very different. With the army team you have any facility you like. The only problem is the new rules for professional players,' he lamented. 'Before, Al Jaish would take all the competition. Now this is a different football. The other teams take good players and pay money for them. But the army doesn't buy because they have good facilities but a low budget. It's difficult for us because I see a player, I want this player, but I can't take this player any more.' The team had also lost something of its military makeup. Only two players now split their time between military and football duty – although Ahmad claims another five wanted to wear the uniform since playing at the club. 'Now the club is down,' he said as kick-off approached. 'Inshallah, we will be big again.'

Ahmad's prophecy wasn't immediately borne out on the pitch. After the crowd, the players and the soldiers present had stood to attention for 'Guardians of the Homeland', Syria's national anthem, in front of a huge Syrian flag, things went downhill for Al Jaish. They were dire and quickly went 2–0 behind. But then something unusual happened. Every decision, it seemed, went in Al Jaish's favour. The small band of Al Majd fans were apoplectic with rage as the full force of the apparatus of the state willed an Al Jaish comeback. When Al Jaish scored, the soldiers celebrated. And then they scored again, and again. The players knelt on the pitch and kissed the grass after each goal as Al Majd tried to work out what had hit them. It was only when the fourth goal had gone in, courtesy of Zambian international Zacharia Simukonda, that they finally gave in. It finished 4–3, and as the players walked off the pitch, the soldiers there to keep order shook their heroes' hands without any pretence of neutrality. Back in the dressing room Zach didn't find this odd in the slightest. 'I didn't know I was coming to the army team,' he explained, sitting in nothing more than what appeared to be a thong. 'There is no difference though between playing for a civilian team and an army team. They don't treat you like army, they are professional.' Outside the dressing room The Colonel was busy taking congratulations from a large, jubilant crowd that had gathered. 'It was a good game, no?' he shouted as I walked past. The conversation was curtailed as yet another man grabbed him and kissed his face, first on the left cheek, and then three times on the right; a sign of true affection. Ahmad Rifat anonymously climbed onto the team bus, in silence, away from the melee and without fanfare. His work was done, even if no one had appreciated it.

In comparison to the next day's game, Al Jaish's unpopularity was only too evident. Al Wehda, Damascus' most popular team, were taking on bottom-of-the-table Al Horriya at the smaller Al Fayhaa stadium. Fans draped in the orange of their team's shirt hurriedly skipped towards the ticket booths cradling their 100 Syrian pounds for a ticket. The anticipation was no different from a match in London or Turin; children excitedly dragging parents towards the stands, nervous teenagers singing Arabic songs outside the ground. Hope and expectation hung in the air. At Al Jaish all you felt was the heavy hand of the law, of conformity, of order. No one skipped to go and watch Al Jaish play, not any more. The complete collapse of their crowd to one forty-fifth of its past glory proved that, for all the cups and the league titles, Damascus' love was essentially bought, not by flashy foreign players or promises of greatness, but by a tacit understanding that opposing the government and its powerful institutions was unpatriotic. Al Jaish may have stolen the league, but it could do nothing to steal its fans' hearts and minds. Walid, a young Syrian working security at one of the stands, explained it to me. 'Al Jaish is hated,' he said as the match kicked off. Twenty thousand had made the trip to watch the game, even though it had virtually no significance to the home team. 'They are hated because when you are 20 they bzzzzzz, shave your head. If they play for Al Jaish they don't shave your head, you don't have to serve. And then there's wasta . . . ' Wasta is what oils the wheels of Middle Eastern society. It means influence, connections, money. Those with wasta can expect to negotiate the Middle East's labyrinthine bureaucracies with ease, or secure a table at a fancy restaurant, or get off a parking ticket. Everybody else had to wade through a sea of forms and treacle-thick obduracy. No one can expect to get anywhere significant in the Middle East without huge quantities of wasta. 'They have more money,' Walid continued, 'and the referees always give them decisions.' Almost every single football league in the world has its own successful team that its rivals suspect has curried favour with the authorities, but when you hear Arsene Wenger or Jose Mourinho or Sir Alex Ferguson complaining it sounds laughable. In Syria it seemed plausible.

After the impeccably observed national anthem was done and dusted, the Al Wehda band – of three trumpets and a tabla – struck up and the fans sang, until Al Horriya took the lead. And they sang some more. 'Kes akh meck,' they screamed as the Al Horriya team, without any fans there of their own, bowed in front of the nearest Al Wehda stand: 'Fuck your mother.' In Saudi I had been told that a popular football chant was: 'I shit in your father's beard'. I couldn't find any evidence of it because (a) how do you bring it up with a Saudi in polite conversation? And (b) putting the words 'father', 'shit' and 'beard' into Google returned some truly horrific results. Still, Walid and his groups of friends revelled in teaching me the phrases you wouldn't find in your standard Arabic phrase book. Othmar, Luqmar, Imad and Aram all worked at the stadium and were Al Wehda fans who detested Al Jaish and the army. 'I will not go to the army,' declared Omar. 'I'll pretend I am crazy.' We talked about life in Syria as the match ebbed and flowed in front of us, about how, in their opinion, the West had a bad impression of Syria and Islam because of distortions in our media. 'You can see in Syria, we are not all terrorists,' said Assam, a wiry boyish-looking 23 year old studying English. On the pitch players and coaches from Al Wehda were praying during half-time. 'What do you think of Islam?' Aram asked, before answering his own question. 'We are all Muslims,' he said, turning around and pointing his finger to lasso his group. 'We pray every day. But this is the true Islam, between me and Allah. It's personal. Anything else is not praying to Allah. It's for other people to see that you're praying for Allah.' He was right; Syria appeared to be the least outwardly Islamic country I had been to in the Middle East. It seemed less hung up on public displays of faith, much at odds with Saudi or Kuwait or the West Bank, where prayer time meant dropping everything at a moment's notice. Most women walking around the centre of Damascus had long ago dispensed with covering their heads and alcohol was easily available in the city. The previous night I had headed for the Bab Touma area of the old city, the Christian quarter. It was here that several popes were born and Saint Paul lived. John the Baptist also spent some time in the city, in a fashion: his head is allegedly interred in the nearby Umayyad mosque. Walking down through the old city's cobbled streets, I was being navigated through the maze by an Iraqi I had met in an internet café along the way. Mohammad was half Kurdish, half Arab Sunni and had been living in Syria for six months, not to flee the insurgency or its resulting anarchy, but rather because it was cheaper to live in Syria than in the Iraqi Kurdistan, where rents and food prices had doubled since 2003. The Christian area began with the lights from the first off licence. Shopkeepers in tiny, half-room street coves stuffed with bottles of local wines and beers from Lebanon hawked their trade as you walked past. It was 10 p.m. but the streets were packed with glamorously dressed twentysomethings looking for somewhere to go. I headed down a side alley and came across Mar Mar, Syria's hottest club. Behind its huge wooden door designed to keep the noise in, the cavernous venue was empty except for two bar flies supping on bottles of Amstel. 'You can only stay for one drink,' the barman told me apologetically. 'We have dancing and a DJ tonight and the tickets are sold out.'

'Where is everyone then?' I asked.

'We are open until 6 a.m. People don't come until 1 a.m. You are early.'

I settled for one bottle of Barada beer, named after the river that anonymously winds through Damascus. It tasted like watered-down dirty tonic wine. I paid the bill and left, unwilling to wait the three hours for Syria's beautiful people to arrive. As I tried to negotiate back through the old city's impossibly complicated matrix to my hostel cars and people thronged the streets in anticipation of their night out on the town. Syria, like Iran, seemed to have at its core a more liberal, laissez faire social attitude to its regional contemporaries, and appeared, outwardly, to have the most in common with Western values. Yet a mixture of unbending Islamic fundamentalism and political strongmen with a knack of making bad tactical choices – both Assad and Ahmadinejad fall into the latter category – had soured its relationships with the rest of the world to the point that war against both countries had been kicked around as a possibility at the highest level in Washington and London. But whilst the Iranians were growing tired of Ahmadinejad's increasingly erratic behaviour, President Assad still enjoyed some level of popular support if the terraces were to be believed. 'Yes, people love him,' Othman enthusiastically replied when I asked whether their dislike for the army stretched to the president. The rest of the group nodded in appreciation. 'He stands up for Syria. Everyone wants us to get on our knees in front of Israel and America and England. But we won't.' The only thing they were prepared to kneel in front of the West for was the Premiership and the musical talents of Shane Ward. 'Listen, listen!' Othman demanded, pressing headphones into my ear from his mobile. A saccharine sweet pop dirge blared into my skull. 'Shane Ward, "No Promises." He is very popular here. But Backstreet Boys are best.' Everyone in the group nodded in agreement: Backstreet Boys five, Shane Ward nil.

The match had taken a turn for the worse for Al Wehda as they went two down before another remarkable comeback unfolded. Al Wehda hit back with three goals, one offside, one a foul on the keeper, the other a scuffed shot. Scuffles started breaking out between the Al Wehda hooligan faithful as the third goal went in and the clock hit 90 minutes. Al Horriya's players slumped to the floor knowing that another chance at clawing their way out of the relegation mire had gone begging. Al Wehda's fans didn't miss the opportunity to gloat. 'Kes akh tek Al Horriya!' ('Horriya, go fuck your sister!'). As the victorious Al Wehda fans piled out of the stadium into Damascus' early evening, only briefly stopping by the exit to harass players as they came out, it became clear from the two games just how successful and vital the Syrian FA's challenge to the army had been. I'd originally planned on heading to Homs to watch Al Karama play. But I had decided to stick to Damascus and had been rewarded with 12 goals and some of the best attacking football I had seen in the Middle East from a country that still hovered around the 100 mark on the FIFA rankings. Football had become meritocratic. Players were reaping the rewards of their talent and had been cut free from Al Jaish's monopoly to gain freedom over whom they played for. The rewards were being reaped on the pitch too. The FA's overhaul had also heralded a policy of promoting youth. By beefing up its scouting and training structure, and encouraging league teams to play more young Syrian players, the FA has been able to identify more talent and develop it through the ranks. At the 2007 under-17s World Cup, Syria surprised even themselves. After drawing with Argentina, beating Honduras and then losing by a stoppage-time goal to Spain, their tournament ended with a 3–1 defeat to England. At the 2005 under-20s World Cup in Holland, Syria beat Italy before narrowly losing 1–0 to Brazil in the last 16. Many of these players had been groomed for the senior team and were now spearheading Syria's attempt to qualify for their first ever World Cup finals. An excellent draw with Iran in Tehran, followed by another against the UAE, had put them in a good position to make the final Asian qualifying round for the World Cup finals in South Africa in 2010. In the end, they missed out on goal difference. In the last game of qualifying they had to beat the UAE 3–0 in Al Ain. They won 3–1, but time is still on Syria's side. It was a success story that other emerging leagues would be advised to follow.

I still hadn't given up hope on gaining entry to Al Jaish's suspiciously fortified training complex. After the senior team had won its match The Colonel intimated that it might be possible for me to return with the blessings of The General, as long as I didn't bring my camera. I agreed and arrived back where I had started, at the guard booth at the front gate. The soldiers recognised me but, fearing that The Colonel might throw them in jail if they let an undesirable in who had been ejected a few days previously, they barred my path. Remonstrating with the commanding officer didn't work either, until 50 metres away The Colonel's white head poked out of a brand new VW hatchback. I was sure his head cocked slightly in irritation as he spotted me waving furiously from the gate before beckoning me with a cursory handshake. He shiftily looked around, avoiding eye contact as he shook, as if he was about to engage in a highly illegal transaction of some sort. 'Please, please,' he begged, finally meeting my eyes. 'Don't take any photos. Of the field, OK. But anything else. No.' I walked the short distance to the scrubby green field, where the players were waiting. The Colonel had been chauffeur-driven the short distance, before emerging onto the pitch with a large smile and a skip in his step. Ahmad Rifat was there, but sank into the background as The Colonel took centre-stage and started giving the team talk. With his motivational words done, the players started warming up whilst The Colonel sauntered over to the rotting wooden temporary stand I was sitting on and shuffled next to me.

'Who exactly is in charge?' I asked.

'I am the manager. The coach is involved with everything on the pitch.'

'So, who picks the team?'

A pause.

'He does.'

'Do you have any influence on it [matters on the pitch]?'

'Well . . . '

Another pause before the truth willed out.

'I might say before a big game that a player in the side is weak and that he should be replaced with someone who is a strong player, a player who won't be weak. Then after the

season we talk and see which players we will take and which
we leave out.'

It seemed that The Colonel was the true power behind
the throne at Al Jaish, with Rifat merely as a sop civilian
figurehead: A Medvedeu to The Colonel's Putin. Which is
not to say he wasn't qualified for the role of de facto coach.
He himself had been a tidy player in Syria's third tier as well
as an international referee. That was in between the 21 years
he spent as a lieutenant in the army, which included a stint
fighting with the infantry on the Golan front in 1967 and
1973. We sat watching the players circle the pitch as he ticked
off his military career and many battles with the Israelis.

'Do you think Syria would play Israel if they ever both
reached the World Cup finals?'

The Colonel smiled a wry smile. This was a bit of a mean
question. Iran, Syria and Saudi Arabia would be powerless in
the face of the world's biggest, most prestigious footballing
tournament. Qualifying is hard enough and if a Middle Eastern
state forfeited its tie with Israel, not only would it push the
country into the footballing wilderness, it would also spark
riots in Damascus, Tehran and Riyadh. Pretending Israel doesn't
exist matters to many in the Middle East, but playing in the
World Cup finals matters more.

'We'll make a decision when we get there. Israel has some of
our land, the Golan. If they give it back we can have peace and
we can play [but] every day they are killing women, children,
babies, girls, men. How can they live like this? They need
peace too. It's like France coming over and taking a piece of
England. Would you play them after that?'

The Colonel knew he had gone further than a militarily
trained mind should usually allow and quickly changed the
subject, charging off to fetch one of the players. Abdul Razek
al-Hussein was the team's star midfielder and was himself one
of the few players who still chose to join the army as well as
playing for Al Jaish. The Colonel walked him to the rickety
wooden stand. 'You only ask him about football. Not politics,'
he instructed, handing him over into my custody. In the end
he decided to translate for me.

'How have you benefited from Al Jaish's new youth policy?'

The Colonel sprang into action, collecting the response and offering a reply.

'Al Jaish has good facilities, two fields for practice, swimming pool, sauna, professional coach. I have a good chance to show off my technique and fitness. We have here discipline and it is serious. This is why he has come to Al Jaish. Al Jaish is the best in Syria, it is not just my opinion but of everyone, all the journalists.'

It was clear that The Colonel had started to inject his own opinions into the replies.

'Syria will improve with football only if it follows the example of Al Jaish, with discipline, being serious, good training, good money.'

Then The Colonel dispensed with the pretence of answering the questions altogether.

'Yes I think we have a good chance of qualifying for the World Cup if we win the four games, because two teams qualify,' he replied instantly to the question, without even offering it to the confused-looking player.

'What does Abdul Razek think?' I asked again.

'Oh,' he said, relaying the message and garnering a long reply. 'Maybe.'

Despite the team's autocratic tendencies, The Colonel, Rifat, The General – whoever was truly responsible for what went on on the pitch – had started to turn Al Jaish's fortunes around. They had started their own youth programme in the team as well as training talented kids as young as 13. If they didn't make the cut, it was but a short walk to the recruitment office. They won either way. Al Jaish had been forced to change and was starting to show signs that it was finding its feet in the bright new world of professional football. The Colonel offered to drive me back to my hotel. On the journey back he was convinced that Al Jaish would rise again, stronger than before and better adapted for the modern world of cash-rich football. 'We are number one in Syria. Number one in terms of facilities and number one in discipline,' he reiterated as we passed the old city. 'Other clubs will be following our lead.' Who knows, maybe next season they may even be challenging Al Karama for the championship. Which should please The Colonel, if no one else.

With Al Jaish not entertaining the idea of any more visits, it was time to leave along the route I had arrived on, by taxi from Damascus to Amman. Jordan's capital was to be host to the fiercest title run in its history. The country's two best teams, Al Wihdat and Al Faisaly, were three points apart at the top of the table and were due to play the following Friday in a winner-takes-all game. That would make it tense enough, but there was also a political dimension. Al Wihdat hailed from the Wihdat Palestinian refugee camp; Al Faisaly were the team of the Hashemite Jordanians, who were now in the minority and weren't too happy about it. When they played it tended to end in riots and bloodshed, which meant it was pretty much unmissable. I headed for the bus station on the edge of town and pushed through the gaggle of hawkers until I found the service taxi-rank. Imad was waiting as if he knew I was coming, taking my bags instantly without contemplating that I might want to go anywhere else. An elderly Jordanian couple of Palestinian descent and their nephew crammed into the back, him wearing the red-and-white checked ghutra, kandoora and blazer, her in a black cloak. We set off out of Damascus and back into the sentinel gaze of Jebel Sheikh. Imad was silent until we reached the border and its vast, brand new duty free shop. Having grown up with some of the most expensive cigarette prices in the world, Syria's duty free prices were ridiculous. Whereas one packet cost upward of five pounds in the UK, a whole carton of 200 cost two pounds fifty. Imad filled his boots, gleefully buying dozens of cartons. Perhaps, I reasoned, he was stocking up, or buying some for his wife. It wasn't until we walked back to the taxi that his true intentions became clear. He parked in a secluded part of the car park, began ripping the packets out of their cardboard homes and handed them to the elderly couple in the back, who stuffed them in their pockets. The old woman hid more under her cloak and in her handbag whilst the old man pushed more under the front seats. They knew the drill. Four packets of Gauloise Blonde were stuffed into my hoody. Imad hid cartons under the wheel arches, under the spare wheel in the boot, even in the engine. It turned out that taxi driving was only part of Imad's myriad of businesses. His main breadwinner was cigarette smuggling. Over in Jordan he could get double for what he had just paid. The only problem was that we had to firstly hide all the cigarettes, negotiate an unfriendly border and find a carload of unwilling and helpless stooges to be complicit in his scam. There was no way out. I was an hour from Damascus and an hour from Amman. I had to sit tight and hope we got through it. We pulled up at the Jordanian side. The car in front of us was being torn to shreds by customs police whilst the occupants were forced to stand up, legs spread, against a wall. A solitary officer ambled over and poked at the seats with his stick before pulling the bags out of the boot. At first, I thought I'd be safe as he churned through my bag, until I saw the yellow flash of a Gauloise cartoon. When I'd not been looking, Imad had stuffed my bag full of cigarettes and hoped I wouldn't notice. Yet somehow the border guard missed them and waved us on after a suspiciously short shakedown. Imad had a broad smile on his face as he pulled away from Syria, towards the Amman derby between Al Wihdat versus Al Faisaly.

TWELVE

Jordan

Imad's smuggling operation had been a resounding success. He put on his sunglasses and stroked his short, well-kept beard as his taxi took the road south back to Amman. No one seemed to mind that we had been used as fag mules. In its own crazy, illegal way, it represented an act of fraternity. With the cost of living exploding in Amman and Damascus in recent months – neither state enjoyed sufficient oil reserves to meet its needs and were equally at the vagaries of Gulf oil prices as the rest of us – it was hard enough to scratch an existence. The elderly Palestinian couple understood that. The border guard, you suspected, understood it too. Imad pulled up on the side of the main highway on the outskirts of Jordan's capital and sold his contraband to the man who was always waiting for him, at the same spot, every day. He dropped me at the decrepit remains of the Abdali bus station. A new bus station had been built nearby and the hotels, taxi ranks and dive bars left behind that depended on it for sustenance and a steady stream of punters were struggling, desperately trying to entice me into the back of their cars for the two-minute walk downtown. The early spring sun burned my neck as I struggled with my bag towards my hotel. I'd grown to love Amman after passing through it so many times. If Lebanon was the place aggrieved parties went to

fight, Jordan was the place aggrieved parties went to party. Or
relax. Or spy. Anything but open conflict. They were all here.
Israelis pretending they were American, Americans pretending
they were Israelis, Jordanians pretending they were Palestinian,
Iraqis pretending to be Jordanian. It was a place of calm, if not
peace; a place of refugees, tourists and those with enough money
to buy a little temporary respite from the privations of Jenin
or Riyadh or Baghdad – be they recreational or medicinal. It
had the feel of a benign Casablanca. The landscape, too, was
something addictive. Amman is often unfairly characterised as
an ugly city, yet there was something beautiful about the shabby,
identikit flat-topped buildings that stuck out of Amman's 19
hills, and the deep valley that cuts through it, like a mouth of
badly kept teeth. On street corners and atop hills, evidence of
Amman's Roman past presented itself when you least expected
it – a Roman amphitheatre wedged between modern buildings
in downtown Amman; dissolving columns that once held the
roof of a grand Roman palace left orphaned next to a set of
traffic lights.

Yet I had neglected Jordan's sights, always being dragged away
by a football match in Damascus or Jerusalem or Amman. And
so it was this time. The end-of-season dénouement between
Wihdat and Faisaly had been feverishly anticipated by the fans
of Jordan's two biggest football clubs all year. Four months
previously I had been passing through Amman as it froze
during an unseasonably cold winter. In a bar at one of the
city's hotels, the barman – a Wihdat fan – showed me some
of the footage he had captured on his phone of the previous
meeting between the two teams that season. The blurry video
showed the feverish celebrations as Wihdat triumphed 1–0. The
main reason the crowd were going so crazy, though, was that
the Faisaly captain had been sent off and swore at the crowd,
causing pandemonium of a level considered a national security
risk. There were near riots in the stands as the police waded in
to restore order. The barman nodded his head in appreciation
as we watched the shaky video. That victory had given Wihdat
the advantage in the championship but week after week, Faisaly
had matched their results, meaning that the title would go to

the last game of the season in a winner-takes-all battle. It was going to go right to the wire. Or so I thought. After dropping my bag off at the hotel, I climbed the steep steps that took you up to Jabal Amman, the gentrified hill where Amman's best bars, galleries and cafés were found. It was mid-afternoon and the stylish Books@Café was empty and quiet until the barman rushed past me towards the dormant television in the corner and began flicking through the channels. He sat back, enraptured by what he had found. Wihdat were playing in a late-afternoon kick-off against Al Buqaa. Whilst I was in Syria the previous night, Faisaly were busy drawing against Shabab al Urdon, a team that was formed when the directors of Faisaly fell out and went their separate ways. It was the penultimate game of the season and it meant that if Wihdat beat Buqaa, they would go into the final game champions and the last tense, explosive match of the season everyone had been readying themselves for probably wouldn't be as tense or explosive any more, as none of the Faisaly fans would turn up. The last ten minutes ticked by, Wihdat leading by a single goal. I crossed my fingers and prayed for a goal. Buqaa pressed and pushed and missed two open goals. But Wihdat held on for the victory, and with it, the title. Friday would now be a coronation. I wrote a single word down in my notebook. 'Bollocks.'

Tareq Khoury greeted me, like any politician would, with a warm smile and a firm, overfriendly handshake. His office smelt of money. The desk was covered in rich, dark leather, as were the seats and the large bookcases that covered the walls. His shaved head, boyish face, designer suit and penchant for foreign cigarettes gave him the air of a more mature, circumspect West coast rapper. Tareq, however, had far more in common with a much more controversial figure. As an evidently successful businessman, a recently elected MP to the Jordanian parliament and president of Wihdat Football Club, Tareq, careerwise anyway, was more like a Jordanian Silvio Berlusconi. 'There will be 20,000 fans there [at the stadium], to celebrate,' he said excitedly, pulling his seat tightly behind his desk. 'They will all be for Wihdat.'

Tareq, a Christian of Palestinian descent, got involved with the club in the late 1980s, giving money to a community scheme that fed and educated Palestinian orphans. As his business interests grew – importing anything from Ralph Lauren shirts, to food, to oil – so did his influence until at the beginning of this season he was elected president of the club. 'Wihdat club was established in Al Wihdat refugee camp, with Palestinian players but to tell you the truth, there are a lot of Faisaly fans who are Palestinian and most of their players are Palestinian,' he explained when I asked about the background of the club. 'But because of the location it has the look of a Palestinian club. All Palestinians support it as there is no good national team. People look at Wihdat as the national team of Palestine. All Palestinians in Jordan, the USA, West Bank, UAE, Saudi Arabia.' The club was certainly a symbol of Palestinian identity, one of the few in Jordan. It was a tacit agreement that many Palestinians had with the Jordanian government – citizenship and rights that no other Palestinians could enjoy in return for loyalty to the king. Tareq represented a new generation, one assimilated into Jordan but proud of his Palestinian heritage. 'I am originally Palestinian, my wife is Jordanian, my mother, brother-in-law are Jordanian,' he said. 'It's mixed now. Maybe 90 per cent of the Jordanian families are mixed. Now you can't tell that I'm Palestinian or Jordanian [but] I feel for Palestine. We say we are Palestinians so we can save our country so that all people can have Palestine. In Jordan it used to be in the past that there was tension between Palestinian and Jordanians. After the marriage of all families, education, people are more educated. There is no problem. Only with illiterate people and poor people. The poor people don't feel they have anything from this country and think of Palestine as if it could offer them something if they went back because here they have nothing.' It was a far cry from 30 years ago when Jordan became the battleground for a Palestinian homeland. 'It started in the 1970s and 1980s,' Tareq said, pinpointing the time when tensions between Jordanians and Palestinians began to grow, 'when people had influence over Jordan from other countries.'

That period in the early Seventies was one of the darkest chapters in recent Jordanian history. By 1970 the country had taken in two huge waves of Palestinian immigration. The first, in 1948, saw Palestinians flee from what had become Israel. The second, in 1967, comprising Palestinians from the newly occupied West Bank and Jerusalem, helped create a critical mass. With the second wave, and with it the realisation that the Palestinians couldn't solely rely on Arab governments to take on Israel, also came the Palestinian Liberation Organisation, an umbrella of resistance movements determined to fight the Israelis and create a Palestinian state. Unfortunately for the West-leaning monarch of Jordan – King Hussein – the PLO was acting with impunity in his country, launching cross-border raids into Israel and ignoring the authority of his armed forces. Palestinian camps across the country were no-go areas for his troops. Instead, camps like Wihdat had their own security, levying their own taxes and meting out their own form of local justice. The PLO had effectively created its own state-within-a-state. King Hussein had at first appeared unwilling or unable to reassert the state's authority, either out of fear any actions might antagonise what had become a huge proportion of his subjects, or out of necessity. After all, any armed action against the Palestinians would not play well with his Arab allies and trading partners. But on 12 September 1970, King Hussein had to act. The Popular Front for the Liberation of Palestine, a Marxist resistance force, had kidnapped four planes en route to New York. They were flown to Jordan, to the north-eastern city of Zarqa, emptied of hostages and symbolically blown up in front of the world's cameras. The provocation sparked Black September, an assault by the Jordanian army to rid the country of the PLO, whose armed wing had just been taken over by one Yasser Arafat, once and for all. By October King Hussein had been successful in reasserting his will, but not without its human costs. Thousands, perhaps even tens of thousands, of troops and innocent civilians had been killed in the running battles in Amman, Zarqa and Irbid. The PLO eventually fled north, to Lebanon, where their presence once again had a destabilising effect in a country already struggling to deal with an explosive political, religious and ethnic mix. Behind them, though, King Hussein had to deal with a deeply divided population – the Hashemite Jordanians angry at the incursion of foreigners on their land, the Palestinians feeling like second-class citizens and burning with the injustice of Black September's heavy-handed assault on Jordan's Palestinian camps. The enmity was rarely allowed to be discussed in public again. But on the terraces two football teams represented the hopes and fears of each side: Wihdat the downtrodden Palestinians, Faisaly the embattled Jordanians. When they met, it was explosive, a blood-letting exercise that let the low-level prejudices that blighted everyday life go on simmering without being fermented into civil strife. Football provided much-needed, twice-yearly catharsis. 'For Wihdat, 99 per cent of the fans are Palestinian. You won't find any Jordanian fans of Wihdat,' Tareq admitted. 'They [Jordanian Faisaly fans] feel that the Palestinians came to their country and control all the business and are well educated. Some illiterate people think this way. They should be proud that Palestinians are living here and have all their rights like the Jordanians. It's a plus to the country.' The rivalry usually led to chants and then riots after each game, so much so that Palestinian players felt uncomfortable turning out for Faisaly. 'My brother used to play for Faisaly but after he heard what the club and the fans said about the Palestinians, some cursing in the games, he is now with Wihdat,' he said. 'It's the same with Rangers and Celtic or Barcelona and Madrid. Here it is between two countries, Palestinians and Jordanians. Because it is between two nationalities it is becoming a big problem. Me, as the president and MP, I don't feel it is between people who are educated, or think right about the country.'

The match also represented something far deeper, beyond the confines of Jordan's small borders. From Lebanon to the UAE, Palestine's diaspora had long been treated like second-class citizens. In Lebanon's Palestinian camps, it was illegal for refugees to work in most professions, to leave the country or get further education. In Egypt, employment restrictions were levied, in the UAE and Saudi, Palestinians could never become citizens. Their reticence, officially, was that normalising each country's Palestinian population would destroy the raison d'être for future generations to fight Israel for their rightful return. If the next generations felt, say, Lebanese rather than Palestinian, why would they fight for their homeland? Keeping the Palestinians in a perpetual state of flux was a necessary policy decision that kept them hungry for home. There was domestic political expediency at play too. If the largely Sunni Palestinians were given citizenship in Lebanon, it would have huge ramifications on the already politically explosive issue of which sectarian group had the largest population. In the UAE, granting citizenship for the Palestinians would open the royal families up to awkward questions about the other 85 per cent of the country that were foreign-born residents. Yet in Jordan, those official inequalities didn't exist, as long as the Palestinians accepted, inviolably, a Jordanian passport. The fact, Tareq said, that a Palestinian Christian could be elected to parliament in the first place – making him one of 15 Palestinians in the 110-strong legislature – was proof that differences were slowly being bred out over generations. 'Palestinians have full rights and we are happy. I care about Jordan exactly like I care about Palestine, I have the same feeling towards both countries.'

Of course, being elected as President of the country's most popular team wouldn't exactly have been a hindrance to his elevation as an elected member of parliament. 'There are two million [supporters] just in Jordan,' he claimed, quite a boast for a country that has an official population of six million. 'It is the highest number of fans compared to population. We have millions around the world too, 10 to 15 million. When we played in Saudi against Al Nasr club, we had 10,000 fans there [who lived] in Saudi Arabia. More than the local team. In Egypt the same thing happened.' Tareq insisted that buying political popularity through Wihdat couldn't have been further from his mind, but when a third of the electorate sing your name every weekend, it can't be bad for it. 'I'll tell you the truth. What made me go to Wihdat is that if you accomplish anything in Wihdat club you make millions of people happy,' he said just as a board member from the club knocked on the door and let himself in. Tareq handed him an envelope with a cheque for $25,000 in it. A gift, Tareq said, to the players who had brought him the league in his first season. 'I love that. I love to make people happy. It has cost me a lot out of my own pocket. I love it. When I see people are happy and people call me from Korea, the States, Palestine, they are so happy we won the league. I can make millions happy.' Tareq got up to leave and made his excuses. He had important parliamentary business to attend to. He had to just put me straight on one last thing. 'You know Wihdat isn't a refugee camp any more, it's part of the city.' He urged I should go there before heading for the game.

'You will be there?' I asked.

'Of course!' he replied incredulously.

'What will the score be?'

He laughed as we left though the front gate and shook hands goodbye.

'You know, now, I really don't care.'

It was Friday, the last match of the Jordanian season and my last match in the Middle East. The sun shone as it did on most days in Amman as my taxi cut through the quiet roads, emptied of traffic for obligatory Friday prayers. From the top of the hill Wihdat, or the Amman New Camp as it is known, sprawled in front of us. It was still, like the rest of the Middle East was at midday on a Friday. But today was different. As we drove into the camp the still-deserted streets gave signs of what was to come. Everything was green and red. Green-and-red ribbons hung from shop fronts. Green-and-red balloons were tied to signposts. Shop displays had been artfully arranged with products bearing just two colours. Green and red, Wihdat FC's colours. No sooner had I noticed the colours than the taxi screeched to a halt. This was as far as he would go. In front of us the road was full of thousands of men blowing horns and boys waving posters adorned with their favourite players above their heads. Bunting of red and green crossed the street along with the bare electricity cables. Pickup trucks sat stationary in the sea of people, each draped in Wihdat flags whilst the fans in the back improvised with their own costumes. One had made his own league cup out of foil, another wore a green sweatband with Wihdat written on it in Arabic. It was a scene of unbridled joy but somewhere in the centre of the chaos was the office for Wihdat football club, and I had to find it. Tareq had told me to be here by 1 p.m. so that I could meet the team and travel up on the team bus. A small boy wearing a Wihdat shirt took my hand and led me through the maze of stalls and shops and celebrating fans. We came to a long street. What looked like the team bus had been swamped by fans all waiting for a glimpse of their heroes before they left for the match against the old enemy. 'Come back here at seven or eight tonight and then you'll see a celebration,' Mohammad, a bald, dark-skinned 45 year old smoking a cigarette told me as we both surveyed the scene. 'This is all they have in Wihdat,' he shrugged. 'They are poor people, poor Palestinians. For them it is always misery, but Wihdat winning can make them happy.' A gang of small children ran past begging for a photo. I obliged. 'America! America! America!' they shouted back positively. 'Britani sahafi,' I corrected them. They stopped. 'Britani! Britani! Britani!' Wihdat camp was notorious for its anti-Americanism. It's probably the only time since its inception those two countries have enjoyed a positive reaction.

Tareq had been right about Wihdat. This was no refugee camp in the classical sense. This was a town the size of Middlesbrough. The concrete buildings had lost their new built lustre some time back in the early 1980s but they were stout. The roads were paved, the mosques stood up like medieval castles, white and impenetrable, all-seeing watchtowers impervious to the sun, the wind and the rain. Where Wihdat ended and the rest of Amman began was now impossible to make out. It was progress, sure, but the camp's permanence was also a depressing reminder of just how intractable the Palestinian problem was. I managed to push through the crowd and into the club's front door. Just as I got through the doors a man thrust a wad of coloured paper into my hand: posters of last season's victorious title-winning side. In the team manager's office, Wihdat's players had taken shelter from the crowds outside, sitting silently on the sofas that had lined the walls. They waited for the signal, so they could start their journey and plough through the maelstrom to the stadium. On the wall hung a long map of Palestine. In this alternative reality of geographical history Palestine stretched from the Red Sea all the way to Syria. There was no room for Israel. On the windows a collection of schizophrenic posters were displayed. Ronaldo in a Brazil shirt; Queen Rania and King Abdullah smiling; Ronaldinho holding an award in his Barcelona shirt; a baby wearing the black-and-white keffiyeh of Palestinian resistance; Raul mid-celebration for Real Madrid; the Star of David superimposed on the Stars and Stripes, burning. The call came from the bus. The players, all wearing their shirts, got up and silently walked through the dark corridor outside into the harsh sunlight and the deafening roar of the crowd. Car horns blared as their drivers finally got a glimpse of the cargo that would be leading their convoy to the stadium. The rickety team bus crawled through Wihdat as children jogged alongside, giving the two-fingered victory salute and shouting 'Palestine!' It was to be a longer journey than normal. The match had been moved from Amman to Zarqa, 35 miles north-east. Zarqa was famous for just two things. It was here that the Popular Front for the Liberation of Palestine had blown up its hijacked planes in 1970, sparking Black September. It was also the birthplace of Abu Musab al Zarqawi, arguably the most notorious Jordanian citizen in recent times. The Islamist militant founded Al Qaeda in Iraq and was responsible for numerous beheadings, kidnappings and suicide bombings, including the last time suicide bombers targeted Amman when three of the city's hotels were attacked, killing sixty people. Our bus careered through the valleys of lower Amman as the busload of players cheered and sang:

'Allah! Wihdat! Al Quds Arabi!'

God! Wihdat! Jerusalem [for the] Arabs!

The driver, an old man with sunken dark cheeks and a concave chest whom you suspected had been driving the bus since the team's inception in 1956, kept his elbow on the horn, emitting a permanent high-pitch screech whilst singing along, adding his own 'Yallah, Wihdat!' every few breaths. 'The championship gives something to the people of Wihdat,' explained Faisal Ibrahim, Wihdat's captain. He sat at the front of the bus with his young daughter on his lap, watching the trees pass by. 'It is very important for the Palestinians. We are one people, the Jordanians and the Palestinians, but we hope one day Palestine will be for the Palestinian people.' Faisal summed up the difficulty that his generation of Palestinian-descended Jordanians felt. The two identities were being successfully assimilated, which was leading to a more stable Jordan, but was at the same time reducing the number of Palestinians who would seek the right to return to Israel. He felt kinship with the land of his father, his grandfather even. He captained a team heavily identified with the Palestinian diaspora. His shirt was the colour of the Palestinian flag, and his club's badge, worn proudly above his left breast, showed the Al Aqsa mosque. Yet he had a Jordanian identity too. His children would be even further removed from their Palestinian heritage. He was also part of something that was inescapably Jordanian: he was a first-choice defender for the Jordanian national football team. 'I would like to play for the Palestinian team, the national team,' he added cautiously. 'But I can't because I have a Jordanian passport.'

'You need the Palestinian ID,' the team's doctor, Mamoun Harb, shouted through the puff of his strong cigarette. 'You can't have two passports here.'

The bus slowed down suddenly. The police had pulled us over and wanted to see what the fuss was all about. 'They hate us for being Palestinian,' spat the doctor. 'Maybe they like Faisaly.' He had a point. As the team of the king, Faisaly were well supported by the police and military. We waited patiently as the team's manager remonstrated with the stony-faced officer. Eventually, he waved us on our way. Somehow, you knew that Faisaly's coach wouldn't meet the same fate.

We arrived at the stadium and already 10,000 Wihdat fans were inside. The stadium's tiny doors were inundated by a crush of fans wearing white, green and red, each man pressed up against the next one's back in the harsh, early-afternoon sun. They began singing as soon as they saw their team arrive, going quiet as riot police sauntered down the line. They weren't just any normal riot police, though. They were the scariest-looking riot police imaginable, like from some kind of Orwellian future. Wearing all black, huge pieces of kevlar body armour surrounded their chests and backs whilst bulky arm guards and leg protectors made them appear twice the breadth and twice the height of normal men. On their heads they wore black helmets over black balaclavas, to keep their anonymity. Their gloved hands carried black nightsticks, finishing off a look that was not far from a gothic version of Shredder from *Teenage Mutant Ninja Turtles*. A judicious thwack of the stick kept any stragglers in line. They had arrived expecting not just a riot, but war. There was no need. The Faisaly team bus arrived, a gleaming, modern luxury coach with AC and blacked-out windows. It parked next to Wihdat's tiny Mitsubishi minibus, dwarfing it with its opulence. Only a handful of fans cheered the team's departure. This match wasn't for Faisaly. They knew it was a victory parade for Wihdat and only a few dozen of the diehard fans bothered to turn up. By the sullen faces of the Faisaly players, they didn't want to be here either.

Inside the stadium, one half was already full with fans jumping up and down and singing, shaking black-and-white headscarves. I asked one of Wihdat's entourage what they were singing. 'They are singing, "Allahu akhbar! al dowry ahdar!"' answered Ahmad, who ran Wihdat's website. 'It means, "God is great, the league is green."' Oddly there wasn't a single Palestinian flag in sight. 'That's because the police won't let them bring them inside [the ground],' Ahmad explained. Wihdat's faithful sang it over and over again: 'Allahu Akhbar! Al dowry ahdar!' The embattled minority of Faisaly fans looked on sullenly. Usually they would be in fine voice too, pledging allegiance to the king or singing: 'Wahed, ithnain, talagha ya Abu Hussein.' It means: 'One, two, divorce her [Queen Rania] Abu Hussein [the King].' Queen Rania, whom the king married in 1993, is of Palestinian descent. But this time they kept their silence, only showing any anger when

Wihdat's players unfurled a banner heralding their title-winning exploits in front of their small section of fans. Two police officers ran onto the pitch, ripped it out of their hands and escorted them back to the dressing-room. The dressing-room was surprisingly tense as the manager went through his last instructions. Most listened raptly whilst the goalkeeper chose instead to pray next to the tactics board. It being Friday, the fans prayed in the stands too. Officials leant on their knees on the side of the pitch, in the shade, pointing south to Mecca. The players emerged to a one-sided roar. There was no guard of honour for Wihdat; Faisaly were just going through the motions. Minutes before kick-off another roar went up. Tareq Khoury arrived to take his seat at the top of the VIP section. The fans chanted his name ecstatically. He gave a regal wave back, acknowledging his popularity.

The game, predictably, was absolutely dire. With neither team having anything left to play for, it degenerated into an attritional dirge. The fans couldn't have cared less. They weren't here to watch football. Not really. They were here to see their players lift the championship trophy. The sky got dark and the minarets sang again as the game limped to its sorry conclusion. Only a missed penalty by Faisaly gave Wihdat anything to cheer on the pitch. Apart from the final whistle. The staff, substitutes and players' families rushed onto the pitch to celebrate. A makeshift stage was constructed and the players invited to accept their medals. Tareq was there in the centre of things and oddly, it was he who lifted the trophy first. The crowd screamed as he sucked in a few more precious votes. Looking round I realised that the police were hurriedly ushering the Faisaly fans out of the ground. At first I thought this was simply good policing. But then it turned more sinister. As Wihdat's diehard fans sang the name of each player as he bowed in front of the main stand, I decided to sneak out. It was a long way back and I had no idea how I was going to get a taxi. It was only when I had started to take the steps down to the entrance that it became clear the riot police had gone berserk. A wave of well-dressed journalists and dignitaries fell back through the glass double doors. It took everyone by surprise, like a rogue wave on a beach full of sunbathers. The men immediately scrambled past up the stairs to get away from the beatings. Outside, the men in black battered anyone who came near them. It wasn't immediately clear what the trouble was. After squeezing through the doors into the storm, I could see the prone bodies of green and red as the police went about trying to restore calm, screaming indiscriminately and waving their nightsticks at anyone in the crowd who looked at them. Within seconds, the crowd quietened, bruised and tired. A small boy stamped on a green balloon that had no doubt been proudly tied to the windscreen wiper of a proud Wihdat fan's car. It was all the provocation they needed, and they returned to beating fans indiscriminately as they passed. 'You can't be here,' said one of the policemen, looking like a kevlar shogun, before marching me to a 'safe spot' where I couldn't move. 'Welcome to Jordan.'

I hadn't been the only one to be moved out of harm's way. A Wihdat fan protecting his wife and young son stood next to their car watching the chaos unfold. 'They do this because we are Palestinian,' the man told me, refusing to tell me his name. 'All of the police, all of the army, they are with Faisaly.' I decided to make a break for the front gates, past the unconscious figure of a topless teenage Wihdat fan, his friends splashing water in his face to rouse him whilst a policeman prodded the group with his truncheon, intimating that he'd prefer if they undertook their makeshift first aid elsewhere. Behind me the man and his family were being screamed at by another policeman for taking pictures. The mass of green and red moved towards safety and the front gates. Dusk had quickly given way to night and I was a hour's drive from safety. There was no way I was getting back to Amman with 20,000 people all looking for a way back to the capital. Stuck and desperate I spotted a man wearing a Pixies T-shirt. Assuming that a fan of Boston's finest would speak English, I asked him where I could get a taxi. He looked at me quizzically.

'Are you with Wihdat or Faisaly?' he asked, his crew of fellow Wihdat fans crowding around to listen for an answer.

I pulled out the poster I'd been given whilst boarding the bus earlier that afternoon, of Wihdat's title-winning squad from last year, and held it aloft. 'Wihdat.'

'You can come with us!'

Salah and his crew of Palestinian 'gangsters', as they referred to themselves, wriggled through the crowd, through a fence and over waste land before emerging onto the main road grid locked with lorryloads of Wihdat fans. Car horns and police sirens blared in the foreground. Salah's Nissan was parked in a ditch on the side of the road. We squeezed in, four of us on the back seat. The road ahead was full and stationary, but we were safe. 'Hey man, do you smoke hash?' Salah asked. He sparked up a joint as thick as a baby's wrist before waiting for a reply, inhaling deeply and blowing the thick white smoke into the cabin, before passing it to me and turning on the radio to distortion level. We shunted along the celebratory motorcade, with the tabla rattling like a machine gun and the horns of victory blaring around us. Green and red emanated from every vehicle, except the car in front which had a poster of King Abdullah in the back window, a sure sign that the driver was a Faisaly fan. 'He's a son of a bitch!' Salah screamed, bouncing forward and chopping his arm towards the king. 'What about Queen Rania, she's Palestinian, right?' I offered. Salah breathed in a lung's worth of thick smoke, leant his head back and blew it slowly out into the fabric of the roof. 'She,' he started, coughing through blurry, watery eyes, 'she is the biggest son of a bitch of them all.' No one spoke for a few seconds, the nodding heads in the car giving their seal of approval. Wihdat football club was finished for them for another season. It was back to their jobs and their normal lives. For a few short, hot months football would be a distant memory. But soon enough August would be back and Fridays would envelop them once more.

'Come on,' Salah shouted, breaking the silence. 'Sing!'

There was only one song. The six of us replied in unison, through the smoke and over the drums, as the car sped down the dark, unlit highway towards Amman, towards home.

Allahu Akhbar!
Al dawry ahdar!
Allahu Akhbar!
Al dawry ahdar!
God is great.
The league is green.